"A FASCINATING AND DISTURBING STORY."

Library Journal

McKenney was convinced that the man who had led the enemy in the battle of No Name Island in Vietnam was the same man who now appeared on the screen—not a Vietcong or a North Vietnamese Army officer, but an American. McKenney would never forget his name: Bobby Garwood. On the day of the battle, Garwood wore the enemy's uniform. Now here he was on the television screen at the Chicago airport, dressed as a Marine Corps private. For a whole year Garwood had been McKenney's top target in Vietnam, and McKenney had used all the formidable resources at his disposal to hunt him down. He failed, and his failure still tortured him. He had been consumed with hatred then, and he was driven by it now. It made no difference that the man on the screen was carrying a Bible.

For the sake of all Marines whose blood was on Garwood's hands, vowed McKenney, justice would be done.

―――

"Jensen-Stevenson makes a moving, believable case for Garwood as a brave private who proved to be a pawn in his government's game of secrecy and deception."
Ft. Worth Star-Telegram

SPITE HOUSE

The Last Secret of the War in Vietnam

MONIKA JENSEN-STEVENSON

AVON BOOKS ◆ NEW YORK

To Special Forces
Captain William F. (Ike) Eisenbraun
whose ability to inspire was the
measure of the man.

AVON BOOKS, INC.
1350 Avenue of the Americas
New York, New York 10019

Copyright © 1997 by Monika Jensen-Stevenson
Published by arrangement with W.W. Norton & Company, Inc.
Library of Congress Catalog Card Number: 96-24688
ISBN: 0-380-73169-X
www.avonbooks.com

The W.W. Norton edition contains the following Library of Congress
Cataloging in Publication Data:

Jensen-Stevenson, Monika.
  Spite house : the last secret of the war in Vietnam / Monika Jensen-
Stevenson.
   p. cm.
Includes index.
1. Vietnamese Conflict, 1961-1975—Prisoners and prisons, VietCong.
2. Vietnamese Conflict, 1961-1975—Collaborationists—United States.
3. Garwood, Robert Russell. 4. McKenney, Tom C. (Tom Chase) I. Title.
DS559.4.J474   1997   96-24688
959.704'37—dc20   CIP

First Avon Books Printing: September 1998

AVON TRADEMARK REG. U.S. PAT. OFF. AND IN OTHER COUNTRIES, MARCA
REGISTRADA, HECHO EN U.S.A.

Printed in the U.S.A.

WCD   10 9 8 7 6 5 4 3 2

Contents

And Aaron shall lay both his hands upon the head of the live goat, and confess over him all the iniquities of the children of Israel, and all their transgressions in all their sins, putting them upon the head of the goat, and shall send him away by the hand of a fit man into the wilderness.

Leviticus 16:21

Closely allied with the concept of scapegoat was that of the devil. This defense mechanism rejected personal accountability and projected guilt to an object which was conceived as the essence of evil. . . . The assumption that the woes of this world are caused by devils, whether spiritual or terrestrial, is a popular error that continually thwarts realistic analysis.

William Bosch, Author
Judgement at Nuremberg

Acknowledgments

It is impossible to thank everyone who gave me support and help in the writing of this book. First and foremost, my husband and daughter who encouraged me to make it a priority.

I owe a special debt of gratitude to veterans of special operations and the relevant intelligence agencies—Vietnamese, Thai, American, Australian, British—who shared their knowledge and experience about a part of the Vietnam War hidden from ordinary view and who, more important, gave their moral support to the writing of this book. Norman Doney, Mark Smith, Major General Arun Sumitra (current Chief of Thai Defense Intelligence), Harve Saal and his good friends who have asked not to be named, gave me invaluable assistance for which I will always be grateful. I am indebted to Rider Latham whose distinguished services in Asia with British intelligence made his moral support so important. Special mention must go to King Rama IX of Thailand. His friendly, generous, and knowledgeable counseling over many years was outstanding.

I want to thank Vaughn Taylor, Bobby Garwood's long-time lawyer, for sharing unstintingly with me the results of almost twenty years of dedicated and largely unpaid detective and legal work. If I ever had doubts that there still exist in America lawyers who pursue justice over career advancement and wealth, he put them to rest. That kind of integrity may seem even more unusual in a politician, but I am grateful that Senator Bob Smith (R-N.H.) has it and shared some of his findings with me. General Eugene Tighe, the former head of the Defense Intelligence Agency, now deceased, provided the road map for me to pursue this story at the very beginning, when official government policy dictated that the truth about Bobby Garwood remain buried. This book owes much to General Tighe's belief and determination that an innocent soldier had the right to be exonerated and honored for what the general called "exceptional courage." I owe General Lam Van Phat, the last South Vietnamese military commander of the Saigon area, who testified courageously from his own prison experience, a similar debt of gratitude. Bill Garnett Bell, the former Chief of Operations, Joint Casualty Resolution Center, shared not only his knowledge of the intricacies of the Viet Cong and North Vietnamese prison system during and after the war, but also generously helped me to communicate with former South Vietnamese military and intelligence professionals. There were others convinced of the need to tell Bobby Garwood's true story. They offered valuable contacts, research time and skills. John Holland and Quyen Le must be singled out for their very important contributions. I look forward to the day when it will be possible to thank publicly senior officers in Hanoi whose sense of military honor overrode their political concerns in order to provide independent confirmation of the details of Garwood's fourteen years in a hitherto undisclosed secret prison system of the Democratic Republic of Vietnam.

1: Remembrance Day

November 11th, 1991, Crystal City Hilton, Washington, D.C., Annual Meeting, Vietnam Veterans Coalition

I sat at the speakers' table and noticed him come through the door. He surveyed the large room with some distaste and just a touch of embarrassment. Several hundred men and women were milling around breakfast tables.

He had never attended a gathering of Vietnam vets before; meetings such as these made up a world he had always heard about with sadness. He hurt for all those guys in their camouflage dungarees and bush hats, growing bald and paunchy, because they seemed unable to move past the memory of the time they spent in Vietnam. To him they were like the Wall, the Vietnam Veterans Memorial in Washington, which he had never seen and never intended to see: the veterans, it seemed to him, offered themselves up, in perpetuity, as symbols of defeat.

Still, he saluted the flag and sang the national anthem with his usual spirit. He had finally recognized that this was a subculture with its own ceremonies, celebrities, and jargon. But he definitely did not feel part of it—it was

1

too emotionally complicated. He still remembered with puzzled pride the wartime nickname he had been given without his knowledge: "Colonel Smooth." Until the day before he left Vietnam in September 1969 he had no idea that this was the image his men had of him. At a farewell party, his senior sergeants presented him with a small marble Buddha and a note that said he reminded them of the Buddha, because he "always stayed calm, no matter how tense the situation . . . he was unshake-able." He thought now: they had no idea just *how* tightly wound he had in fact been underneath. What had made him so seemingly sure of himself had nothing to do with being smooth. It was something much simpler: the belief he had firmly held since his first tour in Korea—that he was just a Marine doing what Marines do.

He had come to Washington to find a man he had hated for twenty-three years. He knew it was unlikely that his old nemesis would be here, but it was always possible. The Colonel, still obsessed by his search, blanked out the meeting, the speakers, the awards. Not encountering his man among the crowd, he would ask my help in tracking him down—Robert (Bobby) Garwood, a former Marine private, captured in Vietnam in 1965. Garwood returned from Vietnam in 1979, six years after the peace agreements were signed, only to be court martialed and found guilty of collaborating with the enemy. He figured in a book I wrote.

Greeting people after my speech, I again became aware of the visitor, a ramrod-straight, imposing figure in a dark suit, waiting patiently, an intense look on his face. He made no move to speak. Only when I began to move away did he step forward and take both my hands in his. He began to weep silently. The silence stretched on and on. Finally he said, "I am Colonel Tom C. McKenney. You must know how to reach Bobby Garwood. I directed an official mission to assassinate him behind enemy lines, because I believed what they told me. Would you tell him that I will crawl on my hands and knees to beg his forgiveness?''

2: No Forgiveness

There was no forgiveness in the Colonel's heart when Garwood suddenly appeared on a TV news report following his shame-ridden return.

"They've let the traitor come home. After all those months we spent trying to hunt him down and kill him, here he is, getting off a plane in Chicago." McKenney's eyes were fixed on the television screen. Even though he thought the words and said nothing, the anger that boiled up in him was visible, dark, and ugly. It stunned his Bible study group in Wickliffe, Kentucky. They had just finished a discussion and were chatting over coffee or watching the evening news, but now they fell silent. The change in their Bible-class teacher was almost frightening. Some knew he had seen combat in Vietnam.

There was so much more he had never spoken about, never been allowed to speak about. He had once directed some of the assassinations that eliminated thousands of South Vietnamese suspected of working with the enemy. And that was only half of it.

Tom McKenney's mind flashed back ten years, to June 5th, 1969, and the aftermath of the battle of No Name

4

Island in Vietnam, when he had gone to interview the survivors. He imagined once again the battle scene they described. In his mind he saw the wreck of what was left of a platoon of K Company, Third Battalion, First Marines, and the mutilated bodies of the young Marines made him wince. He could hear the screams of some of the injured while the enemy taunted them in English, "Marines, you die tonight—no sweat." He remembered the strange, listless way the few American survivors repeated the phrase, "they had us whipped."

McKenney was convinced that the man who led the enemy on that raid was the same man who now appeared on the screen—not a Vietcong, or a North Vietnamese Army officer, but an American. McKenney would never forget his name: Bobby Garwood. On the day of the battle, Garwood wore the enemy's uniform. Now, here he was on the television screen, at the Chicago airport dressed as a Marine Corps private. For a whole year Garwood had been McKenney's top target in Vietnam, and McKenney had used all the formidable resources at his disposal to hunt him down. He failed and his failure still tortured him. He had been consumed with hatred then, and he was driven by it now. It made no difference that the man on the screen was carrying a Bible.

For the sake of all Marines whose blood was on Garwood's hands, vowed McKenney, justice would be done.

3: Drummer Boy Dreams

For as long as he could remember, Tom Chase McKenney wanted to be a soldier. The first question he recalls putting to his father went something like this: "Can I be a drummer boy when I grow up?" His father answered, "I hope not." He was only three at the time, inspired by a picture of rag-taggle American revolutionary soldiers carrying two drummer boys on their shoulders as they waded across an icy stream in the middle of winter. That brief exchange between father and son seems to have little relevance to Vietnam; yet it reveals the personality of a small boy who, from that moment forward, never changed his mind about wanting to become a soldier, and who became so single-mindedly a Marine that he would go way beyond the call of duty to live up to his own personal code. That such a code, based on traditional American values, might be twisted to make him, finally, a man committed to assassinating fellow American soldiers, denying them a trial or defense of any sort, would have been inconceivable to the boy's family and his mentors.

Everything in McKenney's early life contributed to the building of old-fashioned character. His parents, grandparents, uncle, aunts, and cousins all lived within a sixteen-mile radius of his family home in Kentucky. They believed passionately in education, the more classical the better, and the discussion of ideas. They instilled in McKenney the sense of being blessed to live in a country where so much was possible and to have had ancestors who created it through blood, sweat, and tears. With this privilege went the responsibilities to do one's best and to be patriotic. McKenney's father added something else: "Always choose the most difficult path, it's sure to be the right one."

McKenney was taught to believe and trust his country's government and elected leaders. Even when he learned that some leaders were unworthy of their offices and that few seemed to match the brilliance and moral fiber of his political and intellectual hero, Thomas Jefferson, he never stopped trusting the highest levels of government.

Growing up in Lexington in the 1930s and during the war was like a dream. The city had a small-town feeling, with long, white fences and stonewalled roads everywhere—even downtown. The population was fifty thousand, a figure that hadn't changed much in 150 years, and when McKenney walked down Main Street he recognized almost everybody. Prosperity depended on tobacco, whiskey, and horses. The town's leaders deliberately resisted industrialization. Lexington was secure in its identity, deeply rooted in history.

Founded in the nation's earliest expansion from the eastern seaboard, Lexington soon became known as the seat of culture and civilization on the raw frontier. Every Kentucky schoolboy learned it was once called the Athens of the West. McKenney still thought of it that way. Where the Viaduct intersected with Main Street there was a bronze statue with direction markers called the Zero Milestone. To McKenney, it was the center of the universe.

Lexington was decidedly "Old South" in its values

and customs, a kind of time capsule where women wouldn't dream of going to shop without dressing properly, which included wearing gloves. Gentlemen tipped their hats, stepped aside, opened doors, and walked on the outside of the lady. Gentility was an absolute virtue and honor a tangible thing. Business deals were sealed with a handshake. A gentleman's word was his bond.

The city was also a place where a boy could go to jaw with Will Harbut, the groom of the greatest horse of the century. At least that's what everybody in Kentucky thought in those days of the mighty Man o' War. Lots of famous people came trekking through Lexington to see Man o' War, known to racing fans as Big Red, but few impressed Will Harbut and few got the chance to see the horse he called "d' mostest hawse." McKenney was there, though, when Will made an exception for the man he figured was a bigger stud than even Man o' War— the father of the Dionne quintuplets. Taking Dionne round the stable after hours, Harbut shrugged off the famously prolific father's effusive thanks: "Heck, I wanted the horse to meet *you*," he said.

Man o' War's name evoked all the heroic military role models that haunted Lexington's town squares and the University of Kentucky, where McKenney's father, one of the founders of 4-H Clubs of America, taught agricultural science. The boy picked up the pride Lexington felt in its military history beginning with the conflicts with Native Americans. In his own childhood, they were still called the Indian Wars. McKenney was reared on stories that don't make American school books any more: heroic tales like that of Bryan Station, where the women saved the fort by risking their lives to go for water. Names forgotten now were banners in his school days: Blue Licks, the last battle of the Revolution; New Orleans, the last battle of the War of 1812, where Kentucky and Tennessee volunteers along with a small force of Marines fought with valor; Mexico City, captured by a small contingent of Marines after they put a thirty-thousand-strong Mexican army to flight; and other names that lacked a Shakespeare to write them into permanent legend—Perryville and Chancellorsville, San Juan Hill and Belleau Wood. Each rang in his ears like a call to arms. The idea that America could ever involve itself in a war without honor was unthinkable. In his mind victor and vanquished were honored equally. It did not occur to him until much later that no honor was ever accorded to vanquished or victorious Native Americans no matter how bravely they had fought.

Lexington was steeped in Civil War history, and intensely Confederate. Banks closed on Robert E. Lee's birthday and Confederate Memorial Day was observed on May 10th. At football and basketball games, people stood for "Dixie" *and* "The Star-Spangled Banner." It was ill-mannered and unpatriotic to remain seated for either. There were two statues in the courthouse yard, both of Confederate generals idolized by McKenney: John Hunt Morgan, the dashing cavalry commander, and John C. Breckinridge, the great-grandfather of Colonel Jim Breckinridge, who would later become McKenney's good friend. John C. had commanded the Third Kentucky Confederate Brigade, better known as the Orphan Brigade, because after Kentucky was invaded and had formally joined the Union side in the Civil War, the brigade never received replacements. He had been vice president under President Buchanan and had run against Lincoln in the last presidential election before the Civil War. After commanding the Orphan Brigade, John C. became minister of war for Jefferson Davis. What particularly thrilled young McKenney about Jim's great-grandfather was that he was the only Confederate cabinet minister who did not go to prison. He escaped to Cuba in an adventure so heroic it sent shivers down the boy's spine just to think of it. That Breckinridge had been on the losing side did not detract one iota from his glamour.

McKenney carried the name of his own ancestor, Salmon P. Chase, who, in 1864, at the time of Breckinridge's Confederate exploits, became chief justice of the U.S. Supreme Court. Chase flirted with impeachment by frequently dueling over matters of honor.

McKenney was a great reader of history and the classics, but nothing he read ever filled him with more wonder than the history of his own family and the families of his friends. His reading reinforced an upbringing that taught him that honor, duty, and country were the only principles to live by. It was common knowledge to McKenney and his friends that a portrait of Jefferson Davis in his Union colonel's uniform still hung in West Point's Washington Hall. They also knew that Benedict Arnold's name had been chiseled off the chapel plaque that honored America's revolutionary heroes in that institution. They understood the difference. Davis acted on principle; Arnold sold his country for cash. In his later life McKenney would often think his was perhaps the last generation (even in Kentucky) to care about such things as honor, principle, and duty.

There was a downside to such dedication, but this never occurred to Tom—not until late in life, when his military career was over. That the Civil War had ruined the lives of the majority of men who fought it, on both sides, was not something young McKenney considered: John C. Breckinridge, an exception, was the kind of man he wanted to emulate. Breckinridge gave his all for the Confederacy, but once the Confederacy was defeated, he devoted himself to the Union. He had come back from Cuba when it was safe to do so, and had brought up his son to respect the Union he had tried to defeat. His grandson, J. C. Breckinridge, became a famous Marine Corps general, father of the fleet Marine force concept, serving in the Spanish American War and World War I. Breckinridge's great-grandson, Jim, would serve in Korea and Vietnam, wars that brought him close to Tom McKenney.

* * *

McKenney would later think that his overriding desire to become a Marine—because the urge to become a soldier had soon translated itself into a specific attachment to that branch of the armed services—started with his admiration for the Breckinridge clan. A greater influence, however, may have come from his reading. When McKenney was eight or nine he read *Mack of the Marines in China*. Mack was an idealized sergeant, and after reading about him, McKenney wanted nothing more than to be a Marine sergeant and go to China. Later he read *Leatherneck*, the publication for enlisted men put out by the Marine Corps. *Leatherneck* was full of stories about men who, in the words of historian Andrew Geer, "had the will to win and curses on the man or unit who lacks it; the moral stamina to stand and fight when all seems lost; the courage to charge a hill when death warns to stay."[1]

His family environment was not at all military, certainly not warmongering. McKenney's father tried to stem his son's fervor for soldiering. "There is an ugly, inhuman side to it," he told Tom, "that men who have been through it can never forget." He told of his experience during World War I, about reaching under a fallen comrade to turn him over. The wounded man had five or six machine-gun wounds, and his fingers slipped into the bullet holes "as they would into a bowling ball."

Young McKenney listened to such admonitions, but they had little impact. He idolized his father, "the most self-disciplined, reliable, and honorable man I ever knew." But what impressed him most about the elder McKenney, who was blind in one eye, was that he had tricked World War I recruiters into signing him up despite his handicap. He had simply memorized the eye chart. At the time he had just signed a lucrative contract

[1] Andrew Geer, *The New Breed: The Story of the U.S. Marines in Korea*. Nashville: Battery Press, 1989.

with the Cincinnati Reds, and he figured if he was good enough to pitch professionally with one eye, he was certainly good enough to shoot with one eye. The fact that he was giving up the possible fame and fortune of a baseball career meant nothing next to doing what he saw as the honorable thing.

From his father, McKenney learned that if he worked harder and got up earlier than the rest of the crowd, he would succeed. McKenney liked this challenge. His creed became: "When it gets too tough for everybody else, it's just right for me and my guys." It did occur to some of his friends that perhaps the only institution that could provide constant challenge to such a young man was precisely the one he wanted to join—the Marine Corps.

McKenney was fifteen years old when World War II ended, a conflict, with its clear delineation of good and evil, that had a big impact on him. He would have given anything to be six years older, like his next-door neighbor Bill, who joined the Marine Corps as soon as he was able, in 1943.

McKenney's cousin Floyd was the person he most wanted to emulate. When war broke out Floyd was thirty-three, old enough to sit it out. What's more, his health was precarious. As a highway patrolman, he had stopped one night to offer his help to a man walking along the roadside. The man, an escaped convict, shot Floyd in the stomach and left him for dead. Bleeding profusely, he drove himself to the nearest hospital. McKenney always figured that this incident alone proved Floyd's mettle. When his cousin joined the USMC, first talking reluctant recruiters into giving him the okay, and then choosing the tough path of a "recon" (reconnaissance) Marine, McKenney was overwhelmed.

Floyd was the oldest in his platoon in boot camp. The other men called him Pop or Grandpa and knew instinctively that he was the one they could count on. Floyd, along with a small team, was assigned the dangerous work of reconnoitering small islands held by the Japanese. One morning on one of those islands in a "safe" area, Floyd stepped on a mine. When he awoke he found himself in a strange, silent world, on board a ship headed for home. There were no medevac planes in those days. The ship, part of a convoy that adjusted its speed to the slowest landing ship among its vessels, and zig-zagged to confuse enemy submarines, progressed only fifteen knots a day.

Once home, he traveled from hospital to hospital, but there was little remedy for someone who, Tom's father said, "was torn asunder and broken, but didn't even get the Purple Heart because he did all his bleeding on the inside." Like McKenney's father, Floyd tried to impress upon him the reality and horror of war even though he didn't talk much about his own wounds. But Tom McKenney determined that somehow he was going to make it up to Floyd. He believed fervently that men like Floyd, and all the thousands of others who had fought and died during the war, had saved the nation and deserved its gratitude.

4: Tindeltown Beginnings

There were no white fences or stonewalled roads in the Tindeltown trailer park in Indiana where Bobby Garwood grew up. Neither were there any male role models for Bobby except his father, Jack, whom he admired for keeping their large family together but whom he was never able to please. Family life was rocky. The elder Garwood had married a young Jewish woman in an intolerant town that made life unbearable for those who went against the grain. Jack Garwood began to think life would be easier if his wife gave up Judaism. The way he saw it, "the open sky is the church." The conflict over religion eventually caused insurmountable personal problems. Finally, unable to buck the overt hostility she encountered in the neighborhood without emotional support from her husband, Ruth Buchanan Garwood ran away. Bobby was four years old. His brother Don was two.

That first year without their mother was not so bad. The boys were sent to live with their paternal grandmother, and their mother was in regular contact, something their father knew nothing about. The elder Garwood had been terribly wounded by his wife's flight and he wanted nothing more to do with her. When she tried to get regular access to the boys, he not only took them away from their grandmother, he took legal action to keep sole custody. He never mentioned his wife again. She sent money for them regularly to their grandmother, with whom they often visited. Grandmother Garwood was so cowed by Jack, however, that she told no one about the money. Caring for a severely handicapped daughter, she decided to use it to keep her own fragile household afloat. The effect was devastating, especially to Bobby, who was old enough to remember how loving his mother had been. He could make no sense of what appeared to be total abandonment.

Bobby Garwood and his father had a great falling out. Because lack of cash was always a problem, Bobby began working in grade school. He always had three paper routes. From the age of eleven onward, he was doing hard labor on farms and helping out in a tool rental store, an experience that brought out his aptitude for mechanical skills, a talent that not only insured he could always get a job, but would later save his life. By the time he was fifteen he was making as much money as his father and giving half of it for board and keep.

He had a quick mind, but there was no question of preparing for the kind of higher education his mother had discussed with him when he was just a toddler. Nevertheless, Bobby kept those dreams of going to college.

Along with his mechanical skill went a budding gift for languages. Although he seldom opened his junior high Spanish books, the language seemed to roll off his tongue. But his father gave him no encouragement to study and there was very little time for anything except work. Although Bobby wanted to spend some time relaxing with friends, particularly his steady girlfriend, Mary Speer, his father was very strict and insisted on a ten o'clock curfew. When Jack Garwood married again, Bobby's stepmother made it clear she was boss. It infuriated Bobby everytime she struck his brother Don, who had a bed-wetting problem. Don, in turn, clung emotionally to Bobby, who felt an obligation to protect him.

One day, when she refused to stop hitting Don, Bobby threatened her with a knife and told her never to lay hands on his brother again. That was the last straw for his father, who went to the police and asked that Bobby be put in juvenile detention. There, a social worker offered a suggestion that is given to many young men who get into minor trouble with the law. "Why not sign up with the military?" she asked. Bobby agreed. He chose the Marine Corps because he considered it the best of the services and because his father had taunted him, saying "you'll never make it through boot camp. You're just a wet-nosed, snotty kid." When the Marines accepted Bobby, his father was pleased, told him that, after all, he was a Garwood and bragged about his son's enlistment to friends and neighbors. It was the first time Garwood realized that however difficult it was for his father to show it, he not only cared about him, but was proud as well.

The fact that he was going to war in a strange and exciting place called Vietnam, "in China or somewhere near China," pleased Garwood. He was seventeen. As a member of the Third Marine Division, he was among the first U.S. ground combat troops to be committed to Vietnam overtly, in early March 1965. He was told only that "there was some kind of skirmish, a police action or something, going on over there that involved the Marine Corps." He spent eight months in Okinawa cooling his heels along with five thousand other Marines while Washington made up its mind. There his talent for automobiles led to courses in supply, mechanics, and motor transport, and he ended up as a motor-vehicle operator. He loved everything about it. He said, "I thought that's where I belonged. I was very good at it and that's where

I wanted to stay throughout my tour—in motor-vehicle transport.''

Garwood loved being a Marine and he understood precisely what made a good one. He understood that along with the pride went a certain amount of rowdiness. ''What we called a good Marine,'' he would tell a U.S. congressional committee many years later, putting it in Marine Corps slang, ''is go out and whip butt and not get caught at it but still everyone had to know that you were as bad as you were supposed to be.'' A good Marine, he explained, would occasionally end up in a barroom brawl, but make it back to base safely. ''If that didn't happen once in a while, then you were a candy ass or a brownnose.'' Garwood made certain that he did not fall into that category. He accumulated a number of nonjudicial punishments (from his commanding officer) for speeding, being late for formation, and returning just slightly past the midnight curfew. In Garwood's case such minor infractions, which resulted in small fines, extra duty, and confinement, seemed almost like an unconscious attempt to keep from being promoted. He liked being a private, and shied away from any awards or promotions. Later he said that he was actually afraid of moving up in rank because he did not want the responsibility that came with it. That seemed to go along with the need he had for men to look up to. ''Actually,'' he said, ''I had to be very careful not to be accused of being a brownnose.''

In Forest-Gump style, Garwood went overboard on required assignments, a trait that got him into serious trouble near the end of his stay in Okinawa. Because of a series of oversights on the part of the noncommissioned officer in charge he was not relieved from one driving assignment. When he was not pulled off, he assumed that he was expected to continue driving until he dropped or the vehicle broke down. He just knew that he was not going to question orders. Seventy-two hours into the job he fell asleep at the wheel and crashed into a civilian bus. No one was injured except Garwood, who went through his windshield and sustained fairly serious head injuries, resulting in severe headaches and problems with his vision. He panicked. He did not want to be put out of the Corps or, worse, taken out of his military specialty.

When he got out of the hospital he was shocked to find that charges had been filed with a recommendation that he be court martialed for destroying the civilian bus, damaging government property, and totaling a Marine vehicle. He was scared to death.

His assigned counsel requested an audience before the commanding general to explain the circumstances of Garwood's accident. The commanding general dismissed the charges, noting that the fault lay with the NCO who had not relieved Garwood of his duties after a reasonable period of time. Despite Garwood's total vindication, the incident would have lifelong repercussions. Later, a slanted account of this incident, hinting that he had been guilty after all, was entered into his records and would be used against him.

When he reported back to his platoon at Camp Hague, they were on red alert to embark. Garwood's first sergeant called him in to tell him, that because they wanted to do more medical tests to insure he was medically fit, Garwood was to remain in Okinawa and be reassigned to Headquarters Company, Headquarters Battalion, Third Marine Division, at Camp Butler. It was a plum assignment but Garwood was unhappy to be separated from his friends. He missed their camaraderie.

Hoping he might be able to rejoin his old unit if he downplayed recent events, he said nothing about his medical record when, along with headquarters, he embarked for Vietnam. Through the circumstance of his accident he became part of the advance landing team sent to set up Third Marine Division headquarters in Da Nang, Vietnam.

In Vietnam he did bring up the subject of wanting to rejoin his old platoon with his new first sergeant. The sergeant just laughed. There was a shortage of drivers at headquarters. He told Garwood, "if you want to visit them, they're right next door. When you're not on duty, visit them as much as you want."

When Garwood arrived in Vietnam he fell immediately into the kind of safe and easy work most enlisted men only dream about. His first job was driving a six-wheeled, canvas-covered vehicle commonly known as a 6BY in all the military services. He fit in immediately, getting along well with the officers he chauffeured from the compound to the city of Da Nang and the nearby ridge of hills where several Marine companies were based. He had an overwhelming, understandable need to win approval. Those officers who frequented the bars and brothels of Da Nang found that Garwood would not only drive them at all hours of the night; he also had the right answers whenever they were stopped by military police.

His job insulated him from the civil war that was going on all around him, between the government of South Vietnam and the Vietcong (VC) guerrillas, who were supported by the communist government of North Vietnam. The Marines were in the center of I Corps Tactical Zone, the northernmost military region of South Vietnam. The South Vietnamese government controlled the cities; the VC controlled the countryside. Garwood, whose compound was outside the Da Nang air base, knew little about the hazards most of his fellow Marines faced. Their job was to protect the airfield against VC infiltrators and mortar attacks and defend the ridge of hills west of the field. They were severely limited by rules of engagement, which prevented them from shooting unless they were shot at and stipulated, among other things, that they had to broadcast their destination even when moving through territory known to be controlled by the VC. This meant the Marines were in constant danger of being ambushed or booby trapped. Across the Cau Do River, a mile south of Da Nang, the area was dominated by VC except for a thin ribbon along Highway 1, which stretched from the air base to Marble Mountain, a landmark about six miles away.

A few months before his tour of duty was due to end Bobby Garwood got what he thought was a lucky break when he landed a job as one of the drivers for Major General Lewis Walt. In June, Walt, the junior major general in the Corps, had taken over as commander of Marines in I Corps. Since almost all Marine combat units were based in this tactical zone, he effectively commanded Marines in Vietnam. The only Marines in Vietnam not under his command were embassy guards, advisers to the Vietnamese units, those on Military Assistance Command Vietnam (MACV) staff, and some with U.S. Aid for International Development.[1] Although Walt had begun his career as a commissioned officer, he had the leadership style of a "mustang." For that reason he was respected by most of the enlisted men. Garwood was on cloud nine.

The new job came as a result of a bad break, and the lucky consequences made Garwood think he was in good

---

[1] General Walt commanded a new Marine organization, the Third Marine Amphibious Force (III MAF), which replaced the older series of Expeditionary Forces. The name Expeditionary Force had unpleasant connotations for the Vietnamese because it sounded like the old French colonial Expeditionary Corps. III MAF was born in May 1965 when the Joint Chiefs of Staff relayed presidential approval for the deployment to Da Nang of a Marine force / division / wing headquarters to include commanding general Third Marine Division and First Marine AirWing. This was followed by the highly successful amphibious landing at Chu Lai, which included seven of the nine infantry battalions of the Third Marine Division, supported by most of the Twelfth Marines, the artillery regiment of the division, a large portion of the First Marine AirWing, and intelligence units. From May 7th to May 12, more than 10,925 tons of equipment and supplies were unloaded and moved across the beach at Chu Lai.

company at last. He had been assigned to the standard, once-a-year thirty days of temporary additional duty. This meant he had to deal with a pretty nasty bunch of local kids who kept trying to come over the wire patch into the base to steal, beg, harass, or perhaps worse. When the kids were thwarted, they threw stones. He thought he had devised a pretty clever way of driving them off, with pellets of clay fired from a sling-shot made from an old inner tube. Then, by mistake, he hit a Marine sergeant going by in a jeep. Garwood's temporary additional duty was immediately canceled; he lost rank for sixty days and was fined $1.98 per day, in addition to having his pay docked. His cushy job at the motor pool was gone as well, and he sat around unemployed most of the time except for the occasional tune-up job. Then everything seemed to go right again.

One of General Walt's drivers, a top-ranking sergeant E-5, went on emergency leave. That left Walt with only one driver, also an E-5, who was needed for high-security trips. An additional driver was required for lower echelon jobs like routine trips to the field to inspect new troops or equipment. There were no spare drivers around. Garwood, the simple private who was being punished for doing his job too well, got the assignment. Like all of Walt's drivers, he was officially assigned to G-2, the intelligence section. This was done for reasons of security. Walt's comings and goings were known to only a small group of G-2 officials. The job normally required at least two tours of duty and an impeccable record. Garwood was determined not to botch this one by becoming over-enthusiastic.

Driving the man in charge of Marines in Vietnam was akin to working for God. The perks were plentiful and General Walt was fair. He liked his men to have a good time. Garwood drove him to the parties Walt liked to throw for the guys at China Beach. There would be pigs roasted in discarded fifty-five-gallon fuel drums, and

iced-down beer filling the 6BYs. The General would strip
to the waist and swim and play volleyball with the rest
of them. What was most gratifying for a young Marine
of Garwood's background was that the respect Marines
had for the General rubbed off on his driver. When he
drove Walt and his ever-present aide to the Joint Command Center, accompanied by two jeeps—one in front
and one in back—he would wait outside the war room
and drink coffee with the sergeants. Often while running
errands for the General he was obliged to carry a brief-
case handcuffed to his wrist.

General Walt insisted on respect for the people who
worked for him. One day Garwood got dressed down by
a captain who spotted him waiting for Walt with his feet
on the dashboard and his jacket off, outside the Joint
Command Center. Immediately the captain yelled, "Marine, get out of that fucking jeep right now!" When Garwood obeyed, the captain demanded to know why he
didn't salute. Just at that moment Walt came back from
his meeting. He turned on the captain: "When you see
one of my drivers, you will give him due respect." Garwood also appreciated that later Walt attributed the captain's short fuse to his having just come back from the
battlefield. Then he reminded Garwood to uphold certain
standards as driver for the commander of I Corps. But
the General did not humiliate Garwood before others.

There was an easiness between the General and the
private that Garwood believed was due to Walt's having
never forgotten that he came up through the ranks. This
easiness allowed Garwood to feel comfortable in situations he would not have imagined being part of just a
year before. In the room adjoining the war room, for
example, he could catch glimpses of red points and blue
pins on the big situation map. He never actually saw C-
section, the most secret situation room, but he knew it
was lead lined. He felt that he was a small part of this
very important and highly secret side of the war effort.

He had come a long, long way from Indiana. Often, it seemed to him, the General would make on-the-spot decisions about the course of the war after conversing with Washington directly on the very specialized communications equipment hidden in the two staff cars that were always available for Walt. The bumpers actually functioned as antennae. Walt never discussed business with him, but Garwood had a good idea of what was going on, and there were conversations about the minutiae of the war—the small human elements and the personalities they encountered together. When the two were on the road, Walt wanted to know everything about Garwood. He was interested in his father, and especially in Garwood's reports of a newly reopened relationship with his mother.

That was another part of his life that was finally shaping up. After having spent most of his life separated from her through the bitter manipulations of his father, he was now corresponding with his mother regularly. He had been able to spend his last stateside leave with her in California, where she had also put him in touch with other members of her family. As a result he had been able to spend weekends with his uncle Carl Buchanan while he was training at Camp Pendleton. His mother gave Bobby confidence in what he was doing. She was proud of him and told him he followed in family tradition. Two of her brothers fought in Korea. One died in a Chinese prison. He also found out that she had been married before she married Jack Garwood. Her first husband, a pilot during World War II, was missing in action. There was only one worrisome note. She had a brain tumor and did not know if it was cancerous. But her doctors were optimistic that she would live at least long enough to see Bobby again after his tour of duty. Once when Walt heard about the mother, he asked if Garwood felt half Jewish. With the fervor of someone discovering that a whole new rich culture and religion belongs to him,

Garwood told him that under Jewish law he was fully Jewish.

Garwood sensed that Walt's questions were motivated by a need to know that he could depend on the people who worked for him. Walt, naturally, was fully aware of the dangerous environment he traveled in. Garwood, too, knew that in the event of an ambush, it was his job to defend the General, and he was fully prepared to do so but thought it unlikely to happen. On a more mundane level, Walt was a stickler for promptness. Garwood would say later, "If you were supposed to be there at five-thirty, you'd better make it five o'clock. If you didn't meet his specifications, you were out." Walt made it clear that Garwood did meet his specifications and this became a source of comfort and sustenance to Garwood in trying times ahead. For Garwood was to miss an appointment to report back to the General's headquarters by fourteen years. On September 28th, 1965, less than two weeks before he was due to go home, he vanished.

5: Man of War

In the early 1960s, as the United States sank deeper into Vietnam, Major Tom McKenncy realized that it was becoming exactly the kind of situation for which he had trained and had a special affinity. The United States was helping the democratic South Vietnamese from being taken over by the communist North. He did not care that many did not share his views. In a way he had been waiting for Vietnam all his life.

His abiding regret was that he had come late to the war in Korea. He had done a tour of duty right after high school, and then gone to the University of Kentucky. When the Korean War broke out at the end of his first semester, he was desperate to join up again, but could not break a promise made to his father that he would finish school first.

By the time he got back into the Marine Corps as a second lieutenant, the Korean cease-fire was already in effect. By August 1954, he was assigned rifle platoon leader of Third Platoon, H Company, on the front line of the Panmunjon Corridor in Korea. Some would dismiss service in Korea after the armistice as noncombat, but the fact was that the entire First Marine Division was still in an official combat zone.

When he returned home in 1955 McKenney was disillusioned. He believed politically inspired foolishness and the nonsense perpetrated by deskbound meddlers had effectively lost that war for the western allies. Hard-won victories had been thrown away at the negotiating table. "Desk types" would become his pet peeve. The only part of the war that had lived up to his sense of honor was the Marine Corps, and in his opinion, it was the Corps that saved South Korea. Forty-two Marines were awarded the Medal of Honor for valor—twenty-six of them posthumously. It was a particular point of pride for McKenney, and for every Marine he knew, that only one Marine in 570 was taken prisoner. The average for other U.S. servicemen was one in 150. Later a U.S. congressional investigation would single out Marine POWs for praise: "[Marines] did not succumb to the pressures exerted upon them by the communists and did not cooperate or collaborate with the enemy. For this they deserve greatest admiration and credit." Later, during the Vietnam War, when given the dirty task of hunting down POWs accused of collaborating, McKenney would be influenced by what was presented as Bobby Garwood's dishonoring of such a distinguished record.

McKenney went back on active duty in 1965, the same year Bobby Garwood arrived in Vietnam as part of the first contingent of shock troops. The war allowed McKenney to resume the active Marine Corps career he had given up seven years earlier.

For a short period after he had returned from Korea, he never expected to take off his uniform. He was one of fifteen hundred handpicked Marines to join Test Unit I, a special program directly under the command of the USMC commandant. Test Unit I's purpose was to bring the USMC into the nuclear age. It had been heady stuff for a young lieutenant, affording a unique opportunity to work with legendary Marines he had idolized since World War II. More important, Test Unit I introduced him to reconnaissance—a specialty that soon became his passion. Reconnaissance taught special skills in operating behind enemy lines and a sophisticated knowledge of clandestine service and weapons. He was sent to Special Forces School at Fort Bragg, North Carolina, graduating first in his class, and when he returned to Test Unit I he took command of Charlie Company, the only first lieutenant given that opportunity. (He had been automatically upgraded to first lieutenant in December 1954 after eighteen months of service.) Charlie Company was a laboratory for concepts that would change modern warfare: enlarged and relatively independent infantry battalions; the use of assault units where they were needed, instead of abreast in an unbroken line; and the helicopter assault. It foreshadowed the type of clandestine warfare that would be used in Vietnam and elsewhere.

When Test Unit I was disbanded in the summer of 1957, McKenney was convinced he had worked on future doctrine with the best and most enlightened Marines. These men were real leaders, who cared passionately about the enlisted men under them. This gave McKenney an unshakeable and stubborn confidence in the moral rightness of orders coming down the chain of command. He dismissed criticism that such dedication as he felt was peculiar to the Marine Corps and somewhat reminiscent of the fanaticism of the wartime Axis powers.

Like all other Test Unit I alumni, McKenney was promoted to captain and given a choice of assignments. He took command of the security detail at a nuclear weapons project at Fort Campbell, Kentucky. Despite the fact that the job gave him a security clearance of Q—higher than Top Secret—he found it boring and unchallenging. But the base was also the home of the Army's 101st Airborne Division. McKenney wanted airborne training and qualifications, and figured the Marine Corps could only gain by sending him to the Airborne school, something no Marine, to his knowledge, had ever tried before. He admired its toughness. You had to learn a lot in a hurry, and it was intensely physical.

When the Marine Corps finally agreed to pay for his training, he was elated. Not so the school instructors. He heard through the grapevine they were appalled that not just a Marine, but a captain, was trying to hog in on Army territory. Known to be "big, mean guys," they competed for the honor of making the Marine quit. It didn't help that McKenney, because of his rank, was the senior man in the class and troop commander every time they had a formation.

McKenney remembered that first day as one of the toughest of his life. Lining up for personal inspection, he thought he was well prepared. He knew Field Manual 22–5, the Army drill manual, by heart. He did *not* know that the 101st Airborne had its own "customized" drill routines. So when they fell out that morning, the very first thing he did was wrong. The instructor addressed him by his number, not his rank: "Get a gig, number one. You did that wrong." "Get a gig" meant punishment: jumping in the air, doing a layout into what's called the leaning rest or push-up position, landing on hands and boots, and doing ten or twenty push-ups— depending on the whim of the instructor. All this on gravel, which cut the hands and scarred the boots. This kind of punishment was called an "on the spot correction"—humiliating because it had to be carried out before the whole formation. There was something wrong with everything he did, and by the time he moved onto physical training, right after personal inspection, he had already done two hundred push-ups and was barely able to do the twenty more required. But he would be dammed if he quit. McKenney remembered: "For about two weeks they killed me. I mean they nearly killed me! But finally they realized I was not going to quit, and more important, I wasn't going to give them any back talk."

McKenney finished first in his class, a position usually

designated Honor Graduate. But not this time. This time number two was made Honor Graduate. A new title for Marine Corps Captain McKenney was invented: Outstanding Graduate. It hadn't been used before, and it hasn't been used since.

But that was the late 1950s—a sort of peacetime. A small number of U.S. covert units were already undertaking secret operations in Vietnam and elsewhere but they were largely Army and CIA controlled. The Marine Corps was facing political pressure to downsize. On the face of it there was no place for the kind of Marine McKenney wanted to be. When his tour of duty was up, he resigned from active duty but remained a very active reservist. He wanted to be prepared for the next overt war against communism—one he expected would take place in East Europe—so he attended Force Reconnaissance School at Coronado, California. Force Reconnaissance is the Marine Corps equivalent to the Navy Seal program.

At school he learned how to "recon" a beach for obstacles and mines, exit from a submarine, scuba dive, and other skills involved in launching an amphibious assault, as well as parachuting, marksmanship, survival, and self-defense. McKenney's wife Marty liked to say that Tom was never really out of the Marine Corps, even though he went back to school on a National Science Foundation scholarship in botany and zoology, and then taught at a branch of the University of South Carolina, all the while fulfilling his many reserve duties. In 1964, he was promoted to major. It was hard to tell which work took precedence.

He was offered one challenge that both interested him and seemed more in tune with the profession he loved more than teaching. The Central Intelligence Agency (CIA), learning of his outstanding record at Special Forces School and other special operations training, tried to recruit him. Special Forces was then under the jurisdiction of the CIA. He was tempted, because he believed that the caliber of the country's intelligence could win or lose the next war, but he declined. The style of the CIA and its agents did not appeal to him; they had none of the clear-cut virtues and code of behavior of the Marine Corps. This was his first brush with an organization that later seemed to rival the Corps in institutional priggishness. He had no idea then that despite never joining the Agency he would later carry out its secret policies without question, and unwittingly betray his deepest convictions.

When McKenney volunteered for Vietnam in 1968, even close friends were puzzled as to why, with a large and happy family, he would choose to go to war again. Marty McKenney, his wife, had only one answer when people asked her how she could let him do it, again, at this stage of their lives. "What else would one do?," she would say. Commitment and loyalty were bred in the bone. They never questioned that he should go.

McKenney arrived in Vietnam in September 1968. The Marine Corps had already suffered more casualties in what was then still considered just a conflict than in any war except World War II, but he felt that these sacrifices had made control over the critical northern boundary of South Vietnam possible. In January 1968 the war had escalated dramatically. In what was known as the Tet offensive, North Vietnamese regulars and VC guerrillas had launched a coordinated assault on every American base and village and town throughout South Vietnam. The ancient city of Hue fell into communist hands with the massacre of thousands of innocent Vietnamese. The Marine Corps' job was to retake Hue. They did so in twenty-six days of bloody, house-by-house fighting. Hue lay in ruins. Five thousand enemy soldiers were killed and three thousand Marines and soldiers of the allied

Army of the Republic of Vietnam (ARVN) were killed or wounded.

In McKenney's view, the North Vietnamese "shot their bolt" in pushing for the same kind of rout they had achieved against the French at Dienbienphu in 1954. Since then the enemy had remained in the jungles and rice fields, striking quickly at isolated enemy units, and then just as quickly pulling back to wait for their next opportunity. Tet was different. The People's Army of North Vietnam (NVA), numerically the fourth largest in the world, had come out into the open to launch all-out attacks with divisions and corps, mortars, artillery, and armed vehicles. The only problem was that the offensive was a military failure. What the NVA intended to be the Americans' Dienbienphu McKenney believed would prove to be their own Waterloo. The American media, on the other hand, presented Tet as a victory for the North Vietnamese. For this McKenney gave great credit to the communist propaganda machine. Twenty-five years later some North Vietnamese veteran generals would finally admit to their American counterparts that Tet was a military defeat; nevertheless, it provided decisive impetus to the antiwar movement in the United States, which saw it as evidence that America was making very little progress in its so-called war of attrition. In the fall of 1968, McKenney ignored the propaganda and felt certain that Tet was the beginning of the end for the Vietnamese communists—provided the U.S. used the right strategy, based on good intelligence. All of his instincts, honed by the reconnaissance training he had received, told him that this was where the Americans had thus far been deficient.

McKenney did not know yet that Vietnam had the largest CIA contingent in the world outside Washington; that it commanded huge resources, including several of its own airlines, hundreds of political experts, economists, linguists, and interrogators—even social scientists and psychiatrists. But in the months following Tet, as he prepared for Vietnam, he had puzzled over the fact that the CIA, whose task he did know was to anticipate enemy activities, had failed to pick up advance warnings of the imminent offensive. This he considered the most elementary and essential kind of intelligence during war.

The Marine Corps mission had been broadened considerably as a result of Tet. Much of the new strategy and many of the new goals would be cloaked in secrecy and carried out by men skilled in special operations and reconnaissance. It was his reason for being there. Looking down at the lush countryside from the commercial Boeing 707 that brought him to Vietnam, he had a hunch that the NVA and the VC, because of their huge losses during Tet, would soon revert to guerrilla tactics, which meant a replay of the terrorist campaign waged before the offensive.

Da Nang beneath him looked like a tourist poster, and this last leg of his Continental Airlines flight came complete with stewardesses and breakfast of heated Big Boy sandwiches, coffee, and terrible cookies. He seemed to be a customer of some cheap travel agency, with combat listed among the attractions. The undeclared war in Vietnam he supposed would be the fulfillment of his career, but in fact it would take him close to spiritual destruction. It would lead him far from the code of warfare he had admired when he was growing up. He would become obsessed with the betrayal of men who offered up their lives here. Eventually he would count himself among the betrayers.

McKenney kept a running account of all that he saw, did, and learned about the war and the country. Diaries, letters, and notes that were sometimes made in an improvised code, all these would become a way of reinforcing his memory. Events drew him into the most secret operations. It would be years before official documents were declassified that substantiated his own personal records.

On a midmorning in September 1968, Tom McKenney arrived at III MAF headquarters, which was situated in an old French compound in Da Nang East, between the Da Nang River and the South China Sea. He was tired, dirty, and bearded, but anxious to start work. He had not been told what his job would be. He reported to the adjutant major and while waiting to be given his assignment, he moved his seabag into a dirty room on the second floor of an open "sea hut," the acronym for Southeast Asia hut, or regulation quarters. There he was assaulted by the heat and fecal smells that hung in the heavy air. The sickly odor of diesel fumes adding to the fetid mix came from the landing craft tied up at the ramp just outside the compound at the edge of the river. He expected the usual long-winded processing through the bureaucratic rigamarole that was part of every military task he ever undertook, but he was slightly miffed that no one had come to interview him. He had been promised his choice of a reconnaissance assignment when he signed up for this tour of duty. Early in the afternoon, someone finally showed up and said he was to join G-2, the intelligence section. It had been moved since Bobby Garwood was there in 1965, from one pleasant old French colonial building to another that was, for McKenney, evocative of the antebellum South. When Garwood was assigned to G-2 as one of General Walt's drivers, it had still been part of the air base on the other side of Da Nang, just south of Red Beach. Later, McKenney would marvel at the twist of fate that set his own life and that of Garwood, his future prey, on such parallel trails. On the southwest side of the compound, where the river met a pathetic little village, children begged through the wire fencing. They no longer threw stones at Marines.

There were too many Americans now, and children had discovered they were a soft touch.

His specific job was order of battle officer for the southern provinces in I Corps, which made him responsible for identifying and knowing enemy units and leaders, and reporting their whereabouts. He would have access to information gleaned from the most secret surveillance activities conducted by the United States and was given a very high security clearance.[1] McKenney had access to C-section, the most secret situation room in G-2, located directly across from the office of the man who headed the unit, a full colonel known simply as the G-2. Here highly trained specialists in electronic surveillance eavesdropped on the enemy, often via spy planes, and communicated continuously with secret radar sites that guided U.S. bombers to their targets. The situation room was also at the receiving end of White House messages to generals and certain senior officers, through a communications system known as the backchannel net, which was free from tapping and interference.

As order of battle officer, McKenney went into C-section daily. He needed to monitor the visual display of enemy unit locations. These were in constant flux. This gave him an unusual perspective on the American operations in Vietnam. He realized with growing disbelief that the war was being fought from Washington. He had heard stories from his friends before coming to Vietnam that General Walt, who had commanded Marines in I

---

[1] McKenney's clearances in Vietnam included Top Secret, Q, Code Word/Signal Intelligence (Sig Int), and Military Assistance Command Special Operations Group (MACSOG). Clearances were related to job, not rank. Even a general would only have the clearances he needed. Most Marine generals would not have had the MACSOG clearance that McKenney had because they did not work with MACSOG. An enlisted cryptographer would have a "Crypto" clearance; a general would not. At the time there was probably not a general in I Corps with more, or more sensitive, clearances than McKenney.

Corps before McKenney's arrival, received on average three phone calls from the White House every day, instructing him on field decisions. The war, he began to understand with horror, was being politicized for domestic consumption. This often had disastrous consequences for the men.

McKenney's good friend Lieutenant Colonel Herbert J. Bain had been unlucky enough to fall victim to this political parochialism during the early days of the war, when Washington had decreed that U.S. soldiers could not fire their rifles unless they were fired upon first. Bain was a battalion commander when a shaky hospital corpsman volunteered to stand watch as rifleman in a defensive perimeter. When he accidentally fired his rifle, Walt's predecessor, Brigadier General Frederick J. Karch, on orders from Washington, ordered Bain to relieve the hospital corpsman's commander, a captain. Bain refused, saying, "He is a fine company commander, and relieving him will end his career as a Marine." Karch answered: "All right, Colonel, then I am relieving you." Bain was sent back to Okinawa to finish his tour. He appealed to General Wallace Greene, the commandant of the Marine Corps. Although he sensed Greene and other superiors respected the way he had stood up for the innocent captain, Bain was nevertheless stripped of his battalion command. It was the end of his military career.

McKenney saw how Washington made an almost daily mess of the war, causing countless casualties, because of such rigidity. He had always known that wars were begun for political reasons; but once entered into, he believed they should be prosecuted on military principles. Washington seemed divided on whether to push for victory or peace talks and on how to approach either goal.

The kind of high-level, long-range interference that was being seen in Vietnam would normally provoke him to discussing it with friends among the senior officers. But he was beginning to function in a world so secret, he locked everything he learned into a separate compartment of his brain. In this world the rules were so stringent that if he suffered a medical emergency, he could not even be anesthetized without supervision by appropriate intelligence personnel. The information he carried in his head could compromise the U.S. war effort, he was told, if squeezed out of him by the enemy. So he stored his frustrations deep in his subconscious, where they festered, waiting for an outlet. Within weeks he was given a means to act on what he believed was the most flagrant violation of the trust between men at war.

McKenney began receiving intelligence briefings on all activities going on in I Corps within weeks of his arrival, a good indication that he was on the fast track to the kind of reconnaissance job he really wanted. He was disappointed that his immediate boss, the G-2, seemed not to have a good handle on the job and had problems dealing with men under him. Nevertheless, McKenney met other men there whose quiet competence, integrity, and hard work reminded him of the men he had worked with in Test Unit I.

Major Stan Sydenham, his assistant and close confidante, was a West Point graduate and career officer. Sydenham was another victim of Washington's direct and unprecedented interference in the running of a war. He had only recently been transferred to the Marine Corps as punishment for a crime he did not commit. Sydenham had been second in command of an Army battalion that raised the ire of Brigade Commander George Patton III when it failed to clean up debris—used ammunition cases, ration boxes, etc.—while fighting its way through a Vietnam rubber plantation. Patton, the son of the famous WWII general, was hosting a high-ranking visitor from Washington. When they went out to observe the battle, the visitor noted that the battalion failed to clean up after itself. This apparently wounded Patton's pride and he vowed to get rid of the battalion commander. When that proved impossible, because the man had "connections," Patton zeroed in on Sydenham. In the military slang of the time, Sydenham was "shit canned." McKenney thought this might be the only time in all of military history that a commander kept his job while his second was relieved. What happened to Sydenham violated an ancient and sacred principle: that the commander, and the commander alone, is responsible for all that happens or fails to happen in his command. And besides, everyone knew that no one stopped to clean up a battlefield while the battle was still in progress.

McKenney considered Sydenham outstanding as a soldier and as a man. The Major became McKenney's right arm, and was to succeed him as order of battle officer. With the help of the efficiency reports McKenney later wrote for him, he would, against all odds because of the blot on his record, be promoted to lieutenant colonel the following year. At III MAF, the two worked closely together and were briefed on many classified matters simultaneously.

These briefings took place in the Marine counterintellingence (CI) office at III MAF, a narrow little room with several desks and a lot of padlocked file cabinets. "There was always an air of mystery about that place," Sydenham remembered. "There were usually several men who you never saw anywhere else." Like almost everything else in the special operations world, CI operations were known only to a few, namely the counterespionage, countersabotage, and countersubversion people who kept track of the enemy's spies and dirty tricks. It was dangerous business and they suffered many casualties, a fact not generally known at III MAF headquarters. One of their senior sergeants had just been killed during a CI hunt for VC guerrillas masquerading as South Vietnamese officials in towns and hamlets of the III MAF area. This kind of search-and-destroy mission was called an "infrastructure sweep." In this instance, it resulted in the death of a VC district chief as well as the American senior sergeant. McKenney was beginning to take an intense personal interest in the VC infrastructure, which functioned as a sinister shadow government throughout South Vietnam, terrorizing the local population. He believed it must be destroyed if South Vietnam was to have any chance at being a free country. It negated all the good work done by the Americans and the Republic of South Vietnam.

McKenney met regularly with the CI people to discuss the enemy situation and the rocket and mortar threat in the III MAF area. One particular briefing, however, about two weeks into his tour of duty, would take on special significance. It involved American turncoats. That morning McKenney was called in by two CI operatives. The senior officer, John Gunther, was a captain. Both men were mustangs, which made McKenney respect them immediately. They explained that they were passing on intelligence that had come from the CIA, in many instances verified by their own people, and that they had no doubts about its accuracy. What they described to McKenney was the worst perversion of loyalty and patriotism that he could ever have imagined: Americans who had deserted, or who had been captured and then turned, were actually operating with the enemy as advisers against American soldiers. The two CI men made it clear that there was an ongoing operation "to take care" of these traitors. Some had already been killed or otherwise neutralized. The pair showed McKenney a list of names.

One turncoat, they were certain, would be of special interest to McKenney, because he was a fellow Marine. His name was Robert Garwood. He was always referred to as Bobby. As McKenney remembers it, he was given a very general description of Garwood—Caucasian, medium build, muscular, light coloring. He was not shown a photograph. It did not occur to him that this description fit thousands of young Marines. Gunther was the Garwood case officer in the III MAF CI section. He said Garwood had deserted in 1965, and was operating as an adviser to the NVA in McKenney's area of responsibility. The style of the CI men was careful and restrained, but they projected an intensity of feeling with which McKenney empathized. Bobby Garwood, they told him bitterly, was the only U.S. Marine in history who had ever gone over to the enemy.

This briefing was McKenney's first official entry into the world of special operations, a world where everything was compartmentalized, all information was disseminated on a "need-to-know" basis only. Now he was learning a good deal more than he would need to know as order of battle officer. His special-operations training had taught him how the system worked. The fact that he was being filled in on this highly secret "elimination" program meant he would soon have some specific involvement with it. Much later, McKenney would admit that he had probably been given the names of other turncoats. But, because he was the only Marine, Bobby Garwood was the one he chose to remember—with a vengeance.

6: The Making of a Hunter-Killer

Despite Tom McKenney's contempt for the politicians who were running the war, his "the-tougher-it-gets,-it's-just-right-for-me-and-my-guys" attitude, combined with his talent for special operations, made him the perfect tool for their needs, particularly where stealth was concerned. Secrecy had long been regarded as a political necessity in Vietnam, given the nature of the enemy and the American public's likely unwillingness to support the war had they been fully informed. McKenney made it clear that he was totally committed to unorthodox ways of thwarting the enemy. It seemed the best way to frustrate their own knavish tricks. Now he was given an opportunity to prove his mettle. Within weeks of his arrival, he was recommended for promotion to lieutenant colonel by both the reserve and regular selection boards. The regular board's nomination was unusual for someone who had not been on active duty continuously for nine years. McKenney actually felt guilty about being promoted because regular classmates who did remain on active duty were being passed over.

However, nothing dampened his quiet euphoria over a new appointment as intelligence collections and operations officer for III MAF. It followed fast on the heels of his promotion. Finally, he could not only collect information but influence the action as well, particularly one aspect of it that was beginning to obsess him—the Marine who had turned on his own. His obsession had begun with the briefing on the turncoat problem. When the two CI officers told McKenney about the directive to assassinate these men—so highly classified it was never even put in writing—he knew this was the solution for Bobby Garwood. McKenney's job would include overseeing and tasking reconnaissance patrols.[1] McKenney was now acting with the authority of General Robert C. Cushman who, in June 1967, had replaced General Walt as commanding general at III MAF. Discretion was vital. There was never any interference from the commanding general's office.

He worked closely with the First Reconnaissance Battalion, the First Force Reconnaissance Company, and the Third Reconnaissance Battalion commanders. Perhaps because he was a trained Force Recon Marine, he was partial to First Force Recon, a smaller unit than the others that he considered to have the best teams and the best training. It was a kind of snobbery, but he was not above repeating what they said amongst themselves: "Marines look down on the other service branches; recon Marines look down on other Marines, and Force Recon Marines look down on other recon Marines."

First Force Recon Marines were highly skilled at a controversial kind of warfare that, like the turncoat elimination program, was so highly classified it was never put on paper. This warfare involved special hunter-killer operations, where teams, often with snipers, would be sent

---

[1] Tasking meant translating III MAF's overall intelligence goals into specific orders and passing these orders to the units involved. Each order normally contained sufficient detailed instructions to enable recon teams to accomplish their missions as smoothly and successfully as possible.

deep into enemy territory to assassinate selected targets—
initially senior communist officers and couriers, eventually ranking politicos—whose death would seriously
cripple the enemy's offensive capabilities. These kinds of
operations grew out of traditional combat patrols, which
hunted conventional targets of opportunity—vehicles, individuals, or groups in uniform that appeared without
warning in their area of patrol. The traditional patrols,
made up of a four-man reconnaissance team, were not
controversial, however, as the later hunter-killer teams
would be, when assassination of selected targets became
part of the work. In 1965, when McKenney's friend Sam
Owens, then a lieutenant, led some of the first hunter-
killer patrols, the concept was a radical one.[2]

The earlier, relatively noncontroversial operations had
come into their own in 1965, a critical time for III MAF,
hemmed in by strict rules of engagement and lack of
financial resources. By combining good intelligence with
small combat units, the traditional patrols dealt effectively with targets of opportunity, but with only four men
they were too small to search out and engage in combat
with the enemy. At the same time it was not economi-

---

[2] To men like McKenney and Owens these teams had a legendary
history. The precursors of the First Force Recon (hunter-killer) teams
were the Scout-Sniper platoons and the Raider Battalion (an elite group
that conducted commando raids) of World War II and Korea. Both were
under the control of military intelligence, not dissimilar to the way they
were being directed in Vietnam. Both the earlier, World War II units
and the new hunter-killer teams included reconnaissance as an essential
part of their work. The difference between World War II and Vietnam
was in the way these units were used. During World War II intelligence
gathering and direction for such units was under military control. In
Vietnam they were an asset that the CIA's Phoenix program could and
did use. McKenney was officially informed that the directive to assassinate Garwood came from the CIA. This did not mean that hunter-
killer teams were under the command of the CIA. Rather, they got their
orders from McKenney and other Marines like him, who transmitted
the directives they received from above and saw to the operative details
of each mission.

cally viable to have one team collect and report intelligence, when another, larger one was needed to follow up. The more practical solution was to run teams of eight to ten men. These could and often did expand to twelve men.

These expanded recon-combat patrols were at first under operational control of the Third Reconnaissance Battalion, the first Marine reconnaissance unit in Vietnam. By the time McKenney got to Vietnam, they were operationally independent of the battalion structure. Marine officers like McKenney received their orders from an alternative, "plausibly deniable" command structure made up of CIA and high-ranking politicos and military officers. Often CIA men operated in the guise of military officers. The patrols both hunted conventional targets of opportunity such as enemy units or individuals like snipers or couriers in their area of responsibility and assassinated selected individuals.

Hunter-killer patrols always worked closely with Fifth Special Forces and from 1965 to 1966 operated out of Special Forces camps. Unlike other special operations groups, Marine hunter-killer teams stayed together and functioned under one code name, which would change only if compromised. It was a cohesiveness that accounted for their success, or so the participants believed. They became very proficient, frequently getting kills when larger units returned empty handed. They were given superb endurance training. The emphasis was on total sensitivity and alertness to operational surroundings. Owens remembered later that when he was on patrol the hair on his skin would react to the slightest change in atmosphere. His vision became so focused, he could tell what an animal high up in a tree would do next by its slightest movements. Owens could sense with precision where the enemy was or had been in a certain jungle locality, no matter how carefully the tracks had been covered. McKenney thought it was part of Owens's genetic make-up, which was in good part Native American, but Owens maintained it was his Marine training along with his upbringing on a farm in Oklahoma, where money had been so tight that his ability to track a bee to its hive meant there would be something sweet to put on the dining table.

In 1965, Owens's targets generally were enemy soldiers or quasi-military forces working with the VC. This changed progressively, in response to the activities of the communist shadow government that controlled so much of the countryside in I Corps. By the fall of 1968, when McKenney became intelligence and operations officer, hunter-killer teams were already assassinating selected civilian and political targets—suspected of being VC sympathizers—outside the official frame of war, along with traditional military ones. It was the "selected targets" part of the operation that caused international controversy, even though it was common practice among all intelligence services, including those of America's allies. But allies kept these operations secret or presented a "plausible denial" if the public got wind of any of them. The British secret intelligence service, MI6, claimed it would never authorize assassinations. British spymasters held impromptu staff meetings to deny reports that an agent or a group had been licensed to kill. The message for public consumption, made by discreet leaks to select journalists, was that an intelligence service in a democracy would not license its agents to kill. This claim had nothing to do with scruples about summary justice and the dangers of executing innocents; the concern of MI6 was instead political. MI6 officers pointed to the United States as an awful example of how politicians could be provoked, by bad publicity, into placing impossible curbs on their own country's security services. In fact, British military intelligence had no scruples about killing subversives although it was a practical rule to take prisoners when vital information could be forced out of them.

As far as McKenney was concerned, American politicians had already placed impossible curbs on the war effort. He knew there were a lot of soldiers—even Marines—who thought it unfair to shoot someone who was not expecting it. It was something the CIA did, not what combat soldiers should do. For him it was a "dirty business, but you did what had to be done." Eighty percent of the fighting involved small units engaged in what General Walt, the retired commander of I Corps, described as "dangerous, tightly disciplined, meticulously planned activities, wearying and monotonous."[3] These activities were not and could not be revealed to the general public without injuring the most important part of the war effort. McKenney felt the American people would never understand or condone the need for soldiers to be involved in assassinations, because they did not know the whole story. Nor could they be told. Absolute secrecy was a must. But McKenney knew that hunter-killer teams always identified their targets very carefully. He would go quietly furious when he heard his men discussed in terms of "Murder, Inc." by those who had not the vaguest notion of what they were talking about. He remembered the men on hunter-killer teams as being "highly skilled, obedient to a strict code of honor." He knew of no better example than Marine Gunnery Sergeant Carlos (Gunny) Hathcock, a sniper who had been days away from the end of his tour of duty when he volunteered for a mission so dangerous the odds were ninety to one against his making it back.

With only his rifle, one canteen, and a K Bar knife, he had crawled at literally a snail's pace for thirty-five hours across open grassland, from the edge of a jungle where his team waited, to a Vietnamese compound near the Laotian border. He had not eaten or slept and drank water

---

[3] Lewis W. Walt, *Strange War, Strange Strategy: A General's Report on Vietnam.* New York: Funk and Wagnalls, 1970.

only rarely. He narrowly escaped NVA patrols guarding the area and came face to face with deadly bamboo vipers coiled in the grass. Stinging ants made his camouflaged body their home. The target had been a Vietnamese general whose assassination, right within his own headquarters, was meant to demoralize and throw his troops into confusion.

Miraculously, Hathcock succeeded in hitting the target's heart from a distance of eight hundred yards. To do this, he had to be hypersensitive to how the prevailing wind, sun, barometric pressure, and humidity affected the flight of the bullet. Calculating wind velocity required a quick and highly focused mind. All factors had to be finely tuned on a minute-by-minute basis. For this extraordinary mission of courage and self-sacrifice, Hathcock received a hero's welcome from the small band of men he worked with. That was all. No public recognition was possible. McKenney was determined that, at least on his watch, such men would not be betrayed.

In addition to the Marine units he worked with, McKenney was closely involved with most of the special operations groups organized under the Military Assistance Command Special Operations Group (MACSOG).[4]

---

[4] MACSOG was formally established in January 1964 as a Joint Unconventional Warfare Task Force assigned on paper to Military Assistance Command Vietnam (MACV). In reality, it was an independent organization that answered to a top-secret section of the Joint Chiefs of Staff. This section was headed by the special assistant for counterinsurgency and special activities. In its first year, this was USMC General Victor H. Krulak. Special operations group (SOG) missions were submitted seven days in advance to be considered by the secretaries of State and Defense and the National Security Council, which advised the president, although some latitude was given to SOG commanders in the early years of the war. The use of sophisticated satellite communications equipment allowed special operations units to maintain a rapid communications link with Washington. This became a severe disadvantage to the men on the ground because it was often used by President Johnson to cancel or modify upcoming missions whose ef-

These were units that "could not risk political oversight" and were highly classified. Among the most important to McKenney was Command and Control North (CCN), one of three centralized command posts[5] in different parts of the country of organized resistance activities—unconventional warfare, psychological operations, and other intelligence and operational activities. They were experts at hunter-killer operations. Their teams did the most long-range "over the fence" reconnaissance, in places like

---

fectiveness could by their very nature be appraised only by men who were on the spot. Few military commanders were allowed details on SOG operations but these activities were usually reported to MACV headquarters, which, however, had no authority to approve or veto them. As the war progressed and Washington became more confused and ambiguous about its support for unconventional warfare, an administrative vacuum seemed, to the men on the ground, to be created. This was progressively filled by the CIA, which already had an administrative "special" relationship with the Army's Special Forces and Command and Control outposts. SOG personnel were handpicked, crack U.S. special operations experts from all branches of the armed forces and civilian intelligence agencies who believed in fighting guerrillas with counterguerrilla warfare. It also included South Vietnamese Special Forces soldiers, ethnic Chinese-Vietnamese civilians, and other mercenaries. They engaged in missions against the entire NVA command structure and logistical network, but it was the territories directly across South Vietnamese borders that were of most interest to SOG reconnaissance teams. Cross-border operations were regularly conducted to disrupt the Vietcong, Khmer Rouge, Pathet Lao, and NVA in their own territories; keeping track of all missing Americans and conducting raids to assist and free them; training and dispatching agents into North Vietnam to run resistance movements; "black" psychological operations such as establishing false broadcasting stations inside North Vietnam; and the retrieval of sensitive allied documents and equipment lost or captured during combat with enemy forces. (Summarized from Harve Saal, *SOG: MACV Studies and Observation Group.* Volume 1: *Historical Evolution.* Ann Arbor: Edwards Brothers.)

---

[5] Command and Control North Was based at Da Nang, Command and Control Center (CCC) at Ban Me Thout, and Command and Control South (CCS) at Kontum. In addition to their reconnaissance teams, made up of U.S. and indigenous members, each had a battalion-sized indigenous force under American Command.

Laos or Cambodia. CCN had its own chain of command, back to MACSOG headquarters, on Pasteur Street in Saigon. The rest of the Army commands resented them as they resented most special operations units, not just in the way elite units were usually resented, but because they were independent of the tactical and area commanders. But McKenney liked working with them. As a Marine he was not involved in the Army's internal politics.

To him, the special ops people really were special in every way. They were all volunteers, wanting to be the best. They were self motivated, bright, resourceful, and unbelievably courageous. Getting in and out of enemy territory alone was a harrowing affair. Insertions were usually made by helicopter but not always. Those trained in parachute jumping and scuba diving, like Force Recon Marines,[6] often used that method. High-speed truck drop-offs were common in mountainous terrain. Some patrols swam to their destination; others went by foot—probably the most dangerous because it took the longest, and offered the enemy the most opportunities to discover them. All of this was done at night. After insertion in enemy territory, patrol leaders were on their own: every member of a team had to be able to take over the leader's job if he was killed or wounded. Every team member had to know how to control artillery and naval gunfire, call in airstrikes, and operate a radio.

After each mission, patrols returned to the command post for four days, before going out again. During this time they functioned as ordinary soldiers, working on perimeter security, local defensive patrols, and mine

---

[6] Force Recon units were single companies, intended for control by a force, i.e. III MAF. In Vietnam, III MAF gave up direct control of the Force Reconnaissance companies and attached them to the reconnaissance battalions. There was a reconnaissance battalion in each division, which was given the same number as the division, i.e. First Reconnaissance Battalion, First Marine Division. A battalion contained three or four companies.

sweeps. They were never really "off" except for five days of rest and recreation in thirteen months. They received no extra pay, no special thanks, and no medals. Outstanding courage and bravery did not help career advancement, either. The work they did was so highly classified that it usually could not even be written up on their "report cards." Because he continued to involve himself with the actual work of Marine recon patrols, and kept himself informed about the missions of all special ops groups he was in liaison with, McKenney never doubted the integrity of what they were doing. His standards were still those he had grown up with. "Yes, we were doing violent things," he remembered, "but they were controlled, limited, and precise. There was no torture, rape, no unnecessary killing." McKenney's interrogators were not allowed to slap prisoners. Often prisoners, taken by teams he worked with, laughed at their interrogators for being so soft on them. The Vietnamese people who worked with McKenney told him Americans didn't know how to get information from POWs. On the other hand, the enemy, as McKenney soon learned from personal experience, followed a policy of ruthlessness. If they were sent to kill a village headman, they also raped and murdered his wife and children while the rest of the village was forced to watch. Torture was routine for them because the objective was to terrorize the civilian population into cooperating with the communists.

It upset McKenney that his side took many casualties "simply because we were trying to avoid killing innocent civilians . . . who were often not very innocent. Our patrols were normally sent against selected targets like senior officers, couriers,[7] and ranking politicos. They were

---

[7] Couriers were a primary target. They often carried information about imminent attacks, prison camps where Americans were held, and U.S. tactics and planning that could seriously compromise American plans if they reached their destination.

never sent against ordinary citizens, children, or women. Only some were targeted to be killed,'' he said later. ''Many were targeted to be snatched for interrogation. Fed false information, these would then be allowed to escape.''

This restrained behavior did not characterize some of the South Vietnamese recon groups he worked with, however. The provincial reconnaissance units, commanded by ARVN officers with U.S. advisers under CIA control, and comprising Vietnamese, Nhung (Vietnamese of Chinese ancestry), and other mercenaries, did the bulk of the in-country dirty work. They also performed many necessary and courageous operations that could not have been done by Americans. But their tactics and cruelty often matched those of the VC. They were a vital part of the CIA's controversial Phoenix program. This covered the assassination of selected targets, including American deserters. McKenney was willing to carry out the full Phoenix agenda as he understood it: ''to identify the infrastructure, the shadow government of the communists in the south who were terrorizing the countryside, and neutralize [kill, kidnap, or intimidate] them.'' From the very beginning these goals presented no moral dilemma to him; neither did the fact that Marine recon patrols were part of Phoenix assets, if not primary ones.[8]

He saw no contradiction between his enthusiasm for the program and the generally low opinion he had of the CIA bureaucrats who conceived and ran it. He could not stand what he regarded as the mysterious affectations of the CIA men he came across, or their seemingly total

---

[8] Primary assets were the provincial Reconnaissance units, the Navy Special Operations Group (Seals), operating mostly in the far south (Mekong Delta), and the MACSOG patrols, operating out-of-country patrols in adjacent Laos, Cambodia, and North Vietnam, for the most part.

disregard for soldiers. In places where everyone else was in sweaty jungle dungarees, he could always recognize them in their tropical leisure suits, and with their special designer briefcases, and folding stock Swedish submachine guns—definitely not an item of field equipment for a combat soldier. He had little direct routine contact with them. Mostly, the CIA men dealt with counterintelligence officers who would then brief McKenney, as they had on the "deserter" problem. When CIA men did deal with McKenney, he found them arrogant and cocksure. He remembered one self-important operative who would bring reports that he considered "hot." McKenney would send a patrol to check out these reports, risking the lives of men and using scarce assets like helicopters. In one instance, the man in the leisure suit insisted that a "major arms cache" was hidden near a certain village, and demanded action. McKenney's patrol found three rusty and obsolete bolt-action rifle barrels, probably there since the French era. That was the closest to useful information the operative ever submitted, according to McKenney, who thanked him politely and thereafter filed his reports in the "maybe someday" category. Finally, the infuriated operative personally ran to the commanding general of the First Marine Division, O. R. Simpson, to complain that McKenney had ignored "vital intelligence" and requested that he be relieved. Simpson, familiar with McKenney's work, checked things out and simply told McKenney to keep up the good work. The bumptious young operative was on his way back to the States before he knew what hit him. To McKenney this was proof that no matter how amateurish some people or institutions were, the system worked.

McKenney reserved his real scorn for the CIA executives; the ones who made the decisions, but were never seen in the field and never put themselves in danger. Their kind of lifestyle and attitude was later conveyed unwittingly by William Colby, who was then deputy to the CIA station chief in Vietnam: "With the ultimate luxury of being able to call for a helicopter or fixed-wing aircraft to take me where I wanted to go, I could put in a full working Saturday at headquarters, leave in the late afternoon, have dinner and the evening with some province or district advisory team, examine local activities in the morning, and be brought back to Saigon by late afternoon for a swim and dinner, ready for work at headquarters on Monday morning—having happily missed the Saigon Saturday night festivities. . . . There were also shorter daytime visits to the area near Saigon or in the Delta, more carefully arranged field visits by various Washington officials, regional conferences of the provincial advisers attended by Saigon staff, and attendance at assemblies of the military officials."[9]

McKenney could sense the opinion held by men like Colby of the work he and his men were doing: "The American and Vietnamese military could, of course, and did sally forth at day break in search of the major communist units they hoped to find and destroy. Generally, the searches were fruitless."[10] The condescending dismissiveness became apparent early on, and engraved in McKenney's mind a deep dislike and distrust of men so detached from the dirty work they supervised.

And yet he could not see the irony of accepting intelligence and taking instruction on matters like the targeting of alleged military deserters from such men. Admittedly this came through the CI officers he respected. He was confusing the integrity of these messengers with the message they brought. Later he said it was also because he was so totally focused on his immediate special-operations community: really a separate little

[9] William Colby with James McCargar, *Lost Victory: A Firsthand Account of America's Sixteen-Year Involvement in Vietnam.* Chicago: Contemporary Books, 1986.

[10] Ibid.

world, doing things largely unknown to others, much of it not kosher, out-of-country, "we-don't-know-you-if-you're-caught" jobs. Outstanding Army officers moved back and forth between "normal" Special Forces units[11] and the much more secret and what some called the "dirty" groups of MACSOG. Recon Marines could be found working in both as well. McKenney got very emotional about these guys: he loved them. They were not always guys either. One of his very best "agents" was a gutsy little Vietnamese nun, Sister Mary. With her, McKenney did not really function in the normal sense of an agent handler because she came and went as she wished. She was self-motivated and a staunch anticommunist who would bring information on her own, which McKenney would have evaluated and then act on. Sister Mary was particularly effective in drawing his attention to those North Vietnamese or VC who were willing to help the Americans, but who did not want to deal with South Vietnamese intermediaries for fear of being betrayed.

McKenney could block moral questions about who was doing the targeting for Phoenix, or why, because the people who carried out the actual work, like Sister Mary, acted with integrity and honor. He had his own ways of finding out whether they were feeding false information or not. He went "beyond the call of duty" in these highly adventurous special operations. He hated headquarters and spent as much time as possible in the boonies, man-

---

[11] Perhaps the best explanation of what normal Special Forces activities should be has been given by Army Lieutenant General William P. Yarborough. He said such a force should "assist in the development of a resistance mechanism which can operate alone or which will supplement, complement, or precede military operations by uniformed conventional military forces, thus bringing to bear against an enemy aggressor the total physical, political, and psychological resources of a friendly state." (From Ian D. W. Sutherland, *Special Forces of the United States Army 1952/1982*. San Jose: R. James Bender Publishing.)

aging to operate "down-and-dirty," traveling all over the country, walking, flying, in patrol boats and landing craft. Whenever he could, he would participate in one of his pet projects—dropping sensors, called ADSIDs (air-dropped-seismic-intrusion devices), in enemy territory. They were in the shape of darts, weighted on the bottom to make them hit with the point down. The tops were plastic, molded in the shape of local plants found in the area where they were to be dropped. Stuck in the ground, they became part of the jungle vegetation. The shock of impact activated the sensor devices, which picked up any movement nearby, transmitting electronic signals back to Hill 327, the First Marine Division command post. Under McKenney's direction, this highly classified project deposited sensors across all the approaches vital to Da Nang. The mission reminded him of World War I flyers hand-dropping little bombs. He was on a sensor dropping mission in Elephant Valley when significant readings came into Hill 327, unrelated to his unauthorized presence. His companions were still merrily but blindly dropping sensors, unwittingly scattering them among NVA soldiers below. American artillery began to bombard the area as the sensor-droppers left. Later they drank to NVA soldiers who must have been going mad wondering how the Americans knew where they were, in heavy bush, at night.

McKenney irritated a lot of his superiors with all this personal involvement. They did not consider it appropriate for someone of his rank. He had strong support, however, from those in the field. Sam Owens an instructor at the Special Forces School at Fort Bragg more than ten years after McKenney was there, and who as a captain took command of the First Force Reconnaissance Company in the spring of 1969, said "Tom was simply doing aggressive staff work; taking *necessary* risks, getting information impossible to get through normal procedures." Owens felt that McKenney's behavior, which he admitted

sometimes bordered on recklessness, also made him a
more effective intelligence officer. "It was not in the category of craziness among the bad apples in various secret
units; thugs aspiring to be superthugs, glory seekers, and
lovers of violence." Owens knew that special ops, especially the dirtiest special ops, could sometimes create
weirdos. McKenney was slowly and subtly being drawn
into this manic neighborhood, far removed from ordinary
military morality. Assassination orders came from "outside," from institutions he did not respect, outflanking
the chain of command. It was becoming a world where
every ethically questionable action could be justified as
a necessary risk on patriotic grounds.

McKenney became obsessed with Garwood, but he was
very much aware that the issue of deserters went far beyond one Marine Corps traitor. Later he estimated there
were one hundred men on the CI list of targets—largely
in a different category from Bobby Garwood. Most were
"the dopers who didn't want any more combat and hid
out in the villages with whores, thinking they could just
stay high, and report back in when their tours were up
and go home." These men were generally rounded up
by the military police and taken to the brig. It was commonly said that some were killed. McKenney knew this
unreported killing to be a fact even though he had no
professional relationship with military police. He did
have a long-standing friendship, going all the way back
to Test Unit I days, with Lieutenant Colonel Bill Gorsky,
the military police battalion commander. Gorsky had to
conduct periodic sweeps in the villes,[12] searching for
these guys. "If they put up a fight,————." The sentence was never finished. Gorsky spoke of this with regret when he sat chatting with McKenney over a glass
of beer. McKenney, on the other hand, would never, not

---

[12] Slang for local villages or hamlets.

even in later years when other regrets almost overwhelmed him, feel sorry that these deserters had been eliminated.

The most sensitive category of target was the one Bobby Garwood fell into—the political defector. Without seeing any real evidence, McKenney held the belief, common in his small circle, that most of the men in this group were African Americans, convinced by communist propaganda that the United States was waging "a white man's war against their brothers." The presumption was that Caucasian defectors like Garwood had been ideologically radicalized by Vietnamese communist sympathizers to believe the U.S. was exploiting Vietnam and had simply "gone over" to work with the VC and/or NVA. They disappeared from their military units like the dopers. Then U.S. intelligence apparently tracked them into communist territory. Others were reported to have been taken prisoner and "turned." They might have been tortured and otherwise mistreated, but that did not change McKenney's harsh view. You did not turn against your own, particularly if you were a Marine. He remembered the superior record of Marine POWs in Korea and the tough, magnificent standard they had followed.[13]

The very idea of what Bobby Garwood did rankled him. Here was a man, the CI officers told him, who had not deserted from the battlefield, but from a very cushy

[13] A U.S. Senate report on the issue of prisoner of war conduct in Korea had stated: "The United States Marines Corps, the Turkish troops, and the Colombians as groups did not succumb to the pressures exerted upon them by the communists and did not collaborate with the enemy. For this they deserve the greatest admiration." One Marine, during that war, a colonel, former First Marine Air Wing chief of staff with an impeccable World War II record, did succumb. In 1954, a Court of Inquiry determined that he had made a confession only after he "had resisted to the limit of his ability." Nevertheless, Marine Corps standards were so tough, the Court also judged "his usefulness as a Marine officer had been seriously impaired." (From J. Robert Moskin, *The U.S. Marine Corps Story*. Boston: Little, Brown and Company, 1992.)

job in the motor pool. They claimed he had last been seen in the vicinity of a brothel. Some of his fellow Marines were reported as saying he frequented it. Other "evidence" accumulated by the fall of 1968, the CI officers told McKenney, included propaganda statements he had written, asking American Marines to follow his example and join the enemy. Garwood had been seen "leading NVA soldiers and personally turning his weapon against his own former fellow Marines." Added to all this injury was the insult that Garwood was the only Marine to have ever defected. The briefing McKenney got was sparse, as befitted the sensitivity of the subject, and the strict standard of giving out information on a "need-to-know" basis only. It left no room for challenge, allowed no questions about the sources, tolerated no doubts. And it was all McKenney needed to act. He decided, he said later, that "Bobby Garwood was a traitor, a blot on the honor of the nation and the Marine Corps; and that he was to be killed, not captured, and buried where he fell." This, McKenney felt, would protect Garwood's family and nation from shame.

Because he knew how explosive the scandal would be if even a whisper of the assassination of Americans by Americans reached the wrong ears, there would only be two entries concerning these targets in his daily journal. One, written soon after he got his promotion, read: "Recon team sighted a group of NVA/VC with a Caucasian traitor. Unfortunately they did not get him. May have been Bobby Garwood."

Most of those in the small world of special operations who were party to the kill-Garwood directive in 1968–69 did not know the precise origin of the assassination order. This seemed to be of no concern to them because of the "need-to-know" policy. Sam Owens, whose First Force Reconnaissance Company ran the greatest number of hunter-killer missions, said later, "It was just something that was understood." Men who were part of the actual hunter-killer teams would remember, long afterward, that they often thought privately the hunt for Garwood, as distinct from other targets, was initiated by the Marine Corps. Not so McKenney. It was his clear understanding, according to the information he got from counterintelligence, that direction in the Garwood case originated with the CIA and bypassed normal operational and administrative command channels, going to the special operations units who were to do the job[14] either directly or, as in his case, via counterintelligence. Outside the closed world of special operations, nothing was known about assassination programs. It was and continues to be McKenney's belief that even General Cushman, the commander of III MAF and his boss while he was there, was not aware of the assassination programs because "he didn't need to know."

But not all who were party to the directive on American deserters were briefed quite as discreetly as McKenney, or within the strict confines of a small CI office.

---

[14] The Central Intelligence Agency's connection with reconnaissance and special operations units, especially with Fifth Special Forces (Snake Eaters), has often been referred to as "an incestuous marriage." Until 1964, the CIA had run and funded all Special Forces programs. After the Bay of Pigs fiasco in 1961, military operations were officially turned over to the Army, but a complicated funding arrangement allowed Department of Defense monies to be transferred to the CIA so that various programs could operate under more flexible CIA rules. Intelligence gathering, McKenney's official job, was the only openly discussed connection between recon and special operations units and the CIA. In fact, these units, including Marine reconnaissance battalions, despite McKenney's argument that they were "organic" to the USMC, were assets of and took orders from the CIA—especially on the most controversial matters like targeting and assassinations. In 1966, Special Forces had rewritten its charter to place the director of CIA in its chain of command. Members of Fifth Special Forces Group were responsible to their own offices and nobody in the CIA except those at the very top had the authority to give any Green Beret or other military man any orders. It was McKenney's assumption that "the very top" is where the Garwood directive came from.

Army Captain Bobby G. Evans, an intelligence officer at
CCN, which was known to have close ties with the CIA,
independently confirmed SOG's obsession with hunting
traitors. Around the time McKenney received his briefing, photographs of three Marine deserters were shown
at a weekly military intelligence briefing for XXIV Army
Corps, General Joseph Stillwell Jr.'s command, which
was subordinate to III MAF. The briefing came from
"major headquarters" and was attended by Evans and
staff officers from the First and Third Marine Divisions,
but McKenney does not recall attending any meeting
where photos were shown. Asked if major headquarters
meant CIA, Evans steadfastly maintained that he could
not answer that. Some of his friends and fellow veterans
of Special Forces laughingly interjected that this was a
standard reply from those who were affiliated with the
Agency.

Evans's job was to make sure his recon teams had all
the intelligence they needed to work in their assigned
operational areas. For him, as for McKenney, there was
no question that the instructions regarding deserters came
from "major headquarters." They were to be treated "as
the enemy." Evans remembered that specific "kill orders" would have come not from him but from the intelligence operations officer, who had the CCN
equivalent to McKenney's new job. In CCN's case, there
was one such officer for every fifteen recon teams.

McKenney's new position gave him the authority to
translate the directive to treat deserters like the enemy
into specific kill orders. He quickly sent instructions to
First Force Recon Company that every patrol, in addition
to their other assignments, should look for Bobby Garwood and kill him if they found him. He began reading
each team's "after action" reports and studied every bit
of intelligence that might lead to Garwood's whereabouts.

McKenney's relationship with other special operations units was excellent, especially with CCN,[15] where Bobby Evans worked as intelligence officer, and with Fifth Special Forces, because he had graduated from their school and was well versed in their way of planning and operating. This made it easy for him to request that their patrols include the same kill-Garwood requirement as the Marine recon patrols. The requests were always made verbally. McKenney would say something like, "I'd appreciate it if you would. . . ." This was not a big deal, he said, because by the fall of 1968, there was already an understanding among all special operations groups that Garwood was to be eliminated. Some of the men who were aware of this, Evans included, thought Garwood had become the generic term for all traitors.

"There might be a real Garwood, but his name had become the symbol for all those who deserted to the enemy and were helping to terrorize American soldiers," said Evans. McKenney, on the other hand, was always totally convinced Garwood was a real person, not a symbol, and that he was the first and only Marine deserter. There were briefings of the kind Evans attended, where more than one Marine deserter was discussed, but by the time this information reached CI and then McKenney, whatever number there had been was amalgamated into one—Bobby Garwood. Evans and a number of hunter-killer team members remembered that African-American deserters were amalgamated in the same way, but more crudely. They were called Pepper. Evans and ten of the special ops team veterans recalled thinking of Bobby

---

[15] A special clearance was required for contact and cooperation with CCN or any SOG. Anyone who had worked with these groups was required to be debriefed by them before leaving Vietnam and was again sworn to secrecy. All CCN patrol reports came to McKenney daily while he was at III MAF. It is interesting that in CCN patrol reports, names were never used. Each team member was referred to by a number.

Garwood and one nameless "big black American" as Salt and Pepper. The scuttlebutt was that Salt and Pepper often worked together.

It was the understanding of other special operations groups that Garwood was of particular importance to the Marine Corps because he had been one of their own. Unlike McKenney, they knew there were other Marine Corps deserters—a fact that was presumed to be highly embarrassing to the proud Corps. They believed it was for this reason the kill-Garwood order was so important to men like McKenney. Evans, who had himself enlisted as a Marine during the Korean War, did not have McKenney's devotion to the Corps. He even had some sympathy for alleged deserters. He wasn't sure they had all gone over voluntarily: if they had deserted, it was probably because the enlisted Marine "was treated like a dog . . . nothing more than cannon fodder."

McKenney might have had great empathy for the "muddy, sweaty kids facing the target, nose to nose, using the knife," but in a way he was as far removed from what these soldiers went through as the CIA types he was so contemptuous of. Terrible memories would later seriously disturb those "kids" who killed fellow Americans without having been given any justification to do so because it was felt they did not "need to know" the reason.

One Special Forces veteran who had been a sniper remembered how he rationalized the orders "to off any white people you see" by thinking of them all as Russians. Because of this sniper's short height, he was often sent on missions dressed in Vietnamese camouflage—black pyjamas, skin and hair dyed—to ferret out VC guerrillas. He would kill them on his own, or call for the help of his teammates, hidden nearby, if he lost the element of surprise. He volunteered for Special Forces because he had idolized President Kennedy, who called the green beret worn by these men "a badge of courage, a symbol of excellence, and a mark of distinction in the fight for freedom.'' The sniper said later, ''I always thought I was lucky because I never saw any black Russians!''

But for others, the memories would become almost unbearable when, long after the war, some of those who made up the target lists for Phoenix would admit that a lot of Vietnamese were killed who shouldn't have been.[16] No one ever publicly admitted Americans had been targets.

McKenney, in the field, suffered from no doubts. Whatever criticism he had about the men who ran Phoenix, he never stopped trusting their decisions on targets. He was first and foremost a Marine; he trusted the system. He continued to believe his country was fighting this war for the best and most unselfish of reasons. He believed in the guilt of Bobby Garwood and terminal justice. He said later, ''We *had* to get him.''

---

[16] Former CIA agent Frank Snepp said, ''I was in charge of lists of targets. A lot of people who shouldn't have been hit, were hit . . . and it was a sin.'' (From the BBC program *Phoenix Rising*; also broadcast on the program *Witness to History*, CBC Canada, December 12, 1993.)

7: Tripping over Dimes

For Bobby Garwood, back in 1965, the downward spiral began when General Walt flew to a meeting at Phubai with Marine Major General Victor H. Krulak, the Pentagon's chief specialist on counterinsurgency, on September 28th. Normally, driving Walt on low-priority runs was Garwood's responsibility, and he was kept absolutely free of other assignments when the General might need him. Only if the General was traveling outside the Da Nang area was Garwood given other jobs by G-2.

On that day, after securing his twenty-four-hour trip ticket, which always remained with the G-2 staff vehicle he drove, Garwood made a courier run from the compound, on the west side of Da Nang, to the Combined Coordinating Center, on the eastern edge of the city: a five-mile trip across the river and through the city. Garwood enjoyed this kind of routine, which included having a sealed attaché case handcuffed to his left wrist. He had long ago changed the Timex he had purchased at the PX for a song from his left to his right arm so the steel cuffs would not scratch it.

After the courier assignment Garwood drove to the USO in Da Nang. He treated himself to lunch, but did not record this on his trip ticket because it was not some-

63

thing his dispatcher would approve of, but Garwood was now a "short timer" with only ten days left on his tour. He had what was widely recognized as the short-timer's attitude, living in anticipation of his return to the States, and already there mentally. He had begun turning in his military gear. His friend and fellow driver Billy Ray Conley, whose rack adjoined his at the motor pool, told him: "Garwood, you're so short, you're tripping over dimes." When he arrived back at G-2 the dispatcher at the motor pool agreed to let Garwood go finish cleaning his field equipment (782 gear), since there seemed to be no other jobs. The 782 gear, which consisted of cartridge belt, pack, canteen, first-aid pouch, bayonet, and helmet was already broken down and laid out on his bunk. He was about to clean his M14 rifle, which was also disassembled, but was then called back to G-2. A Marine captain, James E. Baier, was in a tearing hurry to get a driver. "I was in a real short-timer's mode," Garwood said later, "so I didn't jump to." Conley, who was hoping to get Garwood's duties after he went home, asked if there was any objection to his taking over the trip ticket. Garwood was delighted. The dispatcher, however, just wouldn't allow that kind of change in the middle of a twenty-four-hour trip ticket without good reason. Conley showed disgust. He was certain the dispatcher was a southern bigot who would "never give us blacks a break." Later Conley would say with a depth of feeling that came from discovering what could happen to American soldiers who went missing: "God looked out for me that day."[1]

When Garwood finally got back to G-2, after covering his gear and rifle parts with a blanket against the all-pervasive dust, he found the captain in a fury. Short timer or not, and even if Garwood did get permission from the

[1] From an affidavit by Billy Ray Conley in the files of attorney Vaughn Taylor, Taylor and Horbaly, Attorneys at Military Law, Jacksonville, North Carolina.

dispatcher, he had left his appointed place of duty. "You may not be as short as you think," the captain growled. Garwood might not only have his tour of duty extended, but he could end up in the brig. The captain pulled a holster with a .45 from a nearby hook, and tossed it to Garwood, along with a K Bar knife: "Do you know where Marble Mountain is?" Garwood nodded, anxious to escape further recriminations, and was relieved to be ordered to pick up a recon lieutenant who needed to go on emergency leave, take him to the airstrip, then return to G-2 section. The lieutenant was stationed at a First Force Reconnaissance base at the north end of China Beach, just south of Monkey Mountain. He would meet Garwood on the stretch of beach that separated Monkey Mountain from the larger and more visible Marble Mountain. Garwood only knew that Marble Mountain, which was at the south end of China Beach, was a landmark about six miles from headquarters, and that Charlie 13 was the road that led to it. That was all. Nevertheless he thought it prudent to say, "I'll find it, Sir." The captain countered, "You'd better." Garwood was too unnerved to point out that it was strictly against regulations for him to go on a run without his full gear, which included the rifle spread out on his bunk in different parts. He took the single .45, a weapon he had never had much success in firing on the range, and left.

Garwood was right to be jumpy about leaving without his full gear. He had no real idea what the captain's instructions would lead to once he left the main road, which was regularly traversed by Marines. Beyond was the unknown and possibly hostile territory around the beach. This early in the war, Marble Mountain still fell outside the perimeter of official Marine Corps responsibility. The fact that both the First Force Reconnaissance Company and Special Forces had recently set up bases there was not on the record. Marines were still divided into different groupings to cover three separate areas and generally moved between them only by sea and air, as overland communication was generally risky. The mission of the Marines was then precise and limited: to defend the American air bases in Vietnam and provide security within strict limitations. Although policy would soon change, Marines were not allowed to patrol beyond the defense areas around the air bases at Da Nang, Phu Bai, and the building site of the planned air base at Chu Lai, a thinly populated stretch of coast about forty-five miles south of Da Nang.[2] The United States was not officially at war. There was political sensitivity to the feelings of the South Vietnamese, many of whom, in the opinion of General Walt, at first regarded the arrival of Americans as a return of the French, who had conquered them by force. The defeat and expulsion of the French from Vietnam had been a source of enormous national pride, in the South no less than in the North. As a result, Americans went to great lengths to avoid any accusations of "neocolonialism." Their fighting men had to obey strict rules of engagement to avoid any appearance of behaving as just another imperialist power. This sacrificed good military sense for political expediency. Garwood could not, for example, fire on the enemy unless he was fired upon first. The enemy, on the other hand, was everywhere and in different guises. American soldiers in the field were taking casualties because so-called i.c.'s, or innocent civilians, were often enemy guerrillas.

Garwood, having had the good luck to land the job as one of General Walt's drivers, remained sheltered from the harsh realities other Marines faced. He had no idea that the beach in the Marble Mountain area was considered too dangerous to travel alone. In fact, the small group of reconnaissance Marines who were based at the foot of Monkey Mountain would have called this "milk run" almost suicidal. First Lieutenant Sam Owens, who

[2] Lewis W. Walt, *Strange War, Strange Strategy: A General's Report on Vietnam.* New York: Funk and Wagnalls, 1970.

would later work with Colonel McKenney and become his good friend, was a patrol leader of one of the two small platoons to which Garwood's intended cargo[3] belonged. Owens, an experienced officer who had come up through the ranks, knew the ins and outs of warfare behind enemy lines. To him this was real "Injun country," hostile to Americans, a place where any civilian you met could be VC. Cam Hai, the fishing village Garwood was approaching, was suspected of being 100 percent VC by Owens and those who reconnoitered the area with him. On October 28th, exactly one month later, they would have proof that Cam Hai was actually an armed camp, housing what amounted in numbers to a VC battalion. Backed by 60-mm mortar fire from the village the VC battalion attacked the newly built Marine Marble Mountain air facility and hospital still under construction, wiping out almost all its helicopters. Afterward they would retreat back to Cam Hai. The small bridge Garwood now crossed to get to his point of rendezvous had already been the object of VC sabotage when villagers floated explosives down the river to blow up the bridge. After the attack on the air facility a month later, Marines sweeping the village would find a network of long-completed tunnels. One of them led directly to the bridge.[4] If he had

---

[3] For security reasons Garwood's passengers were referred to as cargo. The rank of passengers was never mentioned.

[4] Cam Hai would never be pacified and the bridge would remain one of the most dangerous spots throughout the war. Navy Senior Chief Officer Avon G. Hale, who was in charge of maintaining the bridge and who served three tours of duty in Vietnam, from 1967 to 1972, said: "I was at Quang Tri, Dong Ha, Da Nang East, Chu Lai, Cam Duc, the Central Highlands, and in the Mekong Delta. . . . By far the most hostile enemy-controlled place was the village of Cam Hai. . . . In 1969 I maintained the Cam Hai Bridge. . . . In one period of three months . . . they blew the bridge up seven or eight times. . . . My men and I were fired on from the village with both small arms and antitank rocket fire, in daylight, trying to repair the bridge. . . . They blew it up,

been asked, Owens would not have advised that a lone driver be sent to pick up one of his men, although at the time he was working more on instinct and the general belief that even with an accompanying platoon for protection, it was a dangerous zone. The recon unit, unaware of the tunnels beneath its area of responsibility, was still in the process of setting up a small camp with makeshift bunkers and small tents, supposedly hidden from the prying eyes of the enemy by cunning camouflage. "It required someone with recon experience and knowledgeable discretion to pick up one of my men without alerting the enemy to the group's general whereabouts," Owens would say when finally asked, long after, and when it was too late to salvage Garwood's youth and middle years.

Garwood had neither experience nor discretion. He was in that euphoric state known only to soldiers who are days away from finishing up their tour and going home. He was in another world as he sat in his Mighty Mite by the beach where he guessed he had been instructed to go, waiting for the lieutenant and daydreaming about his imminent reunion with Mary Speer, his fiancée. He wondered idly what was holding up the lieutenant. In fact, Garwood had gone about half a mile past the rendezvous.

The view of a small ville was pleasant. Fishermen were mending their nets. Periodically he looked up at Marble Mountain. Its four hundred steps to the top and flanks were off limits to American soldiers. The Vietnamese insisted that it was the sacred site of an ancient temple inside a cave at the summit. The American command

---

and then shot at us while we tried to repair it. My company commander and two other men were killed there in daylight. . . . In September of 1965 Cam Hai was even more dangerous. . . . At least when we were there in '69 there were numerous U.S. units in the area. In 1965 there were none."

officially respected this position. Unofficially, Sam
Owens's small recon platoon had not only reconnoitered
the entire mountain but functioned as hunter-killer patrols
and, whenever necessary, engaged in warfare with the
enemy. The Special Forces camp, based at the other end
of the beach, was involved in similar activity. From their
reports the American command knew that the enemy, exploiting the special dispensation granted a sacred site,
might be using Marble Mountain as a base for spying on
the Americans and launching guerrilla attacks but they
had no idea that it had become an intensely fortified,
well-camouflaged military complex. It would be disclosed later that there was an enemy "hospital"
concealed within the limestone cave at the top, guarded
by statues of Buddha to deceive the "soft-hearted Americans." Even Owens's reconnaissance team had not discovered that inside the very top of Marble Mountain were
caverns that housed both a base of North Vietnamese
guerrilla operations and a fully equipped, if primitive,
casualty station, and even a chilly theater for surgical
operations. The natural fortress serviced Hanoi's fighters
in the South. Wounded VC and NVA soldiers were
brought in under cover of darkness. During daylight, nat
ural fissures in the walls of this cave offered an unob-
structed view of all American activities in the area.[5]

If the boasts of the Vietnamese twenty-three years later
were correct, then Garwood was being scrutinized from

---

[5] American intelligence apparently never became aware of the VC operation inside the top of Marble Mountain. By the late 1980s, the Vietnamese were showing the facility to journalists and tourists. One group
of visitors included the author's husband and Dana Delaney, the star
of the television series *China Beach*. She immediately realized how
vulnerable this observation tower had made American soldiers, and
became visibly sick. A former communist officer told his visitors that
it was "a stupid American policy to leave 'holy places' untouched. . . .
Of course we took advantage. War cannot be fought by handicapping
soldiers."

these secret observation posts as he left the compound and asked the sentries for instructions; as he crossed the bridge; and later, while he sat daydreaming on the beach below. His observers must have decided this was no ordinary grunt; that he had to have a connection with Sam Owens's reconnaissance unit, whose operations, although hidden and more difficult to track, were also known to the enemy. Garwood was driving the division commander's jeep with its specialized communications equipment, and they could see that he was carrying no soldier's rifle. If he was carrying only a small personal weapon, it was "proof" that he was an officer. Those who spied on him concluded they would have a "special prisoner," if they could snatch him. Those first impressions were to remain fixed in the minds of the communist Vietnamese.

Garwood assumed that the strange, silent group of men with antique looking weapons, who appeared out of nowhere and formed a half circle around his Mighty Mite, were South Vietnamese home guard. He greeted them. The answer was a stubborn, increasingly ominous silence. Then one of the younger figures in the group—a boy really—lifted his rifle. Garwood immediately revised his innocent assumption that these were friendlies. First he tried to escape by leaping out of the jeep onto the moist sand. The jump was not smooth. He banged his legs and torso lunging over the gear shift. Blocked by the men, he pulled out his pistol. In accordance with his instructions, it had a round in the chamber and was ready to fire. There was no time to aim so he shot, striking a young man in the face. The head exploded. He wounded another before his adversaries shot him in the right forearm and wrist. One bullet blew apart the face of his Timex and imbedded the watch in his wrist, leaving a lifelong scar. It seemed they had hit an artery, and he was covered with blood. His arm went numb. He could not pick up his gun. His legs buckled. He could no longer resist.

They stripped him down to his boxer shorts where he lay, and carefully went through his identification papers while an old man tried to question him in French. Garwood did not understand him, or the others who were speaking in Vietnamese. The trip ticket clearly confirmed their suspicions. He was on a job for G-2 intelligence section.

The next three weeks were a living hell. Garwood was herded from village to village, in and out of primitive wooden boats, through rice paddies and along slippery trails. He was trussed like a chicken for the pan. Blindfolded so that he had no idea where he was being taken, he guessed from the gradually more muted sounds of American airplanes taking off and landing that he was moving away from Da Nang. Soon he was being shown off as the American who finally got his comeuppance. People pinched him, stoned him, pulled his beard and body hair, and spat on him. Young boys prodded his genitals with bamboo sticks. The farther he was moved from Da Nang, the more abusive his tormentors became. They attacked him with rocks and knives and tried to poke sticks up his anus. His wounded arm received no care. It swelled to the size of his thigh and began to rot and stink. It was a relief when the blindfold was removed and he was pushed face down in a makeshift hootch, hogtied, and strung up to the rafters. He became convinced later that this torturous position had acted as a tourniquet in the days following his capture and had stopped him from bleeding to death. At least it allowed him to sleep fitfully, until children started pushing sticks up his anus again.

After a month of this, Garwood began to regain some alertness. Some instinct for survival taught him to take advantage of his status as a circus animal. He learned to wince at the right time to get the right reaction. This usually gave him a brief respite. He figured that his tormentors would be amused if he tried to sing, so he tried

out his limited repertory of American folksongs. It was
an act of defiance but his captors surprisingly liked it.
They especially liked "Tom Dooley." Everytime he sang
the words "poor boy, you're gonna die," he became
overwhelmed by feelings of helplessness. How could this
have happened to him? He should have been home by
now. And married. And therefore able, as he had carefully planned with Mary Speer, to resume his protective
big-brother role with Don, whose letters showed he was
very unhappy at home.

When Garwood's captors finally considered him docile
enough to be left with just one guard, he made an attempt
to escape. With his arms tied he slipped into a river while
his guard was sleeping. Walking through knee-deep mud
amongst the bullrushes, moving only at night, he bumped
headlong into a group of VC in a boat. On a second
attempt, he was caught by highly professional NVA soldiers, who kept him as they moved silently on remote
paths away from villages and headed toward the moun-
tains. His new home became a bamboo cage at Quang
Da, an NVA prison camp. By then, he was so sick with
malaria, dysentery, and what he suspected was gangrene
that he had given up caring whether he lived or died; he
just wanted to sleep. His captors brought him no medicines for his stinking, swollen arm.

As he moved in and out of a deathlike sleep, he was
pressed to sign a statement excoriating the United States
and asking his fellow soldiers to support the North Vietnamese. He signed when he thought he was close to death
and he wanted the Marine Corps and his family to know
what had happened to him. He figured no American
would believe he had willingly signed such a ludicrously
stilted and extreme communist propaganda statement.
Nor would Marines believe he had referred to them and
to himself as "soldiers." That was something no self-
respecting Marine would do. A Marine was a Marine, not
a soldier. But one result of his signature was that he

found himself dragged back from the brink. His captors began to take care of his injuries. That surprised him. He soon understood why. They wanted information from him.

The psychological and physical trauma Garwood was subjected to was later described by Dr. Emil Tanay, a psychiatrist who had experience in working with World War II German concentration camp victims. Tanay, who would play an important role in Garwood's future, described the kind of trauma Garwood endured at the hands of the VC as one that stripped him of all self-esteem and reduced him to an infantile stage. "Garwood, the prisoner, was completely helpless to do anything about his most elemental needs. He could not eat when he wanted to, go to the bathroom, or escape pain." According to Tanay, the majority of human beings, "when faced with such demoralizing circumstances, give up."[6]

Garwood was too unsophisticated to understand the psychology of what was being done to him. He felt guilty that he had somehow let down the Marine Corps because he had not followed the regulation that a prisoner of war cites only his name, rank, and serial number when taken prisoner. At his lowest point emotionally—which was not when he was closest to death and resigned to it, but when he came back to life and realized that he was completely helpless—his political "reeducation" began.

In Quang Da prison camp Garwood was introduced to the icy smooth Mr. Ho, who spoke flawless British English and began teaching him the "humanitarian policy toward prisoners" of the Vietnam National Front for Liberation. Mr. Ho did not reside at the camp, but came often enough to supervise Garwood's reeducation and to interrogate him. The sessions always took place with Mr. Ho sitting comfortably on a bamboo bench with a backrest, towering over Garwood, who was ordered to sit on a low bench that consisted of three poles strapped to-

---

[6] From the author's interview with Dr. Tanay.

gether. Garwood's chest came to the top of the table, a position that made him feel subservient. In Vietnamese society, as in most Asian societies, those considered lower in social status or in a subservient position are always required to place themselves physically lower than their "betters." The interrogator made it clear that he was always to be addressed as Mr. Ho. Garwood, on the other hand was called Bobby, even though Garwood had always stated his full name—Robert Russel Garwood—when asked. He fleetingly wondered how Mr. Ho knew that back at the Third Division he had been called only by his nickname, Bobby.

It was repeated to him that he had no rights as a prisoner of war or as a human being. He came from a country that had never declared war and yet was "fighting the Vietnamese people." Therefore, he was a criminal and would be treated like a burglar caught stealing in someone's house. If, in time, he learned to repent, he might be allowed to go home. Ho was very interested in Garwood's religious beliefs. Because Garwood was registered as a Methodist, he tried at first to make Ho believe he was a chaplain's assistant, hoping to confuse his interrogators.[7] He did not disclose that his mother was Jewish, or how much she meant to him. That remained in a quiet corner of his heart and offered him consolation when life became intolerable. Something he did not know but perhaps sensed was that the communists adjusted treatment of prisoners according to the precepts of their religion. Catholics were considered more obedient than those belonging to other denominations.[8]

---

[7] Reports that the Vietnamese boasted of having captured a chaplain's assistant reached the First Marine Division. *The Case of Pvt. Robert R. Garwood, USMC*, Final Report, Report to the Assistant Secretary of Defense for Command, Control, Communication and Intelligence (ASD / C³ 1), Volume 1, June 1993.

[8] From the author's interviews with Edna Hunter, who headed the Pen-

But what interested Ho most was Garwood's association with the Marine Corps' G-2 intelligence section. Garwood said nothing about the fact that he had been a driver for General Walt, the commander of Marines in Vietnam, but he wondered if this was something Ho also already knew. The interrogator often boasted that he knew the answers to questions asked; and therefore Bobby's answers would prove whether "he was progressive or unprogressive." Ho had the air of someone who saw himself in a kind of chess match with "them," which seemed to be American intelligence, with Bobby as a pawn.

Between sessions with Ho, Garwood's life continued to swing unpredictably between periods of relative calm and the most cruel psychological and physical torture. He spent more than a week sitting in his own excrement in a hole in the ground, in total silence except for brief periods when guards urinated and defecated on him, and taunted him that he would be buried alive.

He was made to watch while ARVN prisoners were tortured and executed. Garwood was told that he was being given an opportunity to watch the humane and generous policy of the North Vietnamese government toward those who had committed atrocious crimes against their own people. While their fellow ARVN POW's watched, two men were made to sit at a table, while two communist cadre guards stood behind them. Ho, in the role of judge, ordered Garwood to sit with him on the makeshift bleachers above the ARVN prisoners. He explained to him that the POWs were being given an opportunity to repent. If they refused this magnanimous offer, they would be executed. In other words, they were being given the choice of taking their own lives or being killed

---

tagon's POW unit. Hunter interviewed the majority of prisoners who returned from Vietnam, as well as other prisoners who were held in similar camps during the same period.

like dogs. When Garwood said he did not want to watch, Ho told him that it was only a lesson for the criminals. There would be no bullets in the guns.

Bobby watched as the first prisoner stoically lifted the gun he was handed to his temple and blew half of his head off. The second prisoner at the table began to weep silently, refusing the gun handed to him. One of the cadre, with mock gentleness reminiscent of a mother leading her child's hand to mouth, forced the crying man's hand around the gun, lifted it to his temple, forced his finger on the trigger, and pushed down. As the second prisoner's head blew apart Bobby was filled with a hatred so strong, it almost made his heart stop.

When his mother had told him stories about the Holocaust, he had not believed that whole groups of people would allow themselves to be arbitrarily executed without rising up. Now he understood. Some Jews had been like the ARVN POW's sitting below him, utterly helpless. He looked at Ho, who seemed to have forgotten him. The hard-core communist sat as if transfixed in an almost religious glow, his face flushed. The image made Garwood determined that somehow, if only out of spite, he would survive.

8: Handicapping Soldiers

Whenever Colonel McKenney could find the justification and the transportation, he spent time on the ground with the men who were doing the real work, from the Mai Lox Special Forces camp near Khe Sanh in the hostile extreme northwest, to isolated combined action platoons[1] near Hoi An and Chu Lai in the southeastern extreme of I Corps. Traveling by rat patrol,[2] or in borrowed jeeps, hitchhiking on helicopters or tiny observation planes and small landing craft, he did what the men who were fighting the war did. He knew what they faced   things that deskbound staff officers couldn't, and perhaps didn't want to know. He developed a particularly close relationship with Korean Marines who were serving

---

[1] A combined action platoon consisted of a Marine rifle squad led by a corporal or lance corporal and a platoon of Vietnamese Popular Forces. The Popular Forces were the most poorly trained and motivated of South Vietnam's troops. The Marine squads trained them, fought with them, and generally "stiffened" them. Each combined action platoon lived in a fortified hamlet, dug wells, and otherwise helped the locals by day and fought at night.

[2] Jeeps equipped with a mounted machine gun driven at top speed, back and forth along a designated road, to prevent mines from being laid.

in the Go Noi area. Once he went tunnel crawling through an underground passage the NVA had booby trapped and used as a latrine. Twenty-five years later, McKenney's Korean buddies would tell him that, at re-unions, they still laughed at the memory of him emerging from an enemy tunnel, covered in shit.

In other ways, too, McKenney learned very quickly that this was a very dirty war. The enemy's tactics were dishonorable. That was his view of a phantom enemy, hidden within a populace that was often hostile and a constant unknown quantity. Each community, each hut, could and often did conceal enemy soldiers. Women, children, and other civilians were mostly innocent, but could also be expected to booby trap or otherwise harass American soldiers. Often they were not committed to the enemy, but were terrorized into hostile action. He made it a point to concentrate on the many good Vietnamese allies like the Kit Carson scouts,[3] who worked side by side with Americans on the most difficult and dangerous missions. He also, in spite of himself, admired many of the rebel qualities of the enemy.

The VC, in particular, were excellent snipers, creating a perpetual sense of fear; anyone could be hit anywhere, anytime. McKenney, who was an expert marksman with both rifle and pistol, was reminded of Jack Hinson, one

---

[3] Kit Carson scouts were former VC or NVA soldiers working with the Marine Corps. They chose to work with the United States usually after spending some time in a POW camp or South Vietnamese rehabilitation center. These (usually) young men passed through a period of obser-vation, after which they were given a complete issue of equipment and an intensive period of Marine training. On completion, they were as-signed to Marine units like rifle companies. They received normal Ma-rine rations, medical care, etc. They were almost always assigned to Marine units in pairs to share their common language and help over-come any problems of adjustment. Their work was outstanding, General Walt said of them in his book, *Strange War, Strange Strategy: A General's Report on Vietnam*: "There is no way to count the number of American lives saved through Kit Carson scouts; we know only that none have been lost through them."

of his Confederate Civil War heroes, who single-handedly captured a gunboat loaded with soldiers as it navigated the Tennessee River. Hinson simply started to pick off the officers one by one. The Union captain, thinking he was surrounded and overwhelmed by the enemy, ran up the white flag. Much like the VC, Hinson was an unofficial rebel soldier. It wasn't until near the end of the Civil War that the Confederate bureaucracy decided to make him an Army captain.

In his respect for the VC, McKenney was like most recon men. It was a false but almost irreversible myth back home that American soldiers only referred to the VC as they were presumed to refer contemptuously to all Vietnamese, as Charlie or, worse, gooks. This was indeed common slang, but those who were actually involved in matching wits with them often showed their respect as well by referring to them as Sir Charles. McKenney also respected the NVA. "They are good soldiers," he said to anyone who was interested. He especially respected the fact that they always carried off their dead, no matter what the risk, and generally let the Americans do the same without attacking them.

But despite his respect for the enemy, he abhorred their cause and thought the best way to defeat them was on their own territory, with the kind of specialized warfare he had spent most of his professional life training for. He agreed with what President Kennedy had told West Pointers in June 1962: "This war by guerrillas, subversives, insurgents, assassins, war by ambush instead of by combat, by infiltration instead of aggression, seeking victory by eroding and engaging the enemy . . . requires . . . where we must encounter it . . . a whole new kind of strategy." It was also important to operate with the utmost restraint when dealing with the local population, to counter the massive and astonishingly successful North Vietnamese propaganda efforts that depicted the United States as an imperialist aggressor in Vietnam. McKenney was fully confident the majority of South Vietnamese peasants were being coerced into supporting the enemy by wily communists, with ruthless punishment for those observed to be supporting the South Vietnamese government and its American allies. The best strategy, he felt, was to ferret out the hidden enemy and neutralize him.

The most frustrating factor in accomplishing this, and the one that would finally lead him into what many considered morally questionable areas of secret warfare, was his own country's ambiguous position on the war. This had resulted in rules of engagement that seemed to have been written by the enemy, rules that had nothing to do with basic standards of warfare. He had no quarrel with the generally accepted Department of Defense policy that directives issued by "competent military authority" would "delineate the circumstances and limitations under which U.S. forces will initiate and / or continue combat engagement with other forces encountered."[4] He accepted traditional standards of warfare, and even that, for a time, U.S. soldiers were permitted to open fire only when they had been shot at first, but felt allowances were needed for legitimate accidents, as when the hospital corpsman under his friend Herb Bain had fired his rifle accidentally. Bain should not have been removed from command. McKenney was proud of the fact that, for the most part, Marines had behaved with admirable restraint in hostile and provocative situations.

What he could not accept were those rules of engagement established by Washington lawmakers to express their own uncertainties about the war or their opposition to it. There had been controversy about U.S. involvement in Vietnam going back to a period after World War II, when the French were receiving U.S. aid to defend colonialism in Indochina. In Washington, even now, there

---

[4] Joint Chiefs of Staff, *U.S. Department of Defense Dictionary of Military Terms*. New York: Arco Publishing, 1988.

were those who thought the 1964 Tonkin Gulf Resolution, which gave President Johnson war-making powers in Vietnam, was falsely based and wrongly applied. Some senators like Ernest Gruening, or J. William Fulbright, who chaired the powerful Senate Foreign Relations Committee, insisted it meant no expansion of the war. Since President Johnson assumed office upon Kennedy's death there had been several powerful groups engaged in policy decisions. These ranged from those in the Pentagon who wanted a full military defeat of the communists and administrative and bureaucratic intervention in South Vietnam, to those who were trying to work out the theory and practice of hurting but not destroying the North, to those who had never wanted combat troops in Vietnam at all and were trying to pull back on the U.S. commitment as rapidly as possible. They had struggled publicly with each other all year, since the communists launched the Tet offensive, on the future course of the war.

In March 1968 the chairman of the Joint Chiefs of Staff had requested an extra 207,000 men so that the United States could regain the initiative, lost through what was regarded as clever communist propaganda aimed at the American public. That proposal was almost immediately countered by Defense Secretary Clark Clifford, who opposed further escalation on the grounds that it would provoke "a domestic crisis of unprecedented proportions." A compromise was reached: twenty-two thousand more troops, with monthly review of the situation. In McKenney's mind such public argument in Washington, and the recall of America's supreme commander in Vietnam, General Westmoreland, helped the enemy psychologically and resulted in an unnecessary number of American casualties. It was as if medical directors kept stopping and restarting surgical operations by properly qualified doctors. More and more, field decisions were made in Washington because lawmakers set up rules of engagement that made it impossible for commanders to respond to the needs of the moment when they were in battle. The situation was exacerbated by the fact that the rules of engagement were classified so that men fighting the war had to simply accept the debilitating results without possibility of recourse. Those who had access to the actual rules could neither go to the press nor even try to influence Washington because it was illegal to discuss them. Not until 1985 did Senator Barry Goldwater force the Pentagon to declassify the rules of engagement for U.S. forces in Vietnam. Published in twenty-six pages of the Congressional Record, the rules were far more extensive than McKenney and his colleagues imagined.

At the beginning of the war, when Bobby Garwood first came to Vietnam, rules of engagement seemed an expression of excessive political anxiety. They made it mandatory to warn the Vietnamese people by leaflets or loudspeakers before American soldiers entered populated areas. This meant that the U.S. soldier on patrol was constantly exposed to the possibility of sudden ambush. That ambush would come from places where innocent people were living or congregating, and made defensive retaliation difficult. Consequently, the enemy's most common tactic was to use their own innocent countrymen as cover and often as unwilling participants. When McKenney got to Vietnam, the rules seemed to have become codified for certain areas. Marines could still not fire on Marble Mountain, but the enemy shot at passing Americans. Meanwhile, the Korean Marines, unencumbered by these restraints, accepted no casualties from places like Marble Mountain. If they took sniper fire, they simply responded with their own artillery. They were rarely sniped at. McKenney remembered his side took casualties daily.

Then there was the "McNamara Line," a barrier across the demilitarized zone that was supposed to stop

NVA infiltration into South Vietnam. To McKenney, and everyone he knew from private to general, such a totally irrational idea could only have been conceived by a desk-bound bureaucrat who had no idea of what was going on in Vietnam. Every soldier here knew the NVA did their infiltration down the Ho Chi Minh Trail, not across the DMZ. They also knew it cost sixteen dead Marines to clear and build each one hundred yards of the McNamara Line. It would never be finished. Twenty-two years after the American withdrawal from Vietnam, its sponsor and namesake, former Secretary of Defense Robert S. McNamara,[5] would reveal having adopted an antiwar position a year before McKenney arrived there, much too late for such disclosure to make any difference.

Self-defeating rules of engagement did not apply only in populated areas of South Vietnam. There one could make excuses for their existence. They also applied to fighting in the open fields or jungle, making a mockery of American soldiers who were expected to sacrifice their lives in a war that was, presumably, important to their country, but who could never go on the offensive. It may have been only a myth that LBJ had declared "they won't be able to bomb an outhouse without my order," but every soldier and Marine McKenney knew believed it: "It was policy," a friend of his who was a naval pilot said, "to send our pilots on bombing runs so predictable they were called milk runs. One after another was picked off by an enemy that simply stationed himself at the predictable place and time." Similarly, McKenney felt, any warwise American who looked at a situation map[6] of

---

[5] McNamara, often thought of as the architect of the Vietnam War, was appointed secretary of defense by Kennedy. He kept this post in the Johnson administration until November 1967, by which time he had become fully disillusioned with the war. He was replaced by Clark Clifford.

[6] A situation map shows the tactical or administrative situation of a territory at a particular time.

North Vietnam could see that there was only one all-important steel mill. It should have been a primary target. Nonetheless, any American pilot who bombed anywhere within a thirty-mile radius surrounding that factory was automatically subject to court martial. Why? He never found out.

McKenney shared the frustration of young men on the front line, those most directly endangered by these rules. One of them was Lieutenant Lewis Puller, the son of McKenney's friend and idol, General "Chesty" Puller. Puller Junior commanded a platoon in an area called the Riviera, at that time reputed to be the most heavily mined and booby-trapped area in the world. He wrote later that it was "viewed with dread by all but the insane among us."[7] McKenney said, "No one who had never operated there could possibly understand the danger and the courage required just to be there, let alone being there and facing the enemy." Yet Washington had required Lewis Puller, as it did all officers coming to Vietnam, to sign a promise to abide by these rules of engagement that, more often than not, amounted to suicide on a front like the Riviera. Lieutenant Puller thought it odd that warring countries would expect their troops to kill each other in a gentlemanly and humane manner and odder still that the Marine Corps would require its junior officers to undertake such an exercise in hypocrisy.[8] This had nothing to do with the general rules of conduct that apply to all wars, which he had learned from his father, internationally respected as a great warrior and man of integrity.

Unlike Puller, McKenney didn't blame the Marine Corps for hypocrisy. They didn't make the rules. He blamed the politicians in Washington, who seemed to

---

[7] Lewis B. Puller Jr., *Fortunate Son: The Healing of a Vietnam Vet.* New York: Grove Weidenfeld, 1991.

[8] Ibid.

have taken over that part of the job previously the responsibility of "competent military authority." The communists, as far as he could see, followed no code of conduct, traditional or otherwise. They were just hellbent on winning. Terrorism was part of their strategy. He thought of the American situation in Vietnam in the terms of thoroughbred horse racing. In major races for young horses, such as the Kentucky Derby, each horse was required to carry exactly the same weight, including the weight of the jockey and all the tack. If the jockey and his gear weighed less than a predetermined amount, lead was added to make up the exact difference. McKenney felt that this sense of fair play was what the rules of engagement should strive for.

What was happening instead, McKenney told confidantes like Stan Sydenham, was more akin to a handicap race, which involved older, more established horses. In a handicap, the horses with better records carried more weight. A committee of horseracing bureaucrats would decide how much weight a horse had to carry. Did this sound familiar? he asked his friends. In his mind, the racing bureaucrats represented the international diplomats and the politicians in Washington who had decided just how much the American soldier should be handicapped. Back in Kentucky, if the trainer / owner of a horse felt the weight assigned to his horse was too much for him, he withdrew the horse from the race. If he cared more about the money than he did about the horse, he allowed the horse to be overburdened, and the horse might die trying to win. That was happening to Marines, every day, with one big difference. In thoroughbred racing, a trainer or owner who would risk killing a horse this way was regarded as the worst kind of scoundrel. In politics, the same kind of villainy seemed to earn admiration rather than disgrace.

9: Making a Paper Tiger

Unbelievable as it was to him later in life, the briefing Colonel McKenney received on Private Garwood was his first and last. His confidence in the two CI officers who presented the case to him was so complete that he never once questioned the sparsity of evidence or their absolute certainty as to Garwood's guilt. Despite his contempt for the CIA generally, he did not second guess the sentence of death on Garwood and others passed by anonymous judges somewhere in the intelligence bureaucracy.

Such blind acceptance on intelligence matters was unusual for him. Normally, he prided himself on thoroughness, seeking out every clue and leaving no stone unturned. When the target was VC, he was coldly methodical, sensitive to the smallest nuance. A man's history was all important. More than once a VC double agent had been ferreted out by sifting through his known background and putting together bits and pieces that betrayed his real affiliation. McKenney made it a habit never to leave out anything. Yet on Garwood he excluded everything available to him, which he would come to regret, saying later: "I had a high security clearance. I could have tried to look into the specifics of Garwood's disappearance."

Had he done so, he would have been astounded at the number of investigations and reams of documents set in motion by the disappearance of Garwood, a private of the lowest rank, described in government records[1] as simply a motor-pool driver (Military Occupation Specialty 1531). During McKenney's tour of duty, the organizations involved in investigating Garwood included USMC counterintelligence, Fleet Marine Force / Pacific,[2] the FBI, and the CIA. Later the full resources of the Defense Intelligence Agency were brought to bear on the case, which remained open for more than twenty-five years.

By 1968 the effort to justify the kill-Garwood directive was becoming a small industry. Yet the voluminous secret documents that resulted from this activity were full of ambiguity and contradictory views. It took twenty-five years for even a small number of them to be declassified. When they were, it was immediately clear that from the very beginning mistakes made by Garwood's superiors, when they sent him to hostile territory unprepared and improperly armed, were never acknowledged. Neither was the fact that he was only days away from ending his tour of duty.

There was, however, one unchanging constant in all of the reports: an inclination to judge Garwood on the basis of his impoverished and emotionally deprived background. Where others of solid background were given the benefit of doubt, it seems never to have crossed the minds of military and intelligence analysts that Garwood not only might have had some strength of character, but might have found a way to beat what wiser heads decreed

---

[1] USMC Agent Report, November 16th, 1965.

[2] The Fleet Marine Force / Pacific (FMFPAC), based in Hawaii, consists of all combat and support units organized and trained to operate in amphibious assaults with the fleet in the Pacific. Excluded are embassy guards, recruit training centers, schools, supply depots, and Headquarters Marine Corps.

was a system that crushed the toughest resisters. The enemy found many ways to add fuel to the flame.

Most of the information about Garwood once he became a prisoner seemed to be orchestrated and fed to the Americans by the communists. But was it accurate? The USMC was unsure at the beginning. It waffled over Garwood's official status. Some, like his immediate superiors, insisted from the start that he had deserted. Yet they knew that in a matter of days, with his tour of duty over, he could have gone to North Vietnam to meet with the communist leadership, as some American celebrities, antiwar activists, and prominent writers did, without risking a death sentence. It was these officers who later played the strongest role in trying to get him convicted on grounds of desertion and treason. Others in the III MAF hierarchy grudgingly accepted that he was for some time a prisoner who then crossed over. The USMC POW screening board met regularly to determine whether Garwood's prisoner status should be changed to deserter. The majority voted yes, but there was always at least one voice that counseled that evidence of desertion was insufficient.[3] One dissenter wondered if Garwood's Jewish background told against him: anti-Semitism was not then as abhorred, or as openly discussed within the services, and the issue was dismissed as irrelevant. So Garwood was officially regarded as a prisoner of war until his court martial in 1980. ''Had I seen even a fraction of the ma-

---

[3] One example of this occurred in 1971 when the deputy director of personnel of the USMC argued, against the majority, that there was insufficient evidence to establish that Garwood had deserted. General O. R. Simpson, who was then director of personnel and who, therefore, passed on his deputy's recommendation that Garwood keep his status as POW to the commandant, later wrote that he could not remember doing so, but that it was highly likely. In a letter to the author he wrote: ''It would be logical, at the time, for me to recommend . . . that Garwood's status not be changed. . . . I thought long and hard before ever agreeing that anyone be classified as a deserter and thus, in time of war, a 'traitor.' It was an extremely serious situation.''

terial that existed on Garwood in '68 and '69, I might
have questioned the legitimacy of the directive that obsessed me,'' McKenney said twenty-five years after he
left Vietnam. The wrong fraction, however, might have
made him even more determined to see Garwood dead.

In 1968 the record would have told him that the furor
created by Garwood's failure to report for muster at 0730
on September 29th was out of all proportion to his lowly
rank. Such a level of activity was appropriate for a driver
for General Walt, the head of III MAF, but no one, including the CI operatives, ever officially acknowledged
that Garwood had this assignment. Throughout the many
investigations that followed his disappearance, Garwood
was described only as motor pool driver. Bits and pieces
of reports declassified almost thirty years later state that
''a thorough examination'' was conducted that included
interviews with Garwood's friends and acquaintances.

According to investigators, one group of acquaintances
stated that they had seen Garwood the evening of his
disappearance with another group of Marines at the Da
Nang Hotel or USO. They couldn't remember which. He
told them he wanted to make a skivvy run,[4] they said,
and would see them later, but he never showed up. This
report was taken seriously and permanently entered Garwood's record. But no reference was made to Billy Ray
Conley, who testified later that he had tried to take over
Garwood's trip ticket on the day of his disappearance and
that Garwood wanted him to. There was no reference to
Mary Speer, his fiancée, and the fact that he had been on
a high about going home, and had just written to his good
friend Ken Banholzer, also stationed in Vietnam, about
the double wedding they were planning to have in two
months. Speer, who was Garwood's high-school sweet-
heart, had moved from Indiana to California where Garwood and she planned to make a home with Garwood's

---

[4] Skivvy run was slang for going to a whorehouse.

younger brother Don. No one informed her that Garwood had gone missing. After weeks of hellish uncertainty she called Garwood's father to find out what happened. Jack Garwood could only tell her the little he had been told— Bobby Garwood was missing. Mary Speer had a nervous breakdown. She lost touch with Jack Garwood. Private John Geill, who was a tentmate of Garwood's and knew him well, was positive about where he last saw Garwood when interviewed the day after his disappearance: in their tent, when Garwood came in and told him he was going to meet a Marine captain at G-2 headquarters. However, Geill's testimony was not taken seriously or entered into the record because the captain in question, James E. Baier, the assistant chief, administrative officer, Third Marine Division, at the time of Garwood's disappearance, denied that he had told Garwood to report back to G-2.[5]

Baier's assertion would slant the thousands of documents on Garwood that followed. Garwood's commanding officer, Captain John A. Studds, determined that Garwood's absence from the compound was definitely unauthorized. This was a hastily formulated judgment that stayed on the record even after two South Vietnamese agents reported that the VC boasted of capturing a U.S. serviceman who got lost near China Beach. Radio Hanoi broadcast similar boasts. Some local people reported that they had witnessed a firefight between a U.S. soldier and a convoy of VC, after which the soldier had been taken prisoner. These reports were deemed "hearsay" by USMC investigators. Captain Baier, after denying that Garwood had an assignment at G-2, stated that anyway it would be impossible for Garwood to get lost "on the way to G-2 headquarters because it was only half a mile from his tent."

---

[5] Geill changed his story fourteen years later to match that of the other acquaintances who said they saw Garwood the evening of his disappearance about to go on a skivvy run.

The AWOL judgment automatically put Garwood's case under the jurisdiction of the criminal division of counterintelligence, where it stayed until fourteen years later, when the USMC would use it to charge him with desertion. The buzz that he had gone missing during a skivvy run or that he had been captured while visiting a brothel floated around III MAF until it became gospel. In the rumor mills of Da Nang, Bobby Garwood became one of those deserters who thought they could just wait out the time until their tour of duty was over; bad luck had somehow led to his being captured by the enemy. His close associates, like Conley, knew this made no sense as Garwood's tour of duty was virtually over. His superiors, who also knew that Garwood was practically a civilian, failed to note it in the records.

Despite its formally stated reservations about the theory that Garwood had been captured, the USMC launched search operations on an unheard-of scale. It included an aerial search enlisting the help of the ARVN military security services. No deserter ever prompted that kind of response. Although there was no acknowledgment that Garwood was one of General Walt's drivers, the General was personally briefed on Garwood's disappearance. Afterward, Walt himself sent a message informing the secretary of the Navy that Garwood was missing. The equivalent action during World War II might have been for General Patton to inform the secretary of war that one of his foot soldiers was missing. Despite this high level of involvement in the case, there were no leads on the missing man until two months later, when a Marine company found a VC document allegedly signed by Garwood.

Titled "A Fellow Soldier's Appeal," it asked U.S. soldiers to stop "terrorizing the Vietnamese people."[6] The

---

[6] *The Case of Pvt. Robert R. Garwood, USMC*, Final Report, Report to the Assistant Secretary of Defense for Command, Control, Communication and Intelligence (ASD/C^{3}1), Volume 1, June 1993.

USMC itself was not certain it came from Garwood: "The document's signature might well have been made by a rubber stamp and the use of the English language in the letter could lead one to believe that it was not written by a native speaker of English."[7] The other oddity was that some of the documents listed Garwood as being a chaplain's assistant, but there is no indication in available records that USMC investigators considered the possibility that this was a hidden message from Garwood that he was a prisoner, feeding his interrogators false information.

Formally Garwood was now given "presumed captured" status. But the Fellow Soldier's Appeal led to the opening of yet another counterintelligence investigation by none other than the commanding general of Fleet Marine Force/Pacific. The purpose of this investigation was to evaluate the document for "subversive content and authenticity." There was now concern that Garwood might have become "disaffected either by belief, ignorance, or persuasion." For this reason his service record book was reviewed again. Out of that review came perhaps the single most damaging judgment about Garwood, one that colored and shaped all that was to come. In a December 23rd letter to the Marine commandant, assistant chief of staff, G-2, Third Marine Division, J. J. Schutz, one of Garwood's superiors at III MAF, wrote, "Private Garwood's family, and his educational and disciplinary backgrounds demonstrated a possible susceptibility to propaganda and indoctrination efforts."[8] The result of this judgment, based on Garwood's assumed rather than real character, was almost a total, lifelong revocation of his constitutional rights and liberties as an American citizen, as a soldier, and as a prisoner of war. To add insult to injury, each abrogation of rights would

---

[7] Ibid.

[8] Ibid.

be carefully orchestrated by the U.S. government to give
the appearance of falling within the strict framework of
U.S. law.

Soon Garwood's status would change again. In January
1966, fourteen ARVN POWs were released from the
same camp where Garwood was held. They produced a
letter from Garwood to his mother written just a week
before their release. He had asked them to take it to U.S.
authorities.[9] The ARVN releasees informed the USMC
that Garwood was being held in Camp Khu along with
a Special Forces captain, William F. Eisenbraun. They
testified to the cruelty of the camp commandant and
guards. Daily life was brutally difficult, they reported.
The prisoners had suffered from diseases that resulted
from an unfamiliar and inadequate diet. Dysentery,
edema, skin fungus, and eczema were rampant. Many
died. The POWs were moved regularly to avoid detection
by American troops. The VC guards, they said, were particularly abusive to American POWs. For any minor in-
fraction, including conversation with other POWs, the
Americans were psychologically and physically tortured.
They were buried, held for days in a cage with no protection from insects, deprived of food and water, shack-
led, and beaten regularly. Those who resisted the most
were executed. Usually it was slow death by torture.
Hard-core resisters were never released. Garwood, the
ARVN releasees testified, was not excluded in any way
from the VC's brutality and deprivation. As a matter of
fact, only he, four other ARVN prisoners, and Captain
Eisenbraun had not been released with other prisoners
who, after extensive indoctrination, were set free by the
Vietnamese as a gesture of goodwill to celebrate the New
Year (Tet).

---

[9] The USMC acknowledges receiving the letter. Garwood's family says
his mother never received it.

As a result of this testimony an investigative team determined that *Garwood had not intended to defect*. Now he was officially classified as a prisoner of war. However, that information was never made available to the men who hunted him, like Colonel McKenney. The counterintelligence criminal investigation into the circumstances of his disappearance remained open. The investigative team was concerned about a communist press release and a number of Radio Hanoi broadcasts to American servicemen. These announced that "a U.S. Marine captured in a raid at Cam Hai had called on his mates to stop terrorizing the South Vietnamese people."

Fourteen months later another South Vietnamese releasee brought one set of Garwood's dog tags. Garwood had asked him to turn them in to U.S. authorities. He reported that he had been in the same prison camp with Garwood and Captain Eisenbraun. The former South Vietnamese POW had waited fourteen months to turn the dog tags over to the Americans because he knew that he was under VC surveillance and was afraid of retribution. It would occur to McKenney much later that the South Vietnamese reports were disregarded for the shameful reason that these released POWs were "natives."

In January 1968 Private Jose Ortiz-Rivera, U.S. Army, and Corporal Jose Agosto Santos, USMC, two American prisoners of Puerto Rican background, were released from communist captivity. Like all prisoners released during this time they were suspected of having collaborated with the enemy. During questioning by debriefers both reported that they had been imprisoned with Garwood and that their guards told them Garwood had "officially crossed over" to the enemy. They said they had personally seen him participate in a liberation ceremony in May. The two spoke almost no English but said their guards had communicated with them through Cuban advisers working with the North Vietnamese. Garwood, they said, had accepted a commission in the North Vietnamese army, taking the name Nguyen Chien Dau, freedom fighter.

This was given priority over the far more numerous accounts that gave a different picture but came from "non-American" sources: that is, the South Vietnamese. The FBI was called in by the Marines to analyze Garwood's signature on the captured Fellow Soldier's Appeal document, which was known to be a standard enemy propaganda sheet. In a letter to the Bureau referring to the testimony of Ortiz-Rivera and Agosto, they said information had been received by USMC headquarters that "indicated that Garwood apparently defected to the VC during May 1967. Since that date, there have been numerous reports in South Vietnam of a Caucasian assisting the VC in their propaganda and proselytizing programs."[10] From this point forward the investigative teams went on the assumption of Garwood's guilt even though his official status remained prisoner of war.

Contradictory reports about Garwood would become a pattern. Some returning American prisoners continued to claim that he was privileged and collaborated with the enemy. Ironically most of these witnesses were themselves under suspicion of having collaborated. Such testimony was reinforced by Radio Hanoi and a variety of double agents. On the other hand, South Vietnamese prisoners, with one exception, continued to testify that Garwood was a prisoner, like themselves, without special privileges. Later there were even high-ranking South Vietnamese officers who spent time in prison camps with Garwood and testified to his courage and good conduct. But USMC and U.S. intelligence investigators were influenced mostly by one set of documents that Garwood's South Vietnamese prisonmates had no access to. They had his service record, which outlined how he had hit a

---

[10] USMC/FBI correspondence of March 6–18, 1968. *The Case of Pvt. Robert R. Garwood, USMC*, Final Report, Appendix.

sergeant with a slingshot and had been charged in the Okinawa bus incident. And they had the sad history of his early life. Added to hearsay reports of his collaboration, his "official history" forever fixed his guilt with U.S. authorities.

When McKenney joined Phoenix in 1968, secret investigations into Garwood's activities were still being pursued vigorously. Every "live sighting" by Marines and other special operations teams and agents was added to the record. This was intelligence McKenney had access to and trusted, but he did not need it. As far as he was concerned the verdict had been made and the sentence passed when the CI officers briefed him. This was done according to rules that had little or nothing to do with the traditional American justice he had admired when he was growing up, but this did not bother him. Old loyalties were eclipsed by his idealization of the secret world of intelligence and special operations.

It never occurred to him that in his fanaticism he was becoming more like Ho Chi Minh than his childhood hero, Thomas Jefferson. The enemy, too, investigated and judged people secretly without giving them an opportunity to defend themselves. They passed sentence and executed men and women secretly—all justified by thousands of secret documents that were never subjected to proper and objective scrutiny or challenge. Had someone pointed that out to McKenney, he would would have answered that his goal was vastly different from that of the communists. He did not understand until much later that "that was just another way of expressing the communist creed he professed to abhor: 'the end justifies the means.' "

10: Promises to Keep

Colonel McKenney's growing conviction that his main task must be to seek out and destroy Garwood seems in retrospect to have resulted from his increasing frustration with a war so ludicrously labeled by Washington as "full scale but limited." He raged against it as "full scale for the enemy, but limited for the American soldier." The formula might save political skins back home, but it caused untold and unnecessary tragedies that he had to confront each day in Vietnam. There was an overall sense of helplessness, even among the youngest of the enlisted men, who felt that no one in authority seemed to know or care that they put their lives on the line without the freedom to fight this war properly. None of the political higher-ups gave any sign of really wanting to win in the old-fashioned way. Their restrictions were impracticable on shifting battlefields with no visible contours; the objectives were veiled in double-talk. That was also the view hardening in the Colonel's mind, causing some colleagues to wonder "if Tom is taking on the whole damn establishment as well as the enemy." When his recon patrols correctly estimated enemy strength in a given place and time, that information often didn't reach the men at the front who desperately needed it, or it came too late. Like smoke, it seemed to get lost in its ascension through the hierarchy. Too many officers in the rear, McKenney felt, cared only about the way information could be used to advance individual careers.

Somehow Garwood had become a metaphor for wholesale betrayal. He was one clearly indentifiable wrong that McKenney could right with the clean simplicity of a bullet. It was impossible to take aim at III MAF, which he saw in those days as "not a tactical headquarters at all, but a kind of emasculated administrative totem." XXIC Corps (a headquarters organized under III MAF to include the Army combat units in I Corps) looked to him to be responsive only to political struggles in Saigon and Washington, now being waged to the point of irresponsibility with the approach of the U.S. presidential election in November. These political battles offered no definable targets on which he could focus. They were mean, petty, and parochial. And they cost lives. Headquarters Saigon, in a stew over the constant pressure of rocket attacks that might signal a second big offensive like Tet, now launched yet another "study," completely ignoring an extensive survey just completed by the Eleventh Marines, who were taking the hits and knew what they were talking about. The new study, though, would look good back in Washington, besotted with numbers and factoids, and grasping for prior excuses and the kind of statistical justifications that reassure the bean-counters in a well-managed war.

Kham Duc Special Forces camp in the south had just been overrun, as McKenney and his men predicted. It could so easily have been saved. Even at the eleventh hour General Cushman, McKenney's superior, had wanted to send Marines to save the camp, or at least get the men out. He was not given permission. Nothing was more demoralizing to the men than being forbidden to help comrades in need. It was bad enough that they were never allowed to go on the offensive. Increasingly now, they were forbidden to defend themselves or their comrades even when, as in this case, it would have saved many from being killed or taken prisoner.

Now, another Special Forces camp at Thuong Duc was surrounded. The enemy held everything around the camp, including the villages. There were daily executions of local officials suspected of supporting the Americans. The uncertainly showed itself in the people. Half the Vietnamese McKenney encountered now were hostile, the others indifferent. He found the indifference more disturbing.

McKenney was fed up with the leadership within G-2, yet he had to work with it. Despite his promotion, and his authority to task recon patrols with highly sensitive and classified matters, he also had to perform other duties within the military and administrative hierarchy. On top secret matters, like the hunter-killer operations, he continued to function outside the chain of command. Routine intelligence matters were handled by the G-2 section and McKenney, as a lieutenant colonel, reported within the chain of command to the full colonel who was head of G-2. So did his men. Here lay the problem. McKenney prided himself on the character, discipline, and hard work of the officers under him. He could not abide it when they were treated badly.

By October 5th, he had almost had it. The G-2 seemed to be completely unpredictable, as if terrified of upsetting the people in Saigon. He had taken to sleeping in his office for fear of missing any message coming from his superiors, or failing to pass on to them crucial "intelligence." His critics said he was unable to distinguish between crucial intelligence and routine reports. When the chief was unsure, everyone was pulled out of bed to be interrogated. Daily routine reports in hand, he would repeatedly question the poor officer who had written them about their authenticity. Even if the answer seemed to satisfy him, he would, more likely than not, repeat the

same routine two hours later. It drove McKenney crazy.
With the continuous rocket attacks, his men were getting
only three or four hours of sleep a night, if they were
lucky. He noted, "I cannot learn what he expects of me
or what to expect of him. He has alienated everybody in
the section and we have tried so hard to help him. . . .
Over half the analysts have asked for transfers. . . . I
would gladly trade my brand new silver oak leaves for
PFC chevrons and a submachine gun. At least it would
be something I know how to do and I'd know exactly
what is expected of me. Our deputy G-2, Colonel Burroughs, is trying so hard to be loyal to him and help him,
but tonight in the midst of our latest midnight horror
show he [Burroughs] just threw up his hands, picked up
his pistol, and left in disgust." The G-2 was like a Supreme Court justice focusing single-mindedly on a parking ticket. His defenders said he was just another victim
of his own side's indecision.

There was a real possibility of a major attack out in
Elephant Valley that night. Three Marines and two
ARVN battalions were leaving the Special Forces camp
that was under siege at Thuong Duc the following morning. This would leave III MAF a little thin. Nevertheless,
an hour later, the men were summoned by the G-2 again.
McKenney staggered in. This time one of his most
trusted and competent men was on the carpet. Captain
Blake K. Thomas, a rifle company commander, had only
recently been sent to work with McKenney after being
badly traumatized in combat. He had been assigned to
G-2, partly because he needed to heal before going back
to the front. This had not in any way weakened his capabilities as an intelligence officer. Thomas was responsible for reporting on enemy activity in the area. His
judgment, probably because of his experience as a rifle
company commander, had so far been excellent. He had
worked almost all the previous night and had gotten, at
most, two hours of sleep. Now Thomas was being blasted

for reasons that nobody could fathom and his whole career was being jeopardized because the G-2 disliked the answers he was getting.

McKenney was appalled and said so in no uncertain terms. Afterward, Colonel Burroughs, the assistant G-2, gave him a fatherly reprimand for losing his temper. "Whatever the problem," he told McKenney, "in the Marine Corps you do not speak to full colonels in that way." Nonetheless, there were no nightly interrogations for the next little while.

McKenney tried hard not to let his feelings show to the enlisted men; but they knew, and it was demoralizing for them and for him. The Marine Corps was one of the few institutions left where leadership counted. It was expected that officers took charge and, more important, took responsibility. This provided raw young men who came from all over America with confidence to face and defeat the enemy. Time and again, McKenney would see how good officers, like Captain Thomas, evoked an almost disciplelike devotion from young soldiers, similar to the way he felt about Chesty Puller. They became the fathers and older brothers for the teenagers who had, just a few months before, lived the good American life. Now they were facing the toughest challenge a man can face, while friends back home were caught up in the World Series, which the Detroit Tigers would take from the St. Louis Cardinals in seven games.

Officers like Captain Thomas never abused their status. For them, as for McKenney, General Chesty Puller, the most highly decorated Marine in history, was the standard. Everyone knew that Puller had always put the enlisted men fighting at the front first. He had stood up to the highest ranking generals, when necessary, for those who spilled their blood.

This courage seemed to McKenney to be foreign to his seniors at III MAF. His diaries reflect his rising irascibility, even while coldly setting forth his professional activities: the record of a man pursuing his duties but unable to stomach an absence of logic. His seniors, he noted, found time "to go to some damn phony party over in the city with the CIA and the rest of the intelligence community." Hang the fact that a major offensive was in the offing. The Special Forces camp at Thuong Duc remained in trouble: a recon patrol had come back with information that an NVA general, native to the area, had suddenly appeared in the village next door. This information came on top of reports that any Americans who came near the village were being fired upon. It was a good indication the village would play an important part in the NVA's strategy to wipe out the camp. McKenney, in his stiff-necked way, just couldn't reconcile martinis with this looming threat.

He was in charge on a night when a fairly major decision had to be made. At least this gave him an opportunity to use a newly acquired skill. He had learned how to read NVA coordinates in the process of trying to decipher a captured message. He put this together with what he already knew about the recent spate of rocket and mortar attacks, and felt able to predict the enemy's next move. By daylight, the opposing forces had been outmaneuvered. McKenney wanted badly to go to church the next morning, a Sunday. Never terribly religious in the past, he found now that church gave his brain a rest from his professional frustrations. He put the thought of church out of mind. He could not spare the time.

McKenney later thanked God for once that he did not make it to church. Early Sunday, he learned that Lewis Puller, Chesty's son, had been badly wounded in a joint U.S-South Korean operation some thirty hours earlier. He rushed to the naval support hospital in Da Nang, where Lewis lay close to death. McKenney's last meeting with the Old Man, as most Marines affectionately called Puller Senior, flashed through his mind. At that time—it seemed long ago now—General Puller had been sick with worry, and looked vulnerable, almost fragile; his emotional state had been made all the more poignant by his erect and military posture. The Old Man had voiced fears then for his son. Lewis had just volunteered for Vietnam.

In college, Lewis had not been enthusiastic about following his father in a military career and had asked McKenney's advice. Sympathetic, McKenney told him to volunteer and get his service over with. But then Lewis had asked for the toughest assignment in the war, that of combat platoon leader. "No shit-bird job behind the supply lines for the son of a Marine legend," was the boy's attitude. General Puller had been very proud, but fearful. He had some premonition of disaster. Later in Vietnam, McKenney often thought that even though the Old Man put himself in the most dangerous spots throughout his career, the father could not have envisioned the kind of dangerous job the son had taken on. It was a job that had to be done virtually in handcuffs. For the past three months, Lieutenant Puller had led his platoon on regular patrols in the Riviera. A place of sands, bamboo, tall grass, and marshes along the South China Sea, Lewis's tactical area of responsibility was a free-for-all hunting ground, infested by enemy grenades and mortar rounds with trip wires, booby-trapped artillery shells, and secretly armed farmers. It hardly seemed possible, but since the beginning of the August offensive, the VC had stepped up their level of activity there. Enemy snipers were everywhere and McKenney had come across numerous reports of five-hundred-pound bombs set in foot traps.

Lewis had stepped on a booby-trapped howitzer round. It threw him high in the air and literally vaporized a good portion of his body. McKenney arrived at the hospital in the midst of a tropical storm. The senior medical officers explained Lewis's condition and took him to see the patient in the shock research unit with heavy rain thundering on the tin roof and fierce lightning outside the gale-rattled windows. He thought he knew what to expect, but the horror of actually seeing what had been done to the Old Man's son nearly choked him. Lewis looked so pathetically small, his right leg completely gone, the left leg off above midthigh. Parts of both hands were gone too. What was left was burned up to his elbow. In the shock of the first few seconds, McKenney thought he was dead. Then he saw that the color was fairly good. Lewis looked like a broken up little doll, the stump of his trunk and his arms in bloody dressings. The room was drab and water plonked from the ceiling into buckets and bowls. Wordless, McKenney was grateful that Puller remained asleep.

It was unreasonable, he knew, but he felt that he and all the officers here had failed the old General by letting this happen to his son. He knew if Lewis died, his father would not be able to survive it. The Riviera was a mincing machine. It could have and should have been destroyed long ago. McKenney had "incredible intelligence" on the place, particularly on the leprosarium there, which was run by an American VC sympathizer known only as Smith. Because he was a civilian he could not be targeted by hunter-killer teams. By calling it a mission for the sanctuary of lepers, who were treated in Vietnam as outcasts, Smith was able to provide a secret staging area and supply point for the VC. Lewis, like almost every American patrol going in and out of the Riviera, had to traverse a dangerous passageway past snipers who would lie in wait at the leprosarium. The patrols were also betrayed by Smith's spies, who would alert other VC units in the Riviera to their presence. Yet, because of its official "neutral" status, American soldiers never were allowed to answer fire coming from the sanatorium.

October 11th, the day Lewis Puller had half his body blown away, marked the beginning of an ambitious operation to clean up another one of the Riviera's major trouble spots. This was only possible because it was being done jointly with South Korean allies, who were free of the political constraints that handicapped American soldiers. At the southernmost edge of what had been Lewis's tactical area of responsibility was a small village called Viem Dong, controlled by the VC. In the past month, U.S. patrols had taken increasing amounts of hostile fire from it without being able to fire back. Lewis had been part of a joint "cordon and search mission." His platoon was to form a cordon around the village along with other U.S. units. The Koreans would sweep through the village and drive the unsuspecting enemy into the Marines' field of fire. Because of the known toughness—some called it brutality—of the South Koreans, Lewis had figured that the village of Viem Dong would not be likely to play host to the VC in the future.

Lewis had been delighted to go on the offensive, for once, and everything went smoothly at the beginning. Lewis had just gotten his men on line, as part of the cordon, when a squad of green-uniformed NVA soldiers began running out of the village directly in Lewis's path. As he began to fire at them, his M16 automatic rifle malfunctioned, a common experience then for Americans in combat. Weaponless, he headed for company headquarters where the NVA's firepower could be returned by Marines. Then he stepped on the booby-trapped howitzer shell.[1]

When they amputated his destroyed right leg, the corpsman who was working on Lewis asked his father's name. He replied, "Puller." The corpsman then asked, "What does he do?" Lewis answered, "He's a general." The corpsman said, "Army or Marine?" Lewis, a little peeved, answered, "Marine, of course." Tears ran down

[1] Lewis B. Puller Jr., *Fortunate Son: The Healing of a Vietnam Vet.* New York: Grove Weidenfeld, 1991.

McKenney's face when he recalled this: "Lewis had more guts than the law allowed."

Lewis Puller would survive after months of uncertainty, but the psychic scars that accompanied his drastic amputations would take a lifelong toll. McKenney spent most of the first few critical days at his bedside and reporting on his progress to his parents and wife, who was seven months pregnant. Communication from the Marine Corps was terrible and fraught with constrictions. The Pullers had first heard of Lewis's wounding on the CBS news. McKenney had no compunction about breaking the rules here. He used the Military Automated Radio Calls, off limits for casualty calls, to get in touch with Marty, his wife, who would then call the family with frequent reports. This was possible because McKenney had excellent subordinates like Stan Sydenham who were able to carry on for him. And he had the personal blessing of his good friend General Rathvon McC. Tompkins, who was also close to the Pullers.

There was little else McKenney could do. He took out his anger on a young doctor who took pictures of Lewis's wounds from the moment he arrived at the hospital. The doctor's colleagues reported he planned to use the photographs in antiwar lectures after he returned to the States. McKenney had the pictures confiscated. He simply could not understand what he considered the moral treachery of Americans like the doctor, or the active treachery of the man called Smith, who ran the leprosarium as an armed camp against his own country's soldiers.

The Puller tragedy toughened McKenney's resolve to hunt down American traitors who fell under his jurisdiction, like Bobby Garwood, and to do something about cleaning up the Riviera. Neither task had anything to do with honorable warfare, yet they seemed to represent the real killer in Vietnam—this treacherous ambivalence and uncertainty.

In the fall of 1968 more than 50 percent of all casualties in I Corps were from mines and booby traps. The statistics became an effective enemy weapon too. They hurt morale among those pitting themselves against phantoms. A young Marine lieutenant like Lewis Puller had a sixty-day life expectancy. "The booby-trap problem was talked to death, but no one did anything about it, least of all the staff officers safe behind their desks theorizing about nonexistent booby-trap factories," noted McKenney. Any fool knew the materials for making booby traps could be found everywhere: a grenade or a chip of TNT, simple wire, and simple fuse. The enemy was teaching children how to set them. It was a problem that needed to be studied by someone with experience, willing to spend time with the rifle platoons where most of the injuries occurred. Some platoons had very low booby-trap casualty rates. Others, fighting in similar locales, had very high rates. The Korean Marines working the same territory had no casualties. Since nobody in the rear appeared to be bothered, or haunted by the nightmare memory of Lewis Puller's smashed body, McKenney systematically assembled data on all forms of enemy traps. He thought his experience as rifle platoon leader in Korea, though dated, might be something to start with. He had no official approval at the beginning. He knew that the deputy commander at III MAF, General Tompkins, was a great personal leader who built confidence by regularly visiting each of his rifle squads in the field, so later he got Tompkins's approval for the task.[2]

---

[2] McKenney was to discover that the booby-trap problem was created largely by Marines themselves. Almost 90 percent of the booby traps were made with grenades left behind by men on patrol. Unlike their allies, the Korean Marines, American boys had a tendency to be untidy and to leave things behind, such as the grenades with which they had built their defensive perimeters. Considering that each man used five or six grenades in front of the foxholes he dug on almost daily patrols, the amount of booby-trap ammunition made available to the enemy was sizable. Wise to the untidy habits of the Americans, the commun-

None of his seniors knew that less than two weeks after Lewis Puller was wounded, Colonel McKenney began joining the rifle patrols as an "overpaid rifleman." This was not appropriate for someone of his rank. He only got away with it because everyone assumed he was visiting the battalion compounds when he went on his "field studies." He did not disabuse them of the notion. Neither did he write home about it. Supportive though his wife was, she would not have understood. On his first self-assigned mission to an area close to where Lewis Puller was wounded, the patrol camp was ambushed by an enemy unit of women. One Marine took a bullet in the head. That same day in two separate incidents, two more patrol members were killed and three badly wounded by mines. It was not an unusual day. He learned that officers who had never been close to a rifle platoon would often insist on patrols taking place that were nothing more than conditioning hikes with the complication of booby traps thrown in. Exhausted men were sent on one patrol after another to keep them in good form, a ludicrous thesis, since so many came back in no form at all.

The only time he ever had a sense of real foreboding was when he joined Lewis Puller's old platoon for an early morning patrol. He explained it to himself as a case of retroactive empathy. The men had formed up behind the big wire gate of base Camp G, waiting to move out. For security reasons, they found out about their mission—

---

ists invariably moved in after Marines had vacated their positions and collected the grenades. It took only a little trip wire from the grenade to a tree or bush to create a most lethal weapon. Patrols could be and often were devastated by grenades they themselves had provided. And it was not just grenades. It was just as easy for the enemy to booby trap other debris left by American soldiers. One of the first solutions to this problem was to institute a policy of grenade discipline, a laudable idea that should not have required a senior officer to go out on patrol before anyone thought of it.

a joint "sweep" operation with the ARVN—only a few hours before. G Company commander Clyde Woods issued his orders to the platoon leaders and their ammunition, grenades, and rations were distributed in silence. Weapons were cleaned. Then the men had a few hours to sleep in their gear. Now, standing in the hot and humid darkness, tension showed in their faces. Somewhere within the base camp a radio was playing softly. It was Glen Campbell singing "Wichita Lineman." Each must have wondered, as did McKenney, if they would ever hear it again.

At first gray light they moved out single file, weapons cocked, muzzles alternating left and right. That way, if they were ambushed, they would only have to squeeze the trigger and at least half the men would be firing in the right direction. Before each step, the point man probed the sand carefully with a long stick's knife point. He then put his foot in that precise spot, probed again and brought up his second foot slowly. Each man behind stepped carefully in the footprints of the man in front. It required total concentration from the lead man and also keen awareness of the surroundings. McKenney could never put into words what it felt like to miss a footprint or jump a ditch.

Within weeks, McKenney's strange sense of dread the morning he joined Puller's old platoon had been justified. Many of the men of G Company were dead or wounded. Twenty-four of them became casualties when a forty-pound box mine exploded under the amtrac on which they were riding. Captain Woods received severe wounds to his face and upper body in another mission. Lieutenant Kenny Shelleman, who had been a close friend of Lewis Puller's, was shot and killed in an ambush. Neither McKenney nor the small circle of men he worked with dwelled on any of this. To have done so would have paralyzed them emotionally. To survive they buried tragedy in a euphemism peculiar to all wars. In a phrase referring back to the ten thousand-dollar life insurance policy all WWII GIs took out before they went to war, Shelleman, like all those whose lives were snuffed out early, was said to have "bought the farm."

It was after Puller was wounded that Garwood entered McKenney's dreams, a mysterious figure eluding the execution he richly deserved. Awake, McKenney imagined having Garwood brought before him so he could look him in the eye, spit on him, and then personally kill him. If it had been possible to go on patrol with one of the hunter-killer teams after a Garwood sighting, he would have done so. He could not, because unlike the rifle platoon patrols he accompanied to booby-trap country, the reconnaissance teams and hunter-killer patrols stayed in the field four to five days or longer—too long for him to shelve his other responsibilities. He consoled himself with the knowledge that he had the power to direct the hunt, if not act as personal Marine Corps avenger.

Reports of deserters frequently came from Vietnamese agents, whose information was carefully assessed according to previous reliability. A-1 was the ranking for an agent who had always been right and whose information was presumed to be correct; B-2, the most common category, was "a usually reliable source with information that was presumed reliable," and so forth. Agents' reports were combined with reports brought in by Marine and other special operations units as well as "other" intelligence coming from the CIA through counterintelligence or the Naval Investigative Service. One patrol tracking a Vietnamese unit might spot large footprints that could belong only to Caucasians or perhaps Chinese communists, who often had large physiques. If another patrol spotted an NVA or VC unit in the same time frame and vicinity, McKenney could be convinced enough about the possibility of Garwood's being there to attach a special sniper to patrols heading in that direction. If the information seemed really hot, a two-man sniper team might be sent with the sole purpose of hunting down and killing the target.

Information on traitors was taken very seriously when it came from those who had been involved with a personal sighting. One Marine patrol in the early days had strayed into North Vietnam where they spotted a camouflaged team of six Caucasians. Because of the location they considered it a strong probability the six were Russians. No contact was made. This was one of the many elusive sightings of possible traitors. Others were considered hard evidence.

In 1965, Bobby Evans, the CCN intelligence officer who had seen photographs of three Marine deserters soon after McKenney's CI briefing, was a Special Forces sergeant and area specialist when the village next to the Special Forces camp at Min-tan was attacked by a VC battalion, led by a "black American." It was taken as a confirmed sighting because a South Vietnamese Special Forces captain, an acquaintance of Evans who was working with the United States, was not only in the village when the assault was made but also had his camera with him. Hidden under rubble, he took pictures of "The Black," who was then identified as a former U.S. Army master sergeant and adviser with U.S. military command. "The Black," dressed in black pyjamas and wearing a pair of revolvers cowboy style, had told the villagers in passable Vietnamese that he was the assault force battalion commander. Evans personally verified all of this: with a Special Forces B-team,[3] he was on the first resupply aircraft to the village after the assault. But the information had taken a day to wind its way through the

---

[3] An A-team, commanded by a captain, was the lowest level Special Forces team. Each A-team was subordinate to a B-team, the next level up, commanded by a major. Each B-team was subordinate to a C-team, commanded by a lieutenant colonel. C-teams consisted of several B-teams and each B-team consisted of several A-teams. Most of the isolated Special Forces camps in South Vietnam were A-team camps.

ARVN bureaucracy before reaching the Americans. By then it was too late to send the choppers, which normally would move within seconds to cut off the traitor's retreat. An investigation by the U.S. Special Forces A-team was reported through the chain of command to headquarters at Nha Trang and CIA headquarters in Saigon. The response was quick and simple: find the traitor, fix him, and eliminate him. All hunter-killer teams were then instructed to target The Black first if he was spotted with a VC unit.

But The Black never interested McKenney: he was not a Marine. The traitor McKenney did want kept eluding him. Despite tantalizing reports from usually reliable sources, Bobby Garwood seemed always to be too far north; the recon teams were unable to get a fix on him. If CI reported a sighting on Tuesday, by early Wednesday he had vanished from the area.

By early spring of 1969 many of McKenney's other aspirations and dreams seemed to be coming true. He often thought how right his father had been to make him choose the most difficult path. It was now paying off. His friends had warned him early on that his uncompromising attitude could ruin his career, and yet his career was moving steadily forward. He had stood up for his men and supported the kind of warfare the antiwar activists, and later even former Secretary of Defense McNamara, called immoral. By March he was made assistant G-2 (Operations), First Marine Division, where the hunter-killer teams he held in such high regard now became his primary assets. It was pretty much assumed by those in the know that he would take command of the reconnaissance battalion for I Corps in the fall.

He had been called to Saigon in January, during the height of the second Tet offensive, to be interviewed for the assignment of chief adviser to the provincial reconnaissance units of the Phoenix program. The possibility

had excited him because he firmly believed in the goal
of the program and by this time had had plenty of opportunity to see it work, and to direct its USMC hunter-
killer-affiliated projects. His only hesitation was that part
of the job required working with the "leisure-suit types."
He felt more than ever that they knew nothing about the
practicalities of jungle warfare. It was one such type who
interviewed him in CIA headquarters on Pasteur Street
in Saigon, where he had been led after a circuitous route
through back corridors. The interviewer was smug in his
contempt for the Marine Corps colonel before him; and
he seemed childishly secretive, revealing almost nothing
about the job McKenney had come there to discuss. It
didn't take long to figure out that the Leisure Suit knew
nothing about the field end of the job and probably didn't
care. McKenney was annoyed to find later that he had
been summoned for the interview after the assignment
had already been given to someone else. Just as his interviewer neither knew nor cared about the mechanics of
field work, McKenney was in the dark about the program's bureaucracy and politics.

Phoenix was undergoing a radical change, on paper.
Control of the provincial reconnaissance units was being
transferred from the CIA to the South Vietnamese. This
was destined to affect the integrity of the whole program.
Those who were actually assigned the task of assassination believed that when the program was CIA directed,
the lists of targets included only Vietcong Infrastructure,
which could be confirmed by the American special operations soldiers and Marines engaged to do the work.
The fact that they were also told to eliminate American
traitors is curiously erased from this defensive rationale.
It did not occur to McKenney until he was questioned
years later that hunter-killer teams were ordered to hunt
alleged American traitors without the possibility of ex-
amining their guilt. Yet the teams were encouraged to
examine the proof of each Vietnamese target's guilt at

South Vietnamese district and provincial intelligence operations centers. In the opinion of the "shooters," those who "neutralized" or "exploited" the people on the list, it was a professionally run program. It was believed to make few mistakes. It was an article of faith that nobody violated any international convention in killing the targets or exploiting them: they were "proven" provocateurs and spies. This was now beginning to change. Vietnamese people were becoming targets for political, personal, and economic reasons.

South Vietnam had a complicated intelligence and national security system. For political reasons, the Americans did not interfere and often catered to it. A good number of high-level South Vietnamese intelligence professionals were also working for the CIA. Almost every government intelligence and police unit had a twin institution under the control of the South Vietnamese president. A similar system in the U.S. would have meant that in addition to the FBI and the CIA, the president would have had his own FBI and CIA. Most of these units were headed by men who had graduated together from the famous Class 10 at the Vietnamese Military Academy in the late 1950s. Many had then gone on to study Phoenix-like operations at a course given by the British Special Air Services in Malaysia, where communist terrorism had ended with the withdrawal of its communist Chinese leaders. There were basic differences in how the British operations were run and in the conditions of their particular battlegrounds, but what mattered to students from Vietnam was that the British had succeeded. They hoped to get the same results. The cover name for the course was Foreign Area Reconnaissance and Liaison.

Probably only the CIA could keep track of such a complicated system run by powerful men and fraught with rivalries. It was certainly not something that U.S. military men like McKenney, in charge of a small portion of field work, had time to analyze critically. There was, for example, the South Vietnamese Central Intelligence Office, equivalent to the CIA in the United States. The man who headed that agency went under the cover of deputy commander, Saigon Capital Police, and deputy of Special Branch.

One of President Nguyen Van Thieu's closest intelligence advisers, a man who headed what was in effect a very private intelligence agency for Thieu, was Vu Ngoc Nha. Rumored to have been a leader in the Vietminh resistance group, he was remembered by only a few to have actually spent time in prison during the 1950s for those activities. What impressed Thieu, a strong Catholic, was that Nha had given up his Buddhism and converted to Catholicism. Additionally, Nha had headed former South Vietnamese president Ngo Dinh Diem's private intelligence service, known as the Political Research Center. Thieu used him in the same capacity although his private intelligence service had another name. Nha was known to be on the CIA payroll with an office at CIA headquarters on Pasteur Street in Saigon, where McKenney had gone to be interviewed for the job that had already been given away. In fact, Nha acted as secret liaison between the CIA and Thieu. No one doubted he had access to all CIA files. There was strong suspicion that he ordered people neutralized for reasons that had nothing to do with official Phoenix goals.

In July 1969, the following year, Nha and Huyn Van Trong, who worked with Nha in Thieu's prefecture, would be exposed as masterminds behind an espionage ring in a major public scandal that would seriously damage Thieu's presidency. By the end of November 1969, these two along with thirty-seven others would be found guilty of espionage. The U.S. government would then take the official position that it suspected Nha and Trong all along. This would lead many of South Vietnam's political leaders to suspect that the CIA had used Nha to try to bring down the Thieu government as it had brought down Diem's. Nha, they believed, had played a double game with the CIA, and compromised its records. He had been in a perfect position to feed false information into the system on everything, including alleged American deserters like Bobby Garwood.

After the fall of Saigon in 1975, Nha was promoted to general in *Cong An*, North Vietnam's secret service. It was then discovered that infiltration had by no means ended with the conviction of the thirty-seven in 1969.

Another man used by the CIA to try to bring down the Thieu government was Huyn Ba Thanh, the amiable cartoonist of Saigon's popular newspapers *Hoc Binh* and *Xay Dung*. Thanh, too, worked as an agent for the United States with top-level access to CIA headquarters on Pasteur Street. His real status within *Cong An* would remain secret until after the war, when it became vital to shedding light on Bobby Garwood's predicament.

McKenney knew nothing of this, and would not have believed that men like Nha and Thanh were responsible for turning Vietnamese innocents into Phoenix targets. McKenney merely provided the raw input—agents' reports, information collected through prisoner interrogations and the material collected by recon patrols—but he had no jurisdiction over who actually ended up on the lists. In the same way, he was the man who gave the specific kill order for those on the lists who were in his territory. The possibility of mistakes being made, or of corrupt motives resulting in the elimination of innocents, simply did not occur to him.

It more than occurred to Special Forces Lieutenant Mark Smith, a shooter recruited when the program was directed entirely by Americans, in 1967. After the South Vietnamese began making input, he became convinced there were names of innocent Vietnamese on some of the CIA lists.

American deserters were another matter. Smith had no doubt about their guilt even though he never saw their names on any list. He simply believed the stories that he thought were being circulated by military intelligence. He secretly applauded this sensitive matter being handled in such a discreet way. He believed Bobby Garwood, the most prominent and wily of the deserters, was targeted by the Marine Corps for good reason. If he had been given the opportunity, he himself would have gladly neutralized Garwood. Everyone Smith knew in his business felt the same way, and he would have resented any suggestion that this kind of program was either immoral or improper during wartime.

Only long after the war was over and he'd had time to contemplate all that had happened did Mark Smith realize that some of his superiors within Phoenix had themselves questioned the morality of assassinations. It was obvious in the way they tried to distance themselves from the field work. After Smith had neutralized a considerable number of targets his superiors had specified, it was suggested, or insinuated, that perhaps he was getting to like the work too much, that it was time to send him back to the regular army.

Smith prided himself on standing up for the right thing when it counted. He not only personally deleted the names of those he thought innocent from the CIA lists, he took the same action when made aware of innocent Americans who were targeted. Much later in his career, a colleague who was acting as a provincial recon unit adviser in Thua Tin province was felt out by military intelligence about neutralizing an American first lieutenant on a U.S. firebase[4] in I Corps. The lieutenant was allegedly in contact with antiwar groups in America. Mark Smith strongly advised his friend to tell the

---

[4] Short for fire support base, a fortified base camp that contained logistical support, communications, artillery, and mortar fire support for one or more battalions. Firebases were isolated, usually located in the center of a battalion's tactical area of responsibility.

military-intelligence types "to get screwed," and to seek
the help of William Colby, who by then had retired as
head of Phoenix, but could still be influential on matters
like this. Colby apparently pushed the appropriate buttons
because the lieutenant was left alone. Mark Smith, who
had an outstanding battle record, later testified to these
matters under oath.

The certainty of Garwood's guilt among men like
Mark Smith in this period originated with the larger-than-
life stories told about one man, Special Forces sergeant
Issac Camacho, whom they believed had done the impossible. These stories gained credence in the peculiar
circumstances in which they were heard by men in the
jungle cut off from regular contact with a saner outside
world. It was said Camacho had escaped from one of the
toughest VC prison camps in Laos when a nearby munitions dump was bombed by American planes, and this
was certainly verified later. The bombing briefly threw
his captors into disarray. Legend then had it that Camacho trekked his way through heavy jungle and small villages, without weapons in a country where any foreigner
stuck out like a sore thumb, and the locals could literally
smell an American even if he remained hidden. Special
Forces lore had it that Camacho, who was of Mexican
background, passed for an Asian. But that was not what
saved him. He survived because he reverted to the most
brutal and primitive warrior instincts, killing everyone
who got in his way on the way back.

Rumor had it that Issac Camacho was an angry man
when he got back, with a very special hatred for American deserters who were helping to destroy their own former comrades, and that Camacho had informed the U.S.
government about these traitors. The story went that he
had been taunted with the name of Bobby Garwood in
prison and had even caught a glimpse of the traitor in the
distance, dressed in the uniform of the enemy, consorting
with his Vietnamese buddies.

There was only one problem with the legend of Issac Camacho. It was true that Camacho made a remarkable and heroic escape from a brutal Vietnamese prison camp. Navigating roughly by the sun, he found his way back to Min-tan Special Forces camp, eluding at least four armed VC patrols along the way. It was also true that he was angry at those who had compromised him and other POWs. But he did not blame Garwood or any fellow prisoners, or even deserters. In testimony before a Senate committee in 1971, he blamed the politicians whose public pronouncements had fed the enemy's belief that American civilians thought of their soldiers as war criminals.[5] And he blamed the reporters who printed details of his special warfare background after his capture. The VC had used this to torture him mercilessly.

Most remarkably, Camacho's ordeals predated Bobby Garwood's disappearance. Issac Camacho was captured on the day of President Kennedy's assassination in 1963. He escaped in July 1965. Garwood was not captured until two months later.

---

[5] Issac Camacho testified on August 3rd, 1971, before the U.S. Senate Subcommittee on National Security Policy and Scientific Development on the problems of American POWs.

11: To Covet Honor

The First Marine Division command post, to which Colonel McKenney moved in early March, was on Hill 327, better known as Freedom Hill. A large ridge to the west of Da Nang, running generally north-south and blocking the invasion corridor from Dai La Pass and Laos, it was crucial to the defense of Da Nang, constantly probed and periodically attacked by the enemy. His new job had less scope than the one vacated at III MAF but it suited him perfectly. He had none of the irritating administrative duties or the hassles. His new boss, Colonel Anthony Skotniki, could be hot tempered, but he knew the business of intelligence. He also knew how to use McKenney to the best advantage. The only confrontation the two ever had was about McKenney's penchant for going on field trips. Skotniki laid down the law. His new chief of operations could not be chief and go out on patrol, and that included any idea of personally going after Garwood.

In a way the ultimatum was a relief. It allowed McKenney to concentrate on strategy. Besides, the small circle of riflemen he worked with could do the job better. They were younger, outstandingly fit, and perfectly suited to their difficult work. He would sometimes laugh aloud when he read articles about the "stoned generation" back home. They thought they had cornered the market on love and brotherhood. Real brotherhood was here, with the small band of men he compared to King Harry's men—those who went to war, and against all odds defeated the French on St. Crispin's Day. Only Shakespeare had been genius enough to give words to this sentiment when he wrote in *Henry V*: "We few we happy few, we band of brothers. . . . We would not die in that man's company that fears his fellowship to die with us."

No one personified this kind of comradeship more than Captain Sam Owens, whom McKenney already knew from III MAF, and who was now his right-hand man. Owens reviewed all First Division combat POW interrogation and intelligence reports. A mustang, he brought to the job not only the frontier skills he had learned from his father in the small town of Bing, Oklahoma, but also experience and the right attitude. This was the career Marine's second tour of duty in Vietnam and he knew exactly why he was there—"to kill people"—which he did not hesitate to tell people back home during his leave. He was equally prepared to give his life for his country. That was what war was about. He was proud of being good at his job, so good that he had been asked by Special Forces to teach the subtleties of running hunter-killer patrols at their School of Special Warfare, at Fort Bragg. It was an unusual arrangement, worked out between the Marine commandant and the head of Special Forces, to make sure the Army Special Forces teams became as proficient at these operations as the Marine Corps. Owens shared with McKenney a history of excelling in special-warfare skills and striving to be the best Marine possible. They also shared the same view on the CIA. In Owens's opinion, if the CIA suspected someone, they treated that suspicion as certainty. If they made mistakes they made them plausibly deniable. "They were as low as a snake's belly in a wagon track," said Owens. Throughout his career he had headed the Corps "lineal list," the book that lists every USMC officer according to seniority and record of accomplishment,[1] ranking number one among all the officers commissioned with him in 1962. Owens thought McKenney the most professional officer he had ever worked for, more perceptive and focused than the generals at the top.

One of the early Marines in Vietnam, Owens was the patrol leader with First Force Recon Company based on China Beach at the foot of Monkey Mountain in 1965, when Bobby Garwood made his last fateful run. Garwood's intended cargo—the lieutenant he never met up with—was one of Owens's comrades.

Owens had relished living out in "Injun country." He had no illusions about the strength and capabilities of the VC. He understood an enemy who did not have high-tech gadgets, whose craftsmanship included the punji stake, a sharp stick dipped in feces that shot up between an unsuspecting man's legs when a concealed line was tripped. The good thing about having led deep-penetration patrols into the heart of enemy territory was the absence of the kind of restrictions that so frustrated the regular infantry in so-called friendly territory. Living completely by their senses, knowing death as a constant possibility, Owens's comrades shared his sense that they would never again feel so keenly alive. There was a curious dichotomy at work here: a conscious effort not to get too close to the people who might die, combined with a deep alliance that expressed itself in the wish, if die they must, to die only in the fellowship of comrades.

The possibility of being taken prisoner was constant. When that happened, as it did to Owens's radio man,

---

[1] The lineal list, in the library of every command, was published yearly by the USMC office of personnel. Promotion was determined entirely by the number of points each Marine accumulated. No Marine could be placed in command of someone who outnumbered him by even one point.

Russ Grisset, in the spring of 1966, the teams went on with their work but they never forgot those who were lost. After some time, Owens had assumed Grisset was dead because he doubted anyone could survive what Issac Camacho had suffered in a VC prison camp for very long. An additional hazard, and most worrying of all, was the enemy's view that prisoners were not entitled to the protection of international agreements because the United States was waging an illegal, undeclared war.

Then in the fall of 1968, just a few months before McKenney moved over to Freedom Hill, Owens came across surprising evidence that Grisset was still alive. A hunter-killer patrol had killed a VC courier. Checking through the contents of the dead man's bag, Owens found a mimeographed list of American and Vietnamese prisoners, held at a camp never recorded in any American intelligence seen by Owens, and an order transferring them from one camp to another. The original list had been typed on a strange typewriter. The letters looked Cyrillic. Russ Grisset's name was on the list along with a VC report of interrogation noting that Grisset had somehow managed to keep his Marine-issued shoes. His captors had not allowed him to wear them, so he always kept them around his neck. Making special note of Russ Grisset, and that the list appeared to be three months old, Owens passed the names on to his superiors.

It was not until McKenney personally spoke to Owens about targeting Bobby Garwood that something registered in Owens's mind. He vaguely remembered Garwood's name being on the same list but could not swear by it. Details were forgotten. He accepted the directive to kill Garwood without question. Unlike McKenney, he did not assume the Marine private had deserted. He believed Garwood had been captured and forced to go along at first. But he had no doubt that Garwood was involved in leading enemy soldiers against his own. Owens assumed McKenney knew what he was doing.

Much later he would describe it as a kind of tragedy that he was so indoctrinated by the Marine Corps, never challenging anything he was told to do. He had quietly disobeyed only once. In the field, after a losing battle, his superior told him to leave his dead comrades behind because the surrounding enemy would pick off anyone who went back. Owens went back repeatedly, to bring them out one by one. The men under his command did the same. The NVA soldiers watched in silence without firing one shot.

Like McKenney, Sam Owens was well read. He kept up with all the newspapers and magazines in addition to his source materials as an intelligence officer. His priority was Corps, God, and country. It would be ten years after his retirement from the Corps before he questioned anything. In the spring of 1969, although he was not as obsessed with getting Garwood as McKenney, he was just as determined to get the job done.

12: Spring of Hope / Winter of Despair

Honor in the sense that Shakespeare wrote of was not part of Garwood's vocabulary when he was growing up, but he always had a fine sense of right and wrong, of loyalty and responsibility toward those he loved and respected. He never once considered it a duty to take care of his younger brother Don, to turn most of his hard-earned wages over to his family, or to search for his mother despite his father's harsh and absolute opposition.

At III MAF he was the only one to write long, eloquent letters not just to his family and fiancée, but also to close friends. He did this because he valued kinship, affection, and friendship above all else. He knew they did not come cheaply. One of the reasons he was so happy in the Marine Corps was because its creed incorporated all of the values he instinctively admired and because it gave him the fellowship he had always craved.

Now in the prison camps of the North Vietnamese his honor, in every sense of the word, was tested far beyond the experience of men like Owens and McKenney. Like them he had his band of brothers—albeit much smaller than theirs—and did not fear his fellowship to die with them. They were so important in his life, he risked both death and a chance for freedom by not abandoning them.

When they died, he shared with men like McKenney and Owens the primeval need to see them properly buried on home ground. When the enemy denied his impulse to sanctify the dead, he was driven to rectify the violation, no matter how long it took. Later, need for friendship with his own people would become his Achilles' heel, providing a means not only for the VC to apply the cruelest mental punishment in the prison camps, but for both the enemy and some of his own countrymen to exact permanent revenge and ruin his life.

The charges that would be brought against him after fourteen years in captivity were drawn up by commanders of the same corps that had seemed the one safe anchorage in a troubled youth: and the full facts emerge now only through a reconstruction of events by military intelligence chiefs, Special Forces' specialists in highly secret operations, and others with special access to hitherto buried official reports. After the passage of so much time, allowance must be made for fallible memories, but there remain documents and sworn statements that are hard to refute, which back up Garwood's own story and which present a very different portrait of Garwood from the one fabricated to make him seem a traitor.

After enduring three months of interrogation and torture at Quang Da, the first prison camp to which Garwood was taken, his morale was shattered. He was very ill with dysentery and malaria. What he experienced and witnessed being done to South Vietnamese prisoners he could not have conceived of as human before he was captured. He was now living in a six-by-five-foot outdoor cage, four feet off the ground and with no roof, which was in itself a form of torture. The cages were made of bamboo poles strapped together. There were no mats. The rough wood had worn away his flesh and there were festering holes in his hips and buttocks that revealed his bones. These wounds would leave lifelong scars. Periodically he would, for no apparent reason, be placed in a punishment cell, five feet in length and three feet high, with his feet in stocks. He was uncertain about how long he would be allowed to live. More and more he wanted to die in the jungle to escape the horror and pain of the world he found himself in. The worst part of it was the isolation. He had always been a gregarious, outgoing person. It was one of the reasons he had been so willing to do favors for the officers at III MAF. Now he had not seen an American or even another Caucasian since his capture. He continues to believe that if he had remained in isolation much longer, he would have died.

A few weeks before Christmas, Garwood was moved to Camp Khu, situated somewhere between the three provinces of Quang Nam, Quang Gai, and Quang Tu. The camp was brand new, with some structures still being built by South Vietnamese POWs. For the first time he was housed in a thatched-roof structure called a hootch by Americans. At first he inhabited the hootch alone. It was the monsoon season. Dressed in shorts and skimpy shirt, Garwood was stiff with the damp, bone-chilling cold. By now he was almost oblivious to the realities of extreme deprivation. Hallucinating from hunger, his mind was in California with his fiancée, Mary Speer, and his brother Don.

At first, the tall, squinting, phantom-figure in black shorts appearing in the doorway of the hootch seemed part of the hallucination. The apparition leaning on a stick looked like the skeletal figures Bobby had seen of Holocaust victims. Later he would learn that he himself looked just as deathly frail. It was obvious the stranger could not see well enough to respond to Garwood. When Garwood moved closer and looked into his eyes, he knew the emaciated man was another American. Both men began to cry and hug each other, oblivious to the derisive snickers of the communist guards.

The newcomer introduced himself as Captain William F. (Ike) Eisenbraun, Special Forces. He was in terrible

shape. Extremely nearsighted, his glasses had been taken
when he was captured. He was frail and his body was
covered with oozing, chronic wounds from beatings and
swollen with hunger edema. He was bitter because he
had been taken prisoner in what he considered a dishonorable way, betrayed by South Vietnamese comrades. He
had been adviser to an ARVN command post at Pleiku
working out of I Corps. Under attack from the VC, the
entire ARVN battalion stationed in the outpost threw
down their weapons and surrendered. Eisenbraun and two
American colleagues were hiding in a trench when one
of their own ARVN officers pointed them out to the VC.
Eisenbraun had undergone the same forced marches and
humiliations as Garwood. When he refused to answer interrogators' questions he was tortured. He kept on refusing until it stopped making a difference. The ARVN
battalion commander and officers who surrendered and
betrayed him also told the VC everything they knew
about Eisenbraun and the I Corps command structure he
belonged to. They did this during a confrontation between Eisenbraun and themselves set up by the VC, some
weeks after his capture. Eisenbraun was surprised at the
accuracy and extent of the enemy's information. Afterward, he had no compunction about writing confessions
reiterating the same information the VC already had in
their records. It was, he knew, a fallback position sanctioned by military regulations framed after the Korean
War revealed the ruthless and finally irresistible methods
of communist interrogators.

When Garwood realized that Eisenbraun had been in-
terned since early July of that year and how much he had
suffered, he no longer wanted to die. ''I stopped feeling
sorry for myself,'' he said later. Afraid his new friend
might die any minute, he was desperate to keep him
alive. He did not want to be alone again. For almost two
years he helped Eisenbraun, doing whatever he could get
away with, taking over his part of the labor, foraging

food for him, and nursing him. Two years was an eternity; in retrospect, it became one long, endless night of struggle against despair.

The more Garwood got to know Eisenbraun, the more he respected him, so much so that at first he found it hard to call him anything but "Sir." Eisenbraun quickly told him that with only two there was hardly need for a chain of command. It was also the one thing the communists stomped on hard. If they sensed any chain of command, he told Garwood, the two prisoners would be separated. He insisted on being called Ike and always addressed the younger man as Bob, but privately maintained his responsibilities as the officer in command. In Garwood's mind, Ike became the father figure he had always craved. After kinship with his mother, it became the most important relationship in his life. Ike began teaching him how to survive the bewildering and cruel circumstances they found themselves in.

A graduate of the Army's established Jungle Warfare School in Panama, Eisenbraun was a mustang who had volunteered for three tours of duty in Vietnam. One of that small, tightly knit group of Special Forces advisers who came to Vietnam in the early 1960s, he fit the mold of men both Colonel McKenney and Captain Owens held in highest regard. In 1955, as a staff sergeant, he was Issac Camacho's squad leader at jump school, which the communists seemed to know about. In prison, Camacho later said, he was interrogated about it: "Again and again, I was shown Ike's picture and asked to identify him." Issac Camacho said he too had idolized Ike.

Eisenbraun was appalled at Garwood's lack of survival training, telling him bluntly that to have any chance of surviving, he would have to listen and learn. Eisenbraun explained that he would teach him not only because it was his duty as an officer, but also because they were friends. The first thing he taught Garwood was how to look for, recognize, and eat nonpoisonous plants, insects, and small animals—no matter how unpleasant—because they provided the only nutrients essential to surviving the diet provided by the communists. Garwood soon saw for himself that Eisenbraun was teaching him to supplement his diet just as their Vietnamese guards did. It was at least one of the reasons the guards remained healthy on food that at first appeared only marginally better than that of their prisoners. Garwood began to volunteer for work details, cutting and carrying logs used for firewood. He did this even when he was weak and sick so that he could forage for the nutrients Eisenbraun had taught him about. The center of the banana tree and the achua (sour fruit) contained vitamin C. Large green insects provided desperately needed protein. Eisenbraun also taught Garwood which green vegetables and leaves could be eaten as salad.

American prisoners were not allowed to cook their own meals like South Vietnamese prisoners. The VC believed the Americans might try to signal their spotter aircraft with smoke signals from the cooking fires. Eisenbraun told Garwood the VC had watched too many American Westerns. But harsh experience had taught the VC to pipe their own smoke out of the camp in tunnels, using the technique familiar to special operations men like Sam Owens. In the first few weeks of their being together Eisenbraun's weak condition continued to scare Garwood. Since he was the one sent to pick up their rations from the guard kitchen in separate baskets, he made sure that the older man got the greater portion despite his insistence that it be fifty-fifty. Garwood knew that his youth gave him a much better chance of surviving. The outcome of all this foraging and dissembling was that Ike's health improved marginally before "it kind of settled in." It was a matter of optimism for both of them that their health did not get worse and helped them to put up with the daily psychological harassment of their guards.

The two Americans were constantly put on display for the increasing numbers of NVA regulars who were coming through the camp. The guards whose families were suffering from the effects of the war often seemed to be just looking for an excuse to kill them. Neither doubted that their lives could be extinguished at any moment. For a time after the appearance of NVA regulars, though, there was little of the physical beatings, torture, and harassment both had experienced earlier. Eisenbraun was grateful for the reprieve. He guessed there must be political reasons. Perhaps the communists were responding to a move from Washington. He was certain it did not mean a change in basic policy.

Ike had no illusions about the communists. He deliberately resigned himself to the notion that it was likely the two of them would remain prisoners for ten years or more. He told Bobby that was why the younger man must learn to understand their captors; to be able to figure out what was happening to the enemy and consequently to themselves. It was important to get a sense of where they were going when they were moved, which happened periodically, always on short notice. Only by staying alert in every way would they have a chance to get out information to international agencies that their status was that of live POWs. It was the only way they could survive. Ike told Bobby that in the sordid game they were involved in, there was only one hard and fast rule: "No American prisoner ever consciously harms another American prisoner." Going by more realistic rules than the Marine Corps, he said Bobby had done nothing wrong in signing the Fellow Soldier's Appeal under duress. Ike reassured him that he had signed similar documents. "The only people who will pay attention to it are the intelligence units," Bobby remembered him saying, "and they will use it to find us."

Like Colonel McKenney and Captain Owens, Eisenbraun had an unshakeable trust in the American intelligence system. He would not have believed the truth: that Special Forces operatives had, several times since his capture, received hard information on his whereabouts. This information had been quickly transmitted to those who could have authorized a rescue operation, a course of action that was not followed.[1]

Not all of Bobby's conversations with Ike were about the practicalities of survival. There was a lot of talk about home, their families and upbringing, and the importance of faith in God. It was the first time Bobby had spoken to someone who was in Vietnam out of commitment and conviction. Eisenbraun clearly loved his family with a very special attachment to his little daughter, yet he had volunteered for three tours in Vietnam. For all of his cynicism brought about by the South Vietnamese who betrayed him, he had a kind of innocence. He told Bobby he saw the peril the Vietnamese people were in and wanted to help prevent a communist takeover. Eisenbraun believed in the ideals of America, and was willing to give his life if necessary so that Vietnam could have a chance at democracy. He had been betrayed by some South Vietnamese, but Eisenbraun made a clear distinction between those Vietnamese who genuinely wanted democracy and those who didn't care or wanted communism. Until then Garwood had been convinced the Vietnamese, South and North, "didn't want Americans there and couldn't care less if Americans lived or died."

Despite the miserable circumstances, Eisenbraun made Garwood feel secure and safe, and, against all probability, certain that "we were going to make it out of that hell hole." For the rest of his long internment Garwood would remember this time as his one spring of hope

---

[1] From a synopsis of MACV Remarks: 670807 DIC - ON pPRG DIC LIST and *The Case of Pvt. Robert R. Garwood, USMC,* Final Report, Report to the Assistant Secretary of Defense for Command, Control, Communication and Intelligence (ASD/C³1), Volume 1, June 1993.

bracketed by winters of despair. He said, "Everything Eisenbraun told me, I ate it up. Every little joke was funny to me. When he got serious, I got serious. When he felt pain, so did I. When he laughed, so did I. I learned quickly. I don't know what it was but it seemed I had a natural ability to pick up on the Vietnamese language." It was a matter of great pride to Garwood that Eisenbraun told him it was a shame that he hadn't been sent to foreign language school. He was that good. For Ike, Bobby's adulation was probably normal, a part of the same syndrome noted by Colonel McKenney where enlisted men often latch on to older officers they admire. Issac Camacho had done the same with Eisenbraun. Such an attachment was even more understandable in the case of Bobby, who attributed it to Ike that he was still alive and would make it to freedom.

Ike's guidance and tutelage was, at first, an advantage to Garwood. Later it became a cursed gift that denied him any possibility of release from prison because it made his captors certain he was not the low-level Marine he claimed, but instead someone, like Eisenbraun, highly skilled in special operations and sabotage. Later, men with Eisenbraun's training were put in a separate prisoner category by the North Vietnamese, with no possibility of release. Skills he learned here would also isolate Garwood from American prisoners who came to the camps later. His progress in the Vietnamese language and survival and adaptability skills would make him look like a "white gook" and affront fellow Americans. Building on that impression the VC would play a vicious kind of deception that made "gook" interchangeable with "cong." The VC who had been suspicious of his G-2 connection from the day of his capture became progressively more certain that Garwood had espionage training of a kind that could have sinister repercussions for them. Garwood's interrogations by Ho dwelt endlessly on this theme. He never budged from his story that he was a simple private and driver, because it was the truth. They called him *an luc gaao* (hardhead), but seemed strangely impressed by what they considered his intransigence. It was more proof that their suspicions were right. As long as he could talk to Ike, the interrogations, harassment, and even punishments rolled off him.

The South Vietnamese prisoners who were released during Tet 1966 and had reported to Marine headquarters that Garwood was a prisoner were some of the men who had been under Eisenbraun's command. Ike and Bobby were hopeful that word of their incarceration would finally get back to the Americans and that there might be a rescue attempt. But they knew the chances of this happening diminished each time they were moved to another camp. All the camps were much alike, with a kitchen, a camp commander's hootch, a guard hootch, a bamboo fence around it, and separate buildings for South Vietnamese and American prisoners, who were moved constantly to keep from being found and rescued. From Eisenbraun, Garwood learned that the administration of these camps came under the North Vietnamese psychological warfare section.

Both men's spirits were lifted that spring when they were joined by Sergeant Russ Grisset, another young Marine who had been taken prisoner just the week before. Grisset had been Sam Owens's radio man, presumed dead by the Marine Corps until one of Colonel McKenney's patrols killed a Vietnamese courier almost two years later and recovered an order transferring Grisset from one camp to another.

Grisset told Eisenbraun and Garwood that he had been separated from his patrol during an ambush and was then captured. He was not wounded. He surrendered when the enemy surrounded him with insurmountable fire power. To have done otherwise, he told them, would have meant annihilation. But he had not surrendered his shoes. Probably because they were too large to fit any Vietnamese, he had been allowed to keep them although he was not allowed to wear them. He kept them around his neck like a treasured necklace ready to be used at a moment's notice. He was just looking for the opportunity to escape. Like his two new friends soon after their capture, he made two attempts. To the two Americans he looked like an Arnold Schwarzenegger, and it was clear to them that their emaciated frames "scared the hell out of him." When told that Garwood, who now looked like an old man, was only nineteen years old, Grisset's face went white. He did not want to believe that he too would contract the same diseases Garwood and Eisenbraun suffered from.

Along with Grisset came another big change. Where formerly Americans had been separated from the South Vietnamese, they were now being housed together in one gigantic hootch. It did not take long for Eisenbraun to figure out why. He told the other two that the communists were using some South Vietnamese prisoners to spy on the Americans as well as their own countrymen. There were three Americans now and more joined them within weeks. Knowing there was strength in numbers the communists believed Eisenbraun would take command and plan an escape. Eisenbraun was certain that the South Vietnamese who agreed to spy had been promised freedom in exchange. It was obvious to all three Americans that one man, in particular, not only allowed himself to be used in this way, but seemed to enjoy it. His name, Garwood reported later to retired Defense Intelligence Agency chief General Eugene Tighe was Le Dinh Quy, who played informer on his own countrymen as well, which led to the execution of a Captain Nghia, an ARVN artillery battalion commander who had been captured in Pleiku, and whose courageous conduct won the admiration of the three Americans.

When Nghia was first captured by the Viet Cong, he gave a false name and rank. Quy, who knew him and had himself used several aliases, immediately went to the camp commandant and told him Nghia's true identity. This incensed Nghia, who took him to task before the other prisoners, calling him a traitor and threatening to kill him. This only made Quy go to the camp authorities again, charging Nghia with atrocities against the Vietnamese people, which, he said, he had personally witnessed. As a result, the camp authorities held a military tribunal with the informer as major witness against Nghia. The ad hoc tribunal sentenced Nghia to death. Unrepentant to the last, he promised the communists they would be defeated as he was led to his execution. In a last act of defiance, with his hands tied behind him, he bolted, running blindly into the stream next to the camp. Thirty seconds later his body was shredded by eight automatic rifles. Garwood never forgot him. Nghia made him proud to be an ally of the South Vietnamese. From that day forward, both he and Ike actively showed their contempt for Quy. Garwood told Tighe, "perhaps that was why Quy never forgot me." When Quy became one of the communists' early releasees he reported to the Americans that Garwood had collaborated with the enemy in prison camp. Fourteen years later, having become a U.S. citizen and presenting himself as a staunch former South Vietnamese patriot, he testified before a court martial that Bobby Garwood had collaborated with the enemy in prison camp.

In the spring of 1967, after a year of being together, the American prisoners were moved again in what seemed to be a northward direction. They tried to get coordinates from the sun but it was difficult. The triple canopy jungle kept them from seeing the sun except at sunup and sundown. In reality they were being led in circles, which became more apparent with each move. Despite always being led along different trails, the three Americans knew they remained in the same general area because they kept running into the same indigenous people who traded and bartered with their guards.

The third camp was larger, and run primarily by NVA regulars rather than VC. Garwood was by this time almost as proficient in Vietnamese as Eisenbraun, and almost as sensitive to what was happening. Grisset had difficulty with the language. He saw no need to learn it when the other two already had. He also saw no need for scavenging or eating the kind of food the other two tried to persuade him to eat. He did not object to taking food Garwood was able to steal from the guards' food bins although he worried about the consequences to all of them if Garwood got caught. Later Garwood would admit to being guilty of a kind of collaboration with the enemy, if collaboration meant volunteering for any work run that got him near the food bins—like tidying up the kitchen. The better he got, the more chances he took. One night after a severe bout of stomach illness had left Ike unable to eat for two days and nights, Garwood determined to get him some good food. He knew there were extra stores in the kitchen because the camp commandant was hosting a North Korean visitor. At the creek that ran next to the camp he smeared muddy clay all over his body and then crawled low through the gate, right past the guard post and to the kitchen and back. It was one time, he said, "Ike reamed my ass. He told me only a Marine would try a stunt like that." Had he been caught, he would have been shot on the spot. But the little can of French condensed milk he brought back for Ike was worth it.

After the three Americans were moved again in response to an American bombing of the camp, their circumstances changed radically. They were no longer the only American prisoners of war. They were segregated and, for the first time, there seemed a possibility for release. The other American prisoners—Ortiz-Rivera and Santos—were Puerto Rican, which gave them special privileges. Ortiz-Rivera, in particular, seemed healthy as a horse. He was big, looked something like Fidel Castro, and affected the Cuban dictator's mannerisms. He spoke no English. The prisoners were told that Puerto Rico was a colony of U.S. capitalism and that, unlike the other Americans, Ortiz-Rivera and Santos had been forced to come to Vietnam. They had been used. If Ortiz-Rivera and Santos promised to work as agents for the Vietnamese they would be liberated and could return to Puerto Rico.

In May, came word that one of the American threesome—the one who proved himself most "progressive"—would be liberated. The bearer of this message was Mr. Ho, Garwood's frequent interrogator who had let them all know he was a member of the presidium of the intellect committee and head of the South Vietnam Liberation Front. Whether that was true or not, he was clearly a man of importance. "People jumped through hoops when he came to a camp. He always traveled with bodyguards and a doctor," Garwood would say later.

When Grisset and Garwood asked Eisenbraun if he thought Ho was telling the truth about one of them being released, he said it was possible, but only in a manner of speaking. No American prisoners were ever just "released," he said, but there were prisoner exchanges going on all the time. The communists had freed some South Vietnamese prisoners and it was possible that they would let one of the Americans go as a political move. Initially, the three prisoners agreed that if one got out it would give the other two that much more of a chance to survive. Both Grisset and Garwood thought that Eisenbraun, a captain, would be chosen over enlisted men. After Ho's announcement, their rations increased. They got more rice, some pork fat, and fruit occasionally. This was encouraging because it seemed to mean the communists wanted them to look healthy if they were released. But they were moved into separate hootches. It became difficult to talk to each other. They were not even allowed

to eat together. It was devastating. Together, they had
been strong. Now they were vulnerable.

When Ho told Garwood and Eisenbraun that they
would be released, leaving out Grisset, Garwood began
to feel that if he let himself be liberated, he would be
breaking Ike's golden rule: Grisset would suffer. There
was another problem. Ho told Garwood he would have
to travel to villages in the Mekong Delta for a month
showing the appropriate gratitude to the VC and repent
of his and his country's crimes. Garwood, who had only
signed one statement during his incarceration when he
thought he would die, was in a real quandary. It also
seemed as if Ho was saying that Garwood was to be
"liberated on his own." Perhaps that meant Garwood
would be released first and then Eisenbraun would be
sent on a separate "gratitude tour" through the villages;
but more likely it meant that Ike would be kept prisoner
along with Grisset. The thought of leaving Eisenbraun
was unbearable to Garwood. His instincts told him he
would be abandoning to almost certain death the man
who had saved his life.

A liberation ceremony was set up by Ho. It seemed to
Garwood that there was a good chance he would be
tricked, just like a group of ARVN prisoners who had
been "released" the previous Christmas with much fan-
fare, only to be marched back a few months later, to the
derisive laughter of the guards. Anyway he looked at it,
he would be abandoning not only Grisset but also Ike,
who himself seemed certain that trickery was in the offing and that the VC would certainly never release the
senior officer in the bunch. Garwood searched for a way
to reject Ho's offer of liberation without provoking his
wrath. The ceremony was already under way when Garwood brought it to a crashing halt. "I do not feel worthy
of being selected for return to the United States . . . not
until I know more about Vietnamese customs and culture," he announced.

It was not the last time during his imprisonment that moral compunction prevented Garwood from doing something that he had been certain would gain release. Ike approved of the way he handled the matter. That was the only thing that counted. But he paid heavily for his decision.

Ho was paranoid in his reaction: he behaved as if Garwood wanted to stay because he was an infiltrator and had some way of communicating with American intelligence. Still, Ho was very much aware of Garwood's attachment to Ike. Vietnam was a society where one's highest duty was to take care of one's elders. To Garwood, it seemed that maybe Ho respected this in spite of himself.

The VC decision to keep Grisset weighed heavily on Eisenbraun, who at least was given a promise of release, however it might have been hedged. Grisset was desperate to get out anyway he could; and on the verge of doing something that could only result in a horrible death. As the senior officer, Eisenbraun felt responsible for both younger men. A few days later, he made an escape attempt. Garwood remains convinced that this was self-sacrificial. "He wanted to be eliminated without getting the guards' backs up. He wanted to give Russ a chance." Ike was almost blind because the guards had never returned his eyeglasses, and he had to move through mountainous jungle terrain. He managed to get half a mile from the camp before being caught.

His punishment was a twenty-minute beating with rifle butts and sticks of bamboo, deliberately administered within hearing of the silent camp. Grisset and Garwood were held back, guns to their heads. Afterward the guards dragged Ike's unconscious, bleeding body in front of his hootch and put him in stocks. Garwood was determined to nurse him back to health. He had done this once before when Ike had felt dutybound to make an escape attempt with Grisset after failing to dissuade him.

Now, when Garwood was taken over to look at Ike, he knew "this time Ike would not make it." It was the most severe beating he had seen. It had been done to teach Garwood and Grisset a lesson.

When Grisset was brought over, Ike looked up at them both and managed a smile. "Don't quit guys," he said, "don't quit!"

Three days later Ike called Garwood's name. Perhaps out of pity or for some other unknown reason, Bobby was allowed to see the dying man alone.

Ike looked at him. "Bob," he said, "I don't know what they're up to, but they are not going to release you." He stopped for breath. "They are not going to release anybody. Maybe they'll try, again, to take you to a village to use you for propaganda. Next time go along with it. The closer you get to Hanoi, the better your chances. You have none here." Garwood remembered how the older man tried to prepare him. "It's going to be rough for you, Bob. I can't tell you what to do or how to do it. Just remember what I taught you. For God's sake, don't let all three of us die here!" Then, as if he believed Garwood could make it out, Ike added, "When you get out, look up my daughter, and tell her I send her my love."

In a curious way, the guards seemed to respect Garwood's sorrow over Ike's death. Mourning for a comrade seemed to be the one bit of common moral ground between the Americans and the enemy. When Garwood and Russ insisted on burying Ike alone, under the biggest tree near the camp, the guards acquiesced. Garwood was adamant there would be no typical Vietnamese three-foot grave for Ike. They dug it deep and six feet in length. There was no coffin so Ike's two comrades wrapped him in bamboo they were allowed to cut themselves. Ortiz-Rivera and Santos, the two Puerto Ricans in the camp, did not attend the simple, makeshift service of prayers put together by Garwood and Grisset.

A part of Bobby Garwood died on September 27th, 1967, the day Ike died. His friendship with Ike had been a kind of rebirth. It had turned him from frightened teenager into someone able to marshall all of his own inner resources to survive the physical and spiritual debasement of what would be a fourteen-year incarceration. After Ike's death, he became hard, rebellious, and bitter, refusing to go on work details. Ho resented the fact that Garwood blamed him and the guards for Ike's death. Garwood was told that if he could not bring himself to be more "progressive" he was not long for this world.

Four months later, Garwood noted bitterly that Ike had been wrong about only one thing. It wasn't true that none of the American prisoners would be released. Ortiz-Rivera and Santos were liberated. Each wearing a red sash in honor of the occasion and to insure that the NVA would not shoot them, they were ceremoniously put at the head of a small platoon of VC soldiers to do some propaganda work in nearby villages and then released. They had paid the price by consistently and publicly denouncing their fellow prisoners in the camp. Garwood and Eisenbraun, in particular, had been singled out as spies and agents of the CIA. Fourteen years later, Ortiz-Rivera, who could speak no English when he was in the camp, was housed in a separate hootch, and had no direct communication with Garwood of any kind, denounced him again at his court martial—accusing him of being a collaborator and agent of the Vietnamese.

Garwood had no idea, of course, that Ortiz-Rivera denounced him to the Marine Corps as soon as the Puerto Ricans reached their own side. Ortiz-Rivera's denunciation put a smokescreen around the circumstances of his own release, and it confirmed the worst suspicions of CI investigators, who never doubted Ortiz-Rivera's allegation that Garwood had refused repatriation. They counted this as an act of desertion. Therefore, they determined, if he had not deserted in 1965 he deserted in May 1967.[2] Not long after Ortiz-Rivera's allegations, the secret death sentence that so obsessed McKenney seems to have been passed: from that time forward the special operations world accepted as an official directive the elimination of "the traitor, Garwood."

Because of his rebelliousness after Eisenbraun's death, Garwood was separated from his fellow Americans. It was the cruelest punishment his jailers had yet devised for someone who had just lost the most important person in his life. He was devastated when he and Grisset were moved to separate camps for some months. In the new camp he was again separated from other Americans. He was overjoyed when he met up with Grisset again at the next camp. But despite his pleading, he was not allowed to live with Grisset and the other prisoners. As a result he became emotionally isolated from the fourteen new American prisoners who joined them in the early spring of 1968, right after the Tet offensive, at yet another camp, this time S.T. 18.[3] His first impulse was to search desperately for an officer to pick up the leadership gap left by Ike but there was no one who wanted to fill such a role. The ranking officer was Captain Floyd Harold Kushner, a doctor who, because he was a noncombatant, refused to assume leadership. He did not consider himself qualified. Like Russ when he first joined Eisenbraun and

[2] *The Case of Pvt. Robert R. Garwood, USMC*, Final Report, Volume 1. The position taken by various government investigative agencies is unclear. In a confusing analysis, they maintain that Garwood was guilty of deserting on the day of his capture, yet also on the day Ortiz-Rivera accused him of refusing repatriation. The impression given by the final report is that Garwood deserted twice.

[3] S was the communist symbol for prison. The T stood for *trai* (camp in Vietnamese). S.T. 18, Garwood's fifth camp, was actually a larger entity that incorporated some of the earlier camps he was held in as well as future ones he would be sent to. But, in discussing his camp experience, Camp 5 is the only one referred to as S.T. 18.

Garwood, the new prisoners were still healthy and wearing their own uniforms.

The sight of both Garwood and Grisset scared them. Both prisoners were unconscious of how they must appear to newcomers from a relatively rational world. Garwood actually looked Vietnamese. He had always been a handsome man with a particular midwestern casual style. Now, some of his fellow countrymen did not even recognize that he was American when they first met him. Unlike Grisset, he was not only skeletal, but in his forced isolation and association with the enemy, he was beginning to walk and squat "like a gook." He spoke the Vietnamese language fluently but to his own distress, his English was beginning to break up. Most disgusting to many was the food he foraged and ate. His mouth was permanently stained a dark, vampire red from chewing betel nuts. Ike had taught him that chewing the nuts created warmth in the body—something sorely needed in the cold depths of the triple-canopied jungle. He was an affront to the new prisoners. They had no sense of the torture and long imprisonment undergone by the man they found repulsive, and it was inconceivable that the route Garwood had taken was the only route to survival.

Some new prisoners—the Marines in the bunch—faced what others would rather not believe. These, at the start, were full of questions for Garwood. One was Fred Burns, who had been separated from his patrol and captured. Burns was first housed in a hootch next to Garwood. These single living quarters were smaller than previous ones—not tall enough for the men to stand up in—and they were designed rather like a chicken coop. A group of South Vietnamese prisoners were in the same row of hootches. When Garwood and Burns were locked in, Garwood spent the time carefully telling Burns how he had survived. He talked about Ike, and about the tortures and executions, and the character traits of interrogators and guards.

Garwood's briefing of Burns was reported to the camp commander by Quy, the informer who had betrayed Captain Nghia, the artillery captain who was executed as a result.

Garwood was immediately separated from Burns, and the longtime prisoner was forbidden any communication with American POWs without permission. Garwood circumvented that order whenever he could but it became increasingly difficult. Desperate for the companionship of his own kind, he sadly watched his friendship with Burns eroding.

It was a pattern that repeated itself every time circumstance gave him an opportunity to talk to one of the Americans. After Burns moved in with the other Americans, Garwood was incarcerated near the hootches of the guards. He was made to look as if he lived in the same conditions as the guards. There were three perimeters around each camp. The outer perimeter was where the North Vietnamese regular forces were camped; the second perimeter housed Montagnards loyal to the communists. The first perimeter, which housed the guards, was the most important to the VC for controlling prisoners. Within it was a trenchline where the most ideologically hard-core guards—the ones who dealt with prisoners on a daily basis—resided. When there was any threat of a prisoners rescue, these guards were under standing orders to kill prisoners before defending themselves. Like all the American prisoners, Garwood was within this last perimeter—evidence of his real status but by now only Grisset believed he was a prisoner. Garwood wanted desperately to eat with Grisset and the others but was forced to eat in the guards' kitchen. In truth, he lived like the other prisoners, the same hourly bed checks at night, the same slops for food, and the same regulations so that permission had to be asked even to go to the latrine. Since he spoke their language, the guards required him to follow these rules even more stringently. There would not be one time in his entire fourteen years as a prisoner when Garwood did not have to beg permission to go to the toilet in the following terms: "Honorable liberation fighter, may I please. . . ." Under his breath he allowed himself the satisfaction of calling the guards *cong ga det*—dead chicken. Roughly equivalent to a "limp pecker," this was the worst insult one could offer to a Vietnamese male. But it was small consolation and the only pleasure he ever got from knowing the Vietnamese language.

Garwood's mental suffering worsened. He knew he was a pariah among his own, and in their shoes, he would have responded in the same way to someone who appeared to cozy up to the enemy. He sensed that even Grisset—who had never understood the need to learn Ike's lessons—had trouble withstanding peer pressure. Garwood had become the White Gook and the White Cong. He heard both epithets snarled at him by fellow prisoners. His bitter determination to spite the enemy by surviving held him together. Grisset at least knew who he really was and this saved Garwood's own sense of self. He could still help the other prisoners by stealing tiny scraps of food and passing them on through Grisset. He learned sleight of hand to steal bits of rice and other modest foodstuffs while he was on the move. If there was a loose piece of bamboo anywhere near the kitchen, he stuck his hand through the opening to steal what he could while he scurried on his errands for the guards. He discovered an almost foolproof way to steal eggs from the camp's highly valued hens. Sometimes he was even lucky enough to steal a prized chicken and pass it on to Grisset. Whenever he could, he stole small amounts of medicine—especially penicillin—from the camp dispensary for Dr. Kushner to use in aiding the other prisoners. When he discovered Kushner was hoarding the medicine and not giving it to those who were the sickest, Garwood stopped turning it over to him, and thus gained the doctor's enmity. Soon afterward, the camp interrogator accused Garwood of stealing food. When Garwood denied everything, the interrogator told him the camp commandant knew he was lying because Kushner had informed on him.

Soon after this incident Kushner was called in by the camp nurse because Garwood's foot had become badly infected from elephant grass cuts he sustained on food foraging expeditions. Garwood was immediately apprehensive when he saw the surgical pliers in Kushner's hands. Kushner said, "You understand I'm being ordered to do this." Garwood replied, "Just do what you have to do." Kushner then pulled the nail of Garwood's big toe on the infected foot and the nail of his other big toe as well. Later the camp nurse grinned at Garwood and said, "Kushner doesn't like you!" For a long time the "surgery" on Garwood's feet made it impossible for him to go on working parties to forage for food, or run the kind of errands where he could steal food and medicine. But Garwood remained determined to help the others in some small way. Assigned the job of tuning in Radio Hanoi's propaganda program for the Americans, he regularly fudged things so that for a few moments they could listen to the Voice of America.

To many of the Americans, growing apprehensive and suspicious of everything in such inhuman conditions, it appeared as if he gave such hard-won gifts only to spy on them and ingratiate himself with the guards. This feeling was encouraged by the prison commandant and the interrogators, who ordered Garwood to translate their orders and "progressive lessons and interrogations." They took every opportunity to make it look as if Garwood had been converted to communism. He fell into a kind of helpless rage.

Even without mental torture, S.T. 18 was a painful

and dehumanizing physical setting where everyone was sick with hunger edema, dysentery, and malaria. The majority suffered from a host of other tropical diseases as well. The place stank of human excrement, which was left everywhere by men who in a rush of sickness failed to make it to the latrines. Death became routine. Prisoners hallucinated, cried like children for their families, and died. Some, like Fred Burns, just seemed to give up and gradually fade into nothingness. Those with whom Garwood had developed small and fleeting bonds of friendship—all Marines—died. He felt guilty, as if their friendship with him somehow infected them, made them more vulnerable, and caused their death. He became certain the surviving prisoners thought that. And always, without success, he looked for someone senior among the Americans who would take charge; give him instructions; confirm he was doing the right things; tell him how else to prove himself. He needed someone to replace Ike.

Manipulating the prisoners in such a setting was easy for the VC. Edna Hunter, the psychologist in charge of the Pentagon POW program when prisoners came home in 1973, later described their tactic of alienating American prisoners from each other as so thorough that every prisoner who came home felt guilty of having betrayed his own. She said this was particularly true of the group of prisoners who accused Garwood of betrayal. Garwood "the spy" seemed to be the greatest challenge to his Vietnamese jailers. They knew how to fool those in the camps with him and those he left behind at III MAF. He was now periodically required to carry an AK47, its firing pin removed, when he left the camp or when he came back with a work patrol. Sometimes he was required to repair a bullhorn within sight of the other prisoners. He could tell from their reactions that the VC had subtly passed the message to his fellow Americans that he was using the bullhorn to get American troops to lay down

their arms. The An...
more palpable.

According to Gene...
intelligence specialist a...
Defense Intelligence Age...
a priority, Garwood was ...
the Vietnamese: "They saw ...
resistance among the other ...
American prisoners, but for di...
munists were suspicious of Ga...
survival skills and the fact that ...
passing on everything he had lea... from Ike. His
jailers knew that were he to be successful, it would
give the other prisoners a measure of strength and ability to resist."

Ho constantly told him it was inconceivable that he
had learned Vietnamese—which "is well known as the
most difficult language in the world"—in prison. He
must have learned it in "a special school for spies." Ho
suspected that had been the reason for Garwood's close
relationship to Eisenbraun, who was known to be a
special-operations officer. Furthermore, reports were
coming from the communists' own double agents within
the highest echelons of the CIA in Saigon that the Marine
Corps and CIA were increasingly obsessed with Garwood. The enemy knew that even the FBI had been
called into the case. The high-level concern with Garwood did not seem reasonable if he was the lowly private
he claimed. If he was CIA, therefore, it was useful to
keep him alive but segregated, and subject to pressures
and brainwashing techniques that would eventually break
him. To the enemy, it appeared more than probable that
he was, at the very least, a military intelligence officer
who would try to organize a command structure among
the camp prisoners.

In other camps that held Americans, one officer was
usually willing to suffer the consequences of taking com-

the case here. Only after Kushner
more highly educated men refused, did
Sergeant ''Top'' Williams, a forty-eight-
career soldier and World War II veteran, reluc-
ntly take on the job. Of all the prisoners in S.T. 18,
Williams was the most set in his ways and the least able
to understand Garwood. He too would die of malnutri-
tion, disease, and hopelessness.

In the midst of Garwood's troubles with his fellow
prisoners, something happened that seemed to affirm interrogators'[4] suspicions that Garwood was working for
the CIA.

In late spring of 1968 Clyde Weatherman, another
American, joined the group of prisoners. Garwood could
tell immediately the man was in a special category, but
had no idea how closely his own name and reputation
would be linked to the newcomer. Weatherman was
blond and had the same build that Garwood had before
prison camp took its toll. Except for the difference in
hair color, seen from a distance, the two could have been
brothers.

Weatherman also fit the description of a man who later
led an enemy attack against Marines at No Name Island.
This report of treachery would spur Colonel McKenney
to launch his most deadly hunt for Robert Garwood.
Weatherman resembled as well a man who, wearing an
NVA lieutenant's uniform, would be later pointed out to
a number of American POWs in other camps as Robert
Garwood.[5] In obvious good health, Weatherman wore de-

---

[4] There were now two primary interrogators. Ho had been joined by
Hum.

[5] An example of this came from Army Major Mark Smith, the Special
Forces specialist in behind-the-lines operations who later commanded
a regional intelligence service. For years after his repatriation in 1973,
when the North Vietnamese released American prisoners as part of the
peace agreement, Smith nursed a deep hatred for Bobby Garwood, supposedly the man who had been pointed out to him in prison camp as

cent civilian clothes and ate the same food as the camp commandant and Ho. He was housed separately one hundred yards from the camp, outside the perimeter where Garwood and the other American prisoners were held. Even though Garwood was supposed to stay away from American POWs, he was allowed to spend a lot of time with Weatherman, who was billed as a "progressive" prisoner. Garwood didn't believe Weatherman was a prisoner at all.

The respectful treatment Weatherman received from guards, the camp commandant, and even Ho indicated he was a plant who had been infiltrated to work on the "attitude of the other Americans." It was an opinion Russ Grisset shared. Grisset and Garwood managed the occasional furtive conversation when Garwood was allowed to visit the American section of the compound to tune in Radio Hanoi's English propaganda program. Weatherman himself told Garwood that he had escaped from the III MAF brig in Da Nang and that he had a Vietnamese wife and family in Saigon. On his way to meet his wife, he avoided the main roads and was apprehended in a village near an off-beat trail by the Vietcong. Unlike the other Americans, Weatherman asked Garwood a lot of questions about his capture and background the same questions Ho repeatedly asked during interrogations. He talked a lot about the generosity of the VC and hinted that Garwood's life, like his own, could be a lot more pleasant if he collaborated.

Then, in August, Weatherman was allegedly killed in an escape attempt. Garwood was skeptical. He pieced together what really happened and tried to feed it back to the other American POWs. The camp commandant's story was that Weatherman had gone on a working party

---

a VC sympathizer and NVA lieutenant. It was only when he met Garwood and began a series of long and intensive debriefings that he realized the Vietnamese had fooled him and other prisoners in his camp.

to forage for food with four other Americans and one guard. Away from the camp Weatherman had over-powered the lone guard and escaped with Dennis Hammond, another prisoner. The rest of the prisoners, according to the communists, refused to flee.

Two days later Hammond was returned to the camp with a bullet through his calf and, oddly, put in stocks in Garwood's hootch. He told Garwood that he and Weatherman were caught by Montagnard tribesmen loyal to the communists. Immediately after their capture, they were separated by the tribesmen and Hammond was taken down a creek bed; Weatherman was taken in the opposite direction. A few minutes later Hammond heard a shot. Then he heard Weatherman scream. Convinced Weatherman had been killed, Hammond got scared and ran away wildly until he was shot and crippled.

Hammond believed what he was saying but to Garwood, who had much more experience with VC decep-tions, the story stank. Weatherman wanted to get back to his family and told Garwood that Ho had promised him anything he wanted. Having tried to escape twice himself and witnessed attempts by others, Garwood's instincts told him this was VC trickery. No working party ever went out with only one guard. Usually there was one guard per prisoner, each heavily armed with automatic weapons. In this case a lone guard for five prisoners had carried one old, single-shot, bolt action, Soviet-made rifle with only three rounds.

What really persuaded Garwood that Weatherman was not dead and that the escape attempt had been a set-up was that a few days later, the shirt Weatherman always wore appeared on a Montagnard guerrilla who came to the camp. Garwood knew the Montagnards had a strict taboo against wearing or even touching the clothing or other personal items of a dead person. They believed that breaking this taboo would result in the angry spirit of the dead person coming back to seek revenge. So Weatherman must be still alive.[6] It was another lesson Garwood learned from Ike—to familiarize himself with the customs and religious beliefs of the indigenous people they came across. But when he attempted to question the Montagnard, he was harshly interrupted. Colonel Pham Van Thai, the man in charge of interrogations and torture, who happened to be visiting the camp at the time, told him the shirt was none of his business.

Garwood then made a mistake that would have repercussions through all his prison years. During his next interrogation he told Ho that he knew Weatherman was alive. Ho took the news calmly, solicitously offering Garwood some tea. Had Garwood told this to any of the other Americans? "No," said Garwood.

"Well Bobby, now you understand why we can never put you back in with the other Americans," responded Ho. "All along you have confirmed our suspicions. We were thinking you to be CIA when we captured you."

Garwood kept insisting that he was what he was—a simple private, a driver. He recalled: "The more I tried to convince Ho of the truth, the more I convinced him of the opposite." Ho also told him that Quy, whose fingering of Captain Nghia had led to the latter's death, had informed the prison commandant about Garwood's seditious behavior with the other prisoners. Ho added that some of the new American prisoners were informing on Garwood as well, two of whom were soon thereafter put through the liberation ceremony and, decorated with a red sash, then released.

The sedition Ho referred to was the same behavior that convinced most of the prisoners that Garwood was a VC sympathizer. This went beyond irony. Garwood often thought that even if he died in some heroic act of rebellion now, other Americans would never find out the truth.

---

[6] Years later, Garwood would see Weatherman again—healthy and free to move about Hanoi on his own.

In all likelihood they would think it served him right. He consoled himself that at least Grisset knew he had not broken Ike's one commandment—never to consciously hurt another American.

Then, in December 1969, Russ died, too, in a way that made Garwood so enraged he did break the commandment by shoving a fellow prisoner. Russ and Kushner had killed a guard's cat for food. All the prisoners had apparently shared the meat. The guards found tell-tale signs and the prisoners were lined up outside their hootches being interrogated, when Garwood came upon the scene. He had never seen the guards so angry. No one admitted to the deed. Garwood decided the prisoners were subtly making Grisset the scapegoat in the way they stood and averted their eyes from him. The guard commander began to beat Grisset viciously. Garwood panicked that the attack on Grisset would end in death, as Ike had been beaten to death. Enraged at the other Americans for not sticking together now, Garwood ran blindly past the guards toward David Harker, who was standing in the doorway of a hootch. He pushed Harker aside with a shove in the gut: "You let Russ take all the blame. If you'd all kept your mouths shut, this wouldn't be happening." The response from the others was virulently savage. In their eyes he had no right to criticize them and no right to be concerned about Russ. They were so prejudiced against Garwood that they were blind to his relationship with Grisset—a friendship even the guards acknowledged.

When Grisset died, one of the guards told Garwood, "Russ was the only friend you had left."

David Harker had previously enjoyed Garwood's friendship. He had valued the extra food Garwood supplied and, even more, the forbidden information that came when Garwood slyly turned their radios to the Voice of America instead of the required Radio Hanoi broadcasts. After his repatriation, he was to tell a reporter from *People* magazine: "You can't imagine what a great morale-booster that was." But in the camps Harker succumbed to peer pressure and joined the others in treating Garwood as an outcast. It was a pattern he would repeat fourteen years later at Garwood's court martial.

13: Gaming

It wasn't easy for the assassins to follow Garwood's trail. The White Cong, as he was called by some in the closed, small circle of men who hunted him, got a reputation for cleverness beyond belief. Agents reported to U.S. authorities that he spoke Vietnamese so well his VC buddies teased him about it. His accent, apparently, was neutral, like that of the Central Highlands, an incredible accomplishment—if true—in a country full of complicated dialects where more often than not a peasant from the north could not understand a peasant from the south. Garwood, it was rumored, could communicate with both. This skill put Garwood in a very special category, apart from other deserters. McKenney suspected him of working with high-level communist intelligence and of helping to train their spies and infiltrators.

There were numerous cases of Phoenix missions being compromised. The highly secret Phoenix teams of other special ops groups were made up of Americans and Vietnamese. The Marines conducted their own hunting patrols. The majority of other Phoenix teams were largely made up of provincial reconnaissance unit soldiers with American advisers. It had become a highly skilled game to ferret out infiltrators whose job was sabotage. Sam

Owens's friend at the Tra Bong Special Forces camp had lined up members of the South Vietnamese Civilian Irregular Defense Force because they had suddenly decided en masse not to go on patrol. Suspecting two of being VC infiltrators and propagandizers, he had them fall in for inspection and bellowed: "I know that two of you are Vietcong. If you're not gone by tomorrow morning, you're dead." The next morning *three* were gone.

The lack of Vietnamese language skills among Americans made it hard to pinpoint infiltrators. Men with Garwood's reputedly legendary facility were a rarity in I Corps. McKenney considered himself lucky to be able to rely on one of the best—Marine Master Sergeant Bob Hyp, a man who was destined to play a key role not only in McKenney's life, but in that of his pet hate, Bobby Garwood.

Hyp was based at the naval support hospital southeast of Da Nang, near Marble Mountain. There he worked primarily with wounded communist prisoners who might have information useful to Marines. "He had an amazing success rate in getting them to switch their allegiance to the Americans," according to McKenney. "A good number went on to become Kit Carson scouts, valuable additions to American combat units. Many were disillusioned with the communist leadership. Expecting to be tortured—as they would have been in South Vietnamese hands—they were usually hostile at first. Then they saw that they were getting the same treatment as American servicemen in the most sophisticated hospital in I Corps. This made many receptive to Hyp's subtle and humane questioning. Often they were not aware of the secrets they revealed. But they could also trick their interrogators into believing false information. It took language skills and a special kind of psychological and cultural perceptiveness to tell the difference. Hyp had both."

When McKenney became intelligence collections and operations officer, he became acquainted with Sergeant

Hyp. The Sergeant had let him know whenever there was a POW whose information seemed useful. After mid-April 1969, McKenney took the opportunity to work with Hyp on a daily basis when severe bouts of dysentery, later diagnosed as tropical sprue, hepatitis, and several other tropical diseases, brought him to the hospital for a seven-week stay. Instead of going home for treatment, he signed up as guinea pig for a tropical disease study in order to complete his tour. At the hospital he continued with his job as intelligence operations officer,[1] taking full advantage of Hyp's extraordinary skills. One episode involved Hyp and Sister Mary, the Catholic nun who voluntarily acted as a kind of agent for McKenney. It left an indelible impression on him. Hyp was one of those special Marines McKenney considered completely trustworthy. The Sergeant never hesitated to put himself in dangerous situations.

Sister Mary brought news that an NVA regimental executive officer wanted to meet with an American who spoke Vietnamese. Hyp took on the assignment even though it meant entering the high-risk, VC-infested area near China Beach where Bobby Garwood had been captured, alone and at night. Hyp was the only man available who spoke fluent Vietnamese. Another communist offensive was imminent. The NVA officer told Sister Mary he wanted to help the Americans. Fear of being betrayed by infiltrators, with whose work the NVA officer was evidently only too familiar, made him insist that no South Vietnamese be involved. McKenney sympathized with that last request. Betrayal was common in their bizarre world where General Binh, the G-2 of the ARVN in I Corps, had a brother who was a general with the NVA. However, for the very reason that treachery was endemic, McKenney and Hyp had to face the strong possibility that

---

[1] During his seven-week hospitalization McKenney was regularly briefed by Owens.

they were being set up to walk straight into an ambush.

Hyp's decision to meet the NVA officer alone in such circumstances required unusual courage and nerve. The man turned out to be second in command of his regiment and disclosed details of an imminent attack. And sure enough, the enemy hit hard after midnight with rocket and mortar attacks all over I Corps. Thanks to Hyp, the Marines were waiting for them. It was the beginning of the May offensive.

Hyp's bravery[2] and skill led McKenney to trust him completely on everything, including Garwood. Hyp periodically passed on information he heard about the White Cong without embellishment. Like Sam Owens, Hyp never seemed obsessed by the matter. Neither did McKenney discuss the directive to kill Garwood with him. He assumed that Hyp, like everyone else in their small world, knew about it and approved.

All that spring of 1969, Hyp passed on reports that a Caucasian American, presumed to be a former U.S. Marine, was not only leading an NVA patrol with an AK47 slung over his shoulder, he was actively propagandizing in the villages. Dressed in black pyjamas and red sash, the reports said he played a perverse game with his band of Vietcong, trashing the United States, inciting the Vietnamese to take up arms against his own people, thereby increasing the risk to Marines. The red sash, symbolic of communism, was seen as a deliberate slap in the face of Marines. It did not bother Sam Owens because he thought such insignia would make Garwood an easy target.

Rumors of the White Cong in the red sash were reinforced by word from CIA headquarters in Saigon. The

---

[2] On a later occasion, Hyp flew, without hesitation, with McKenney and a wounded NVA prisoner as guide, into a ''hot'' area in the Que Son Valley, where several helicopters had been shot down, to locate an enemy command post.

information came from the Agency's most trusted agent, the charismatic cartoonist Huyn Ba Thanh, who was in reality their secret liaison to President Thieu. Thanh, who used the alias Hai Long, reported that Garwood was actively and publicly leading an enemy NVA patrol. Sam Owens recalled later that there was no briefing of even the limited kind that McKenney got from counterintelligence, just a few challenging words directed at the right people. There was nothing unusual about this. It was the way things were done.

Owens, then a captain, had just been given command of First Force Recon Company, a position usually held by someone of more senior rank. Operationally in charge of Marine hunter-killer patrols, he was now in a perfect position to take care of the White Cong. He automatically incorporated the targeting of Garwood in his patrols' missions.

Sam Owens concentrated a series of patrols in Quang Nghai and Quang Nam provinces, where Garwood had supposedly been sighted wearing the red sash. The patrol leaders came back with word of a large man with a white face and big footprints. Owens now planned a very specific mission to get Garwood, assigning Cowpoke,[3] one of his best hunter-killer teams, for the job. Sometimes, teams would include a Kit Carson scout familiar with the terrain. Not this time. For security reasons, this mission was to be handled entirely by Marines. A few days earlier, the mission leader flew over the area to find a landing zone for the eight-man team. Insertion and extraction of the patrol were the most critical phases of any mission. The situation at the landing area could not be predicted

---

[3] The patrol's name and certain details have been changed to protect the identity of team members for ongoing security reasons. All of the information here was taken from reports of men who participated in a number of different missions charged with neutralizing the man in the red sash.

and helicopters were highly vulnerable to enemy fire as they made their slow descent. The helicopter flight leader and patrol leader carefully worked out the actions they would take if the enemy attacked during landing. If ground fire was received or the enemy was sighted before landing, the team was to proceed on to an alternative landing site. If fire was to commence after landing, the flight leader was to take off immediately. His primary concern was the safety of the aircraft. The ground patrol leader would have to decide whether to stay aboard or deplane and begin action against the enemy. Often a patrol leader chose to take the greater risk that his team's fire power would protect the helicopter's escape.

The rules for such engagements stated that the patrol had to kill or neutralize every one of the enemy before the helicopter could land again to withdraw the team. Sometimes the landing site was booby trapped. This had happened to a team member both McKenney and Owens knew well, a man McKenney had thought indestructible. He had jumped directly onto a booby-trapped howitzer round. Although half his face, one arm, and one leg had been blown off, he had, against all odds, survived for a while. After receiving ninety-two pints of blood in rapid succession, his system could no longer cope and he died.

Cowpoke's patrol leader carefully fixed on several landing sites. Only one was the real thing. The others were designated for mock landings to confuse the enemy. The real landing site, familiar to him, was in an area near a stream where the courier carrying the list of POWs with Russ Grisset's name had been killed. Real "Injun country," it was also the place where previous patrols reported signs of a Caucasian leading a communist patrol. The patrol leader was not told that word had come from division headquarters that Bobby Garwood was in the area. He knew only that they would be looking for a white man leading the NVA. Years later both McKenney and Owens would be appalled to remember that this was, in fact the only description of Garwood given the hunter-killer teams. He surmised that it was probably the fallen Marine, Bobby Garwood.

There was no advance notice for the team's departure. The briefing took place at the very last moment. Usually briefings took place in the patrol operation leader's tent with the company operations officer giving the instructions. This meeting, however, was important enough to take place in the company commander's tent on Hill 34. Sam Owens himself conducted the briefing. Another unusual move added to the tension: McKenney drove over from Hill 327 for the briefing. Because Owens knew how important this mission was to McKenney, he had invited him. McKenney's silent presence told the team that something big was in the works.

"Now gents, this is going to be a tough one," was how Owens began the briefing. The team would be heading to the recon zone for a "first-light landing." The formal term for the period between complete darkness and sunrise was before-morning-nautical-twilight (BMNT), during which there was enough illumination to carry on most ground activities without difficulty: the pilot could land and take off with least risk of being fired on because the enemy could not observe the helicopter or its landing point from any great distance. The landing zone and area to be secured were unveiled. The team was to function as Marines and dress like Marines with standard operating procedures. There would be a point man carrying a 12-gauge shotgun. The patrol leader would carry an M16 rifle. The communications man would also be armed with a rifle and an M76 grenade launcher and pistol. The rest all carried two fragmentation grenades and rifles. Two team members would be carrying smoke grenades to identify landing zones and to break contact.

There was one singular feature. One team member was instructed to carry an entrenching tool, a small, steel shovel with a two-foot long, fold-up handle. It could be used as an effective hand weapon. On this mission, it would serve as a gravedigger's spade to bury the target.

Each man would carry five extra magazines of ammunition. Owens, who had often been in their place, figured if the patrol members could not get command of a situation with 120 rounds they might as well hang it up.

Team members did not need to be told to put all their personal possessions in order on their cot before leaving. That was unwritten policy and would make things easier for all concerned if they ended up as casualties.

It was still dark when Cowpoke boarded the helicopter that had flown over from the Marble Mountain air facility to the base of Hill 34. At BMNT they arrived at the planned landing site, a meadow full of elephant grass surrounded by triple-canopy jungle. The helicopter hovered briefly. There was heavy mist that made landing tricky, but as the mist cleared the helicopter began its descent, and the downwash from the rotors flattened the elephant grass. In less than eight seconds from touchdown, the entire team was running for the shelter of the nearby trees, where they then lay motionless until long after the helicopter was gone. This was the tensest part of the patrol; the easiest time to be ambushed. With no sign of the enemy, the patrol leader signaled his men forward.

They were now totally attentive to their surroundings, moving silently toward the stream they had memorized from the map at the previous night's briefing. There, the patrol leader ordered cover and concealment for six of the men. They positioned themselves where they could see across the stream but not be seen, covering two team members making ready to cross. From the other side, the two would signal and in turn provide cover for the others as they crossed two by two.

Suddenly the stillness turned electric. One of the teammates, moving forward, stepped back quickly, signaling the others that he had spotted an enemy patrol. This was

followed by an even more intense signal: he had spotted
their target, a largish man with fair hair, black pyjamas,
and, most tellingly, a red sash. Now the other Americans
saw him too. The white man seemed to be charging
ahead, making no effort at concealment, although the
Orientals with him appeared much more cautious and almost disconnected from their Caucasian leader.

The emotion among Cowpoke's teammates was palpable. For the first and probably last time in Vietnam,
they forgot about the NVA soldiers on the other side.
Without instruction, and against Marine regulations, eight
weapons aimed at the White Cong's heart and fired. As
he fell to the ground his NVA teammates uncharacterist-
ically scurried away without any attempt to pick him up.
The Marines waited tensely: it was unusual for the enemy
not to answer fire, and unusual for them to abandon the
body of one of their own.

The patrol stayed concealed for many hours, eyes focused on the area where the body of the white man lay.
They all knew of cases where the enemy remained hidden
all day until Americans moved, then sprang an ambush.
And cases where the enemy booby-trapped the bodies of
American soldiers. After this torturing period of stillness,
the patrol leader signaled his man with the entrenching
tool to go to the body. His teammates provided cover as
he cautiously crossed the stream and probed the ground
around the body. Then he prodded the corpse from a
distance. Hoping he had eliminated possible deadly devices, he quickly buried the man in the red sash as fast
as he could. There were other times, much later in the
war, when teams were ordered to check for identifying
marks like moles or scars. Not this time. The objective
was to bury the traitor and erase all evidence of his alleged perfidy. No one should find out that such a traitor
had even existed. On the books Garwood remained MIA.
The Marine noted briefly that even though the VC had
not picked up their fallen comrade, they had taken his

AK47. The only object near the dead man was a sturdy stick.

Whatever feeling of triumph the First Force Reconnaissance Company felt, it was short lived. The man they killed had seemed to fit the general description of Bobby Garwood given to McKenney by counterintelligence although the operative description for the team had been only "that he was white." But he must have been another deserter. Within weeks "Garwood" struck again, more viciously and tauntingly than ever before.

American prisoners held in Vietcong camps in Quang Nghai and Quang Nam provinces heard a completely different story about the killing of the man in the red sash— a man they presumed was a sergeant who had recently gone through the liberation ceremony—from an unexpected source. Ho Chi Minh himself addressed a message to U.S. POWs. The man killed by the Americans, the message read, had been one of their colleagues, an Air Force man who was to be released in a gesture of good will. The Americans had rejected the good will of North Vietnam, said the communist leader. They had not wanted their prisoner and had killed him on his way to be released. For this reason, Ho Chi Minh was sad to report, no more prisoners would be released.

Frank Snepp, a CIA officer who was at the time responsible for the Agency's handling of interrogations of communist prisoners and informant networks, in a later book, *Decent Interval*,[4] claimed there was indeed no great receptiveness to North Vietnam's spring 1969 initiative to exchange prisoners. According to Snepp, the issue of prisoner exchange fell under the aegis of the CIA, which was concerned only with the return of its own operatives

[4] Frank Snepp, *Decent Interval: An Insider's Account of Saigon's Indecent End Told By The CIA's Chief Strategy Analyst in Vietnam.* New York: Random House, 1977.

and officers of high rank. He wrote: "The CIA was particularly inflexible, usually insisting on strict reciprocity, an intelligence operative for an intelligence operative, as if Agency personnel deserved first consideration over any other Americans who might be prisoners of the communists." Snepp's term for the way his employer handled potential POW exchanges was "gaming."

Unreceptive certainly describes the attitude encountered by recently upgraded[5] Army Staff Sergeant John Sexton, who in 1971 was suddenly and without warning released from a VC prison camp near the Cambodian border. The possibility existed that the camp was actually inside a part of Cambodia controlled by communist guerrillas. It was difficult for POWs to decipher their precise location. At first Sexton was accompanied by NVA soldiers who made him walk point, as the Air Force man killed by First Force Recon had been made to do, but he was then abandoned near the small town of Snoul in Cambodia to make his own way back. Sexton, who was dressed in black pyjamas and carried a message from the communists asking for reciprocity for his release, said that once he reached American lines no one on his own side was interested, other than to impress upon him that he was to keep his mouth shut. For a long time he felt that it might have been more convenient for his own side if he had died in prison camp. For years after his return, he could not speak at meetings held by the families of other prisoners without an ever-present government representative to insure his silence. He still feels that his own government had somehow become persuaded that he had been turned by the communists and that was why he had been chosen to be released. His only crime was to have fallen into the hands of the enemy after being severely wounded. He was shot in the head, blinded in one eye,

---

[5] Sexton was a corporal when he was captured. Under U.S. law American POWs were automatically upgraded in rank at certain intervals.

and incapacitated in one arm. His medical care was minimal but he is still grateful that the enemy applied the primitive medicine of setting maggots to clean out his wounds. He suffered torture and interrogation for two years. There was never any proof that he had in any way collaborated with the enemy.

14: Coming Out on Strings

By early summer Colonel McKenney was confident that his side was winning what seemed a war of attrition. President Nixon in the first days of his administration had launched a secret bombing campaign against communist camps in eastern Cambodia. This was followed up by the start of peace talks between the two sides in late January. McKenney felt his president was moving toward peace from a position of strength. It meant that all the sacrifices were worth something. No one thought that the new president, like his predecessor, wanted out at almost any price.

Nixon met with President Thieu on Midway Island and announced afterward that twenty-five thousand men would be withdrawn from South Vietnam. This was the first step of "Vietnamization," a program designed to eventually turn the war over to the South Vietnamese. The idea was a good one as long as it wasn't done too quickly. The Phoenix program had made progress. Many areas under VC control the year before were now back in the hands of the South Vietnamese. This was largely due to the shot in the arm Phoenix got when the CIA began a "blitz" by what it called the Accelerated Pacification Program (APC), a euphemism for expanded

Phoenix activities, at the beginning of November 1968.

The man in charge of APC was William Colby, who had been deputy to Robert Komer, the head of the CIA in Vietnam until then. Colby had already developed an excellent working relationship with General Creighton Abrams, who succeeded General Westmoreland, the U.S. military commander in Vietnam in mid-1968. Now he refined that association. Both men made it known later that they had high moral aspirations for APC, wanting it to function within the framework of traditional standards of war.[1] At the same time, Colby at least seemed aware that excesses were sometimes committed, especially by the South Vietnamese, who, he always maintained, controlled the Phoenix program. Colby later said he never wanted assassinations to be part of Phoenix although he admitted the program had a reputation for brutality. It is generally accepted that twenty thousand Vietnamese were assassinated under its aegis. It is impossible to estimate how many Americans were killed. McKenney has a mental block about the precise number of Americans he knew of being "taken out" during his year in Vietnam. He says the total number could have come close to one hundred.

In his memoir of Vietnam, Colby explained the kind of unwritten kill-Garwood directive that McKenney believed had come from the CIA. "Some units," he wrote, "especially some of the American military, used the term 'Phoenix' to refer to any operation against the Viet Cong Infrastructure or other irregulars, even when the operation had no connection with the Phoenix program at all. In-

---

[1] In a 1968 directive for Phoenix, William Colby wrote "that it was to be a program of advice, support and assistance to the Phuong Hong (Vietnamese for Phoenix)." He stressed that "U.S. personnel are under the same legal and moral constraints with respect to operations of a Phoenix character as they are with respect to regular military operations against enemy units in the field." From William Colby with James McCargar, *Lost Victory*. Chicago: Contemporary Books, 1989.

deed, some of the more lurid accusations heard in public
have turned out on examination to be in exactly this
category.''[2] McKenney's answer to that was, ''I can't
imagine any Marine unit engaged in any Phoenix-style
operation of their own.''

Colby pointed out that Abrams wanted to hear no more
of ''the other war of pacification,'' his allusive term for
Phoenix. APC was to be under the military command
umbrella, Abrams stating that ''the entire effort is to be
one war.'' There were rumors among Special Forces that
Abrams meant by that to show his disapproval of all their
work, that he resented the arrogance of special-operations
people and Phoenix excesses.

McKenney discounted such rumors. He was pleased
that finally the military seemed to be making decisions
along with the CIA. Even MACSOG was now under
Abrams's command. As so often in his career as a soldier, McKenney would be proven wrong in his judgment
of people at the top.

The emasculation of the proud Special Forces, who
preferred the nickname Green Berets, was already un-
derway. An alleged incident involving the killing of a
Vietnamese double agent by Green Berets at the end of
June 1969 would provide those politicians in Washington
who thought the war immoral with the perfect way to
undermine Special Forces. Assassination as a legitimate
tactic of war would be challenged. So would the CIA's
role in issuing the directives for it. McKenney could anticipate none of this. He was too far down the chain of
command and too far removed from Washington to know
who was making policy decisions. He felt secure in the
knowledge that, because of the work he was involved in,
the enemy was nearing exhaustion.

Despite sporadic and sometimes briefly successful efforts, the enemy, he felt, had never really regained the

---

[2] Ibid.

initiative after the 1968 Tet offensive. The best example of this was the second Tet offensive. It began on February 16th, 1969, with widespread rocket, mortar, and ground attacks throughout South Vietnam. The enemy followed their earlier patterns of attack, concentrating on the III MAF area and along the DMZ. The Second NVA Battalion made it all the way to the edge of Da Nang before being pushed back. On February 23rd the ARVN munitions dump directly across from McKenney's quarters was blown up. West of Da Nang the enemy briefly gained control of Hill 327's defensive bunker on the ridge directly above the general's hootch and raised their flag. The action was a microcosm of the entire offensive. The highest point in III MAF's area of operations, Hill 327—Freedom Hill—protected Da Nang from invasion from the west. Raising the communist flag over the American general's hootch made the victory highly symbolic, but the ridge was quickly recaptured, as were all the other enemy objectives. The enemy had been unable to seize and hold any significant objective. There had been only brief moments of glory for the communists, which they replayed constantly for propaganda purposes, apparently believing as did Hitler that if a lie is repeated often enough, it becomes truth.

It was frustrating for McKenney that the sorry psychological state of enemy troops seemed to go unnoticed by the American public. He was in a prime position to monitor enemy discomfiture. Marine reconnaissance patrols infiltrated rear areas, tapped telephone lines, and recorded telephone traffic. The North Vietnamese troops suffered from malaria and hunger, their morale was terrible. They had huge desertion rates. This last item never made the headlines in the American press, but it was such a big problem that the enemy let deserters go virtually unpunished. The North Vietnamese could not imprison or shoot their deserters because they needed them so badly, once recaptured. McKenney had proof that the same men deserted over and over again. They simply got on the Ho Chi Minh Trail and headed north, were found, and sent back to their units.

McKenney felt a funny kind of communion with the enemy when he eavesdropped on their conversations about the communist bureaucratic demand for reports and more reports. It seemed these were ignored or became a substitute for action. The enemy soldiers, the real ones whom he respected, had the same problems as their American counterparts, but with less institutional flexibility to solve them. At least his side was always changing, and the system was still open to men with initiative. McKenney kept the journal of a Vietnamese soldier that his men found on a battlefield. He found it moving. In it the NVA infantryman wrote eloquently of his own despair as he waited, encircled, for certain death. All he wanted was to get home, as did his comrades.

There was still intense combat at the small-unit level. It was a time to be doubly alert. The weaker the enemy got, the more he would resort to terrorism. McKenney was grateful for the countermechanism of the accelerated Phoenix program. He saw evidence that the communists were reverting to the guerrilla tactics that they had been employing since the subsiding of the first Tet offensive.

On June 5th McKenney received a letter from his wife, Marty, reminding him that it was sixteen years to the day that she had pinned lieutenant's bars on him. She also reported that she had just made the last five-hundred-dollar payment on the Kentucky farm they both loved. Their plan was to raise beef cattle after the war. But there was no exultation in McKenney's heart. He was scheduled to interview the survivors of the battle of No Name Island, the patrol base of K Company, Third Battalion, First Marines. He shrank from the demoralizing statistics—forty-eight of fifty-two Marines killed or wounded.

The elusive Garwood again entered the picture at this point. The survivors, at the naval hospital and division rest area at China Beach, told the most horrifying tale about Garwood to date. They made their reports to McKenney in a low key, listless manner. All pride, and even hatred, seemed to have been drained out of them. One young man, face wreathed in bandages that gave him a mummylike appearance said, "They had us whipped." Everyone reported the same thing: the NVA could have killed them all, but the stocky white American with fair hair called them off and they withdrew for no apparent reason when American artillery began to come in.

Security at No Name Island had been lax. In the opening barrage, the lieutenant's foot was blown off. At the outset there was chaos—with the wounded screaming for God's help. One black guy had been dragged outside the wire and mutilated. His comrades heard him cry for his mother's help.

A major factor in the disaster, as so many times before, was failure of the M16 to function in the heat and dust of combat. The lieutenant had inspected all rifles before dark and all were clean. Yet before the battle ended, *every* one failed to fire.

McKenney knew that countless Marines died and were wounded because of Washington's decision to go with the bug-ridden M16 instead of an alternative that worked much better. He had intimate knowledge of how the M16 had been field tested at Quantico's development center in 1966–67 against the much more serviceable and flexible Stoner system. The project officer, a major who had come up through the ranks, had done everything one could with and to a weapon, then written a voluminous report solidly in favor of the Stoner system. McKenney remembered how the major had to sit up all night with his general to rewrite the report in favor of the M16. The commitment to the faulty M16 had already been made in Washington. McKenney felt helpless. He found it appalling that no journalist was interested in a scandal that even now continued to take so many lives.

But he finally had something he was able to act on: the white American who had led the enemy. At the end of the battle of No Name Island, the NVA soldiers stood on the walls, sprayed the wounded with AK47s, laughed with odd, almost Spanish-tinged accents: "Marines you die tonight—no sweat," and similar expressions. Mc-Kenney figured they must have learned the slang from the man who was leading them. That must mean the NVA had been commanded by an American! For the first time he had glimpsed "proof" beyond the mostly ephemeral sightings of recon patrols and agents' reports. The survivors of K-3 platoon didn't know who the traitor was but McKenney knew. Although he was influenced primarily by the fact that the man was white, the description also matched the fair hair and solid build of Garwood, as originally described by counterintelligence. In his mind he began assembling the patrol that would finally get Garwood.

After interviewing the survivors of No Name Island, McKenney concluded that CCN hunter-killer patrols might have more success in getting Garwood than his Marine recon patrols. McKenney's only dealings with CCN teams were through sharing information. After the mission in which yet another Force Recon patrol thought it had killed the White Cong with the red sash, he decided that CCN's smaller, six-man patrols would be more effective. They were more mobile, easier to extract from enemy territory, better equipped than Marines.

And these more compact CCN patrols had the most experience in assassinations. They operated in areas "over the fence," officially off limits to U.S. regular forces soldiers, where Garwood was now reputed to be operating. Being off-limits made these areas more dangerous to the Americans who fought there. If they were taken prisoner they were not protected by international law. On the other hand, they were also freed from the restraints imposed by politicians afraid of bad publicity.

Off-limits meant total secrecy. Every one in special ops knew their work fell under the jurisdiction of the CIA, even though they were technically part of the regular armed services.

It seemed now to McKenney that Garwood was located in just such an off-limits region where no holds were barred—the land-locked kingdom of Laos, used by the enemy but officially neutral. One of the Special Forces most trusted agents[3] had pinpointed Garwood's precise location in an NVA divisional area in Tchepone, Laos, adjacent to I Corps, through A Shau Valley, all the way down to II Corps. This was far from No Name Island, which was located in the delta, south of Marble Mountain. Nobody thought to mention it was unlikely Garwood would be transported by the enemy from one end of such a vast region to another. Common sense would have said the whole idea was preposterous, but common sense was not in common supply.

The assigned patrol was made up of four Americans and two Chinese-Vietnamese called Nhung, volunteers who had many scores to settle with the communists. The official mission was specifically to kill Garwood.

The team was highly compartmentalized. Each member had his own assignment, unknown to the others. Should one team member fall into enemy hands, he could not compromise the others. Only the team leader, who was acting as sniper, and the administration and supply

---

[3] Agents who worked with Special Forces, like those who worked with the Marine Corps, provided crucial information about the enemy's plans and strength. Americans had five categories of agents with "trusted agent" (1) ranking the highest; 2—usually reliable source; 3—source whose credibility is not verified; 4—source who has proved less than credible in the past; 5—source thought to be a double agent. If a letter preceded the ranking it referred to the quality of information. For example, A-1 would signify trusted information coming from a trusted agent, B-1 would refer to trusted information coming from a usually reliable source, and so forth.

technician knew the identity of the target. The role of administration and supply technician, usually a Special Forces NCO with vast experience in the area of operations, was just for this mission played by an old CIA hand experienced in assassinations. In Special Forces parlance, he was called cynically the Public Safety Director.

Whatever the sniper's target, getting him to it and assisting him had priority among other team members, though there were other intelligence objectives as well, like counting enemy trucks entering the area from the North. The planning process was a complicated procedure involving logistics, command signals, radio frequencies, and method of execution, all of which had to be memorized. Planning went backward. It began at the point the mission was expected to be completed. Experience had taught these men that if they started planning from the beginning of the mission they invariably got bogged down in irrelevant details. To McKenney, the CCN modus operandi seemed the ideal response to enemy duplicities, compared with the way the Marine hunter-killer groups were bound by tradition and exaggerated concern for international law and world opinion.

The six-man team heaved a collective sigh of relief when it got its "warning order." This was the green light for the mission. From that point forward they had no contact with anyone not associated with the mission, moving into the isolation area. Here there was no bathing with soap for four days prior to the mission. No deodorant, no aftershave—no "Caucasian" smell that might give them away to the enemy. Their clothes for the mission were washed with sand and beaten on a rock. The Public Safety Director made the final checks, and ensured no one was carrying any letters or anything else that might identify them. He would later take fake letters each man had written, describing how they were on rest and recuperation in Thailand, and mail them from Bangkok.

They were what in Special Forces slang was called a masquerade team: they wore NVA uniforms, tailored and taped at the bulky areas around the knees, ankles, and sleeves. They had heard the baggy, canvas uniforms of the NVA scraping against trees and foliage. No smart recon man made the same mistake. Each piece of equipment in their rucksacks was buffered by socks and other soft items. Their hair was dyed black. Whereas regular Special Forces teams and Marine Force Recon teams used issue camouflage paint, these men had made their own and stained their skin to the exact pallor of the NVA. Their weapons in no way identified them as Americans. They were referred to, and referred to themselves, only by number.

In what follows, this anonymity is respected at the request of survivors who testified to the facts in the following story. Some details, like code names, have also been changed to protect the identity of team members. 1–0 was the team leader followed by 2–0 and so forth. The only identifiable link they had to their country was a piece of silk that bore a serial number and a statement in all the languages of Southeast Asia. This so-called blood chit was for use in extreme emergency and had been modeled on a request for local assistance and the promise of reward concealed in innocent-looking possessions by airmen and commandos in World War II. Only the CIA man, the Public Safety Director, knew the correlation between serial number and person.

Despite the careful planning and compartmentalization, news that their mission was launched apparently leaked. Just before dawn, as the team moved silently away from their forward operations base near the Laotian border, a gong sounded six times, one for each man passing the first nearby village. This simple bit of psychological warfare had recently paralyzed a less-experienced Special Forces recruit. One of his teammates had to bring the unnerved man back to the base. But on this mission, the men were old hands and countered the games played by the enemy. They had, themselves, used similar devices to throw their opponents off balance. They feared no betrayal within their team because they had worked together before. Each man's life had been, at one time or another, saved by one of the others.

Nothing could match the recent harrowing experience of 1–0. He had led a patrol that was dropped in the A Shau Valley by helicopter. Everything seemed in order. The helicopter took off after the drop. Fifteen minutes after its departure, by which time the helicopter had insufficient fuel to fly back to the drop site, seemingly out of nowhere a Vietnamese-tinged voice spoke eerily to the team on a loudspeaker. "Welcome to A Shau Valley, members of Command and Control Detachment North team Anaconda."[4] The voice then named all of the team members.

Quick thinking on the part of the Americans made them winners in the ensuing firefight. They had been betrayed by a Vietnamese teammate. They kept their discovery of his identity to themselves, and pretended to be still on good terms with their false comrade. But now they fed him wrong information and put out false information about him. Word of his "great loyalty to South Vietnam and his membership in the South Vietnamese patriotic front—the Brotherhood of the Sword"— reached the enemy. Within a month he had disappeared. The Vietcong killed off their own man.

The patrol base was situated about as perfectly as it could be in that dangerous area. A weather-worn depression left by the uprooting of a huge mahogany tree, it comfortably housed the six men. Surrounding trees provided cover against air strikes. The uprooted tree provided a quick escape route. Its tough wood was

---

[4] Not the mission's real code name.

impenetrable to bullets. By late afternoon, the best time
to start, 1–0 moved out with 3–0, a Chinese-Vietnamese
Nhung. Both knew this mission could only succeed if
they penetrated the camp and found their target between
1900 and 2100. After 2100 it was usually lights-out for
the NVA and too dark under the jungle canopy to see
anything except the pin points of light from small kero-
sene lamps hung about three feet above the ground to
guide the enemy's trucks. 1–0 and 3–0 moved along parallel trails,[5] keeping the tiny lights in sight.

Surrounded by a thousand jungle noises, 1–0 and 3–0
nonetheless moved in deathly silence. Nothing would
have given them away as quickly as a sound out of tune
with the chorus of the evening. Even the small crack
made when a man stepped on a dry stick could betray
him. They were searching for the line of small, cut, dried,
and brittle branches that was always laid in a circle
around an enemy camp to alert the NVA forward guards.
The sticks were always in the same place, in the same
formation, and the same distance from the guard's positions and the camp itself. 1–0 found the line of branches
and gave a little prayer of thanks for this communist con-
sistency.

Once past the circle of branches, the two painstakingly
checked for mines, booby traps, and punji stakes. The
sharp, notched bamboo sticks smeared with human feces
were a primary weapon in this jungle area. Such booby
traps could be set up in myriad ways to maim and kill.
Some were very primitive, like the huge balls of mud
with spears inside that were hung high in trees and triggered to fall on an unsuspecting soldier below. Some had
romantic names like the Malay-Siam Gate.

1–0 knew there would be five sets of two guards, re-

---

[5] They followed alongside the Vietnamese trails instead of walking on
the trails themselves so that their footprints—particularly 1–0's, which
were larger than those of the Vietnamese—would not give them away.

ferred to as LPs (listening posts), stationed at different points on the compass. He also knew it would be normal to rotate an extra LP in front of a different guard station each night. This was a recent precaution taken by the enemy in response to the success of the Accelerated Pacification Program. Since the Phoenix blitz began in November, 1–0 and his colleagues had scored by infiltrating camps in the area and snatching prisoners.

As he approached the primary LP, 1–0, a few feet ahead of 3–0, stopped and turned his hat inside out. The hat now revealed two pieces of luminous tape. When the two luminous lines merged into one, 3–0 would know he was too far behind. The downward movement the leader was making with his hand told 3–0 to move forward. Then they both waited, absolutely still, observing the Vietnamese LP.

Immediately after the enemy's commander of the relief stopped by to make certain everything was secure in the area, the new replacement guard was killed with a silenced .22-calibre Colt Python pistol. The intruders now had a little less than two hours to find Garwood, kill him, and make their way out by a different route. In two hours the commander of the relief would make his next round.

The two made their way silently through the perimeter zone to the NVA base camp. All NVA bases in this part of the jungle were similar. No fancy bamboo forts like those of the ARVN. Just a series of lean-tos with thatched leaf roofs. Cooking fires were underground; small tunnels carried the smoke up to a kilometer away from the base camp and sleeping hammocks. American bombers would then target the area where they saw the smoke and thus completely miss the camps. 1–0 always admired the communists' ingenuity, their ability to outwit all the high technology thrown against them. "That was one reason I believed so strongly that the war could only be won through the kind of responsive and creative warfare I was involved in," he said. "I respected Tom McKenney for understanding this."

1–0 saw a group of soldiers conversing with several obviously non-Vietnamese men. It was a political education class—another feature of NVA life that could always be depended on. 1–0 easily picked out the Russians. Their body language was arrogant, almost contemptuous of the Vietnamese they were with. He searched for Garwood, whose characteristics he had memorized, dark hair, slender, and almost no facial hair. However, this description did not match that given by the Marine survivors of No Name Island. That man had been "buff" (thickset) and light haired. It would shock McKenney later to learn that although he gave this very precise report to CCN, it was not passed on to the patrol. 1–0 knew that Garwood spoke excellent Vietnamese and was highly respected by his communist comrades. Watching the man he had selected as his quarry, 1–0 was certain that he had found his target. He signaled 3–0. Both were now completely focused on the kill.

When the small enemy group dispersed, the hunters silently followed the man they had identified as Garwood to his lean-to, and crouched nearby until he fell asleep. Creeping inside, 1–0 had almost no light in which to work, and killed the quarry quickly by placing the silenced .22 Colt Python pistol in a precise spot on the back of the neck, in the style of Chinese killings. The Vietnamese shot their victims in the temple. 1–0 planned the style of killing to confuse the enemy when they discovered the body.

One task completed, the patrol could now focus on another. In the period when 1–0 and 3–0 observed "Garwood" and the Russians with the Vietnamese, they discovered that the NVA corps commander had chosen this evening to visit the camp. This was an incredible break. The commander was sleeping in a hammock not too far from the dead man. It would have been easy to kill him.

If they snatched him and sent him back for interrogation, they had a coup of the first order. The man was a potential gold mine of information about the enemy's plans in the area.

1–0 and 3–0 made their way silently over to the commander and immobilized him with a syringe filled with thorazine.[6] His eyes were the only sign that betrayed he was conscious. With a quick motion, 3–0 pulled the hammock down into the arms of 1–0, grateful that the Vietnamese tied their hammocks without knots, looped so that one quick jerk in the right place loosened them. Away from the camp, they got rid of the hammock and 1–0 slung the body of the corps commander over his shoulder. The inert figure weighed no more than ninety pounds. To 1–0, adrenaline pumping fast, the prisoner felt as light as a feather, a good thing because they now had only minutes before the commander of the relief would find the dead guard. As quietly as they came in, they skirted the dead guard and left by the preselected alternate route.

Within twenty minutes all hell would break loose in the camp. But the hunters also knew they had the advantage. The enemy would be demoralized and confused because their people had been killed within the perimeter of the camp. Night time, all recon men knew, belonged to the raiders. That was as true for the Vietcong who infiltrated American positions all over South Vietnam as it was for the Americans and their allies here.

Shortly before 1–0 and 3–0 reached their patrol base, the forest came alive with clicking sounds. This was the

---

[6] Some Special Forces team members remembered using morphine in similar situations. Each man generally carried a vial of morphine in case someone on the team was injured. The team leader carried an extra amount for just this kind of situation, where a prisoner needed to be snatched quickly and silently. With thorazine or morphine, the amount in the vial was just enough to immobilize a prisoner. Too much would kill.

way the NVA spoke to each other in code. It was a code
1–0 understood well, and he adjusted their position ac-
cordingly. A few minutes later he began sending out his
own misleading clicks. The enemy began to move away
from his patrol, responding to the deception.

As soon as the two hunters and their human cargo were
back at the patrol base, 1–0, exhaling first to insure max-
imum soundproofing, whispered the result of the mission
to each man under a poncho. This was to ensure that even
if only one of them survived, detailed facts and the success of the mission would get back to headquarters. Then
he ordered the radio communications man to call for a
helicopter pick-up at BMNT. This time of limited visi-
bility for the enemy was crucial not only to their getting
out but for getting the all important prisoner back to base.
There was no clearing for the helicopter to land—only a
hole in the canopy of trees—which meant they would, in
the lingo of the men who performed this circuslike but
highly dangerous maneuver, "come out on strings."

A 110-foot U.S. Army rappelling rope would be lowered from the helicopter. Patrol members all wore a special harness called a McGuire rig. As soon as the ropes
reached them, they snapped the rope into the rig. Usually
there was not enough time for the men to be pulled into
the helicopter and they were flown back to the base hanging from the ropes, vulnerable to the gunfire from below.[7]
Generally, the enemy aimed at the dangling men rather
than at the helicopter though a well-placed shot at the
machine could wipe out everyone.

---

[7] Most commonly referred to as the spie rig, this special *patrol insertion /
extraction* system had several variations. The variation used by 1–0 had
three rigs that would carry six men. The men hooked their arms around
each other's waists—outside men with one arm extended. This makeshift aerodynamic position helped stabilize them. The spie rig was also
one of the most common procedures used by Special Forces for the
insertion of recon teams. During insertion, men would be deposited in
the heart of enemy territory by descending on a rappelling rope. An
early version of the spie rig was a ladder.

Despite the fact that the enemy was close enough to hear their steps, 1–0's priority was to get the snatched NVA commander back to headquarters even if it meant the team would have to engage in a firefight with an enemy who hugely outnumbered them. The drug injected into the prisoner was so effective that he was still limp except for the frightened look in his eyes. Shoved into a makeshift strait jacket and his own McGuire rig, he was ready to go the second the rope was lowered. 1–0 had ordered a separate helicopter for him so that he could be flown out first. With luck the whole patrol would then follow, but the chances of that happening were slim. The second helicopter would lack the element of surprise, and the team might then have to move on foot.

They were fortunate to be surrounded by tall mahogany trees which, together with the duskiness of early morning, made it very difficult for the enemy to determine where they were. 1–0 knew that if it was possible, the South Vietnamese helicopter pilots, who were affectionately called King Bees, would get them out. In his opinion, they were the best. The H-34 Sikorsky copters they flew had been known to take seventy-six holes in the fuselage and still fly. That was why the South Vietnamese had none of the nervousness of American pilots, who flew the much more vulnerable Hueys. The Americans sometimes lowered their nose and flew away with a man still hanging in the treeline. It was not a pretty sight to see a guy who had been dragged through a forest of mahogany trees on a rope; and that was not as bad as being dragged through bamboo. "The guys who suffered that fate looked like raw meat on a butcher block," one veteran of such operations, Major Mark Smith, said later.

Like clockwork, the helicopters appeared over the patrol precisely at BMNT. Immediately the jungle came alive with the sounds of the enemy. Within seconds, the limp NVA corps commander was raised above the treeline. His makeshift strait jacket dangled him like a

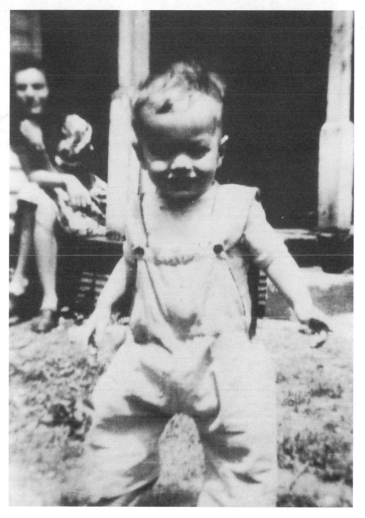

Bobby Garwood with his mother.
(Courtesy: Robert Garwood)

Garwood during the time he was at boot camp.
(Courtesy: Ken Banholzer)

Marine Private Garwood.
(Courtesy: Robert Garwood)

Colonel (then Major) Tom McKenney in 1968 standing by protective bunker, near the G-2 shack at III MAF headquarters on the Tien Sha peninsula, east of Da Nang.
(Courtesy: Tom McKenney)

Sam Owens' home at Trabang.
(Courtesy: Sam Owens)

The Special Forces camp at Trabang.
(Courtesy: Sam Owens)

Two hunter-killer teams before leaving on patrol.
(Courtesy: Sam Owens)

A six-man hunter-killer team just returned from patrol.
Sam Owens is second from right.

(Courtesy: Sam Owens)

ABOVE: Garwood dressed up, but still a prisoner, just before leaving Vietnam. This is a still taken from the Jon Alpert tape.

(Author's photo)

OPPOSITE: Garwood and his sister Linda at the Great Lakes Naval Hospital after his repatriation in March 1979.

(Courtesy: Robert Garwood)

Garwood celebrates his return with family and friends, May 1979.

Garwood and his father in Adams, Indiana, 1979.
(Courtesy: Robert Garwood)

Garwood at the time of his court martial, Automated Services Unit, Camp Lejeune. Garwood was formally assigned to this unit during the trial. His job was to sort and re-route Fleet Force Pacific mail to the USMC Commandant.

(Courtesy: Marine Corps Historical Collection)

Garwood and attorney Bill Bennet before Senate, House Subcommittee on East Asian and Pacific Affairs, June 1985.

(Author's photo)

ABOVE: Tom McKenney and Sam Owens in Columbia, South Carolina, 1994.

(Author's photo)

OPPOSITE: Bob Hyp and Gary Sydow, two of Garwood's debriefers at Okracoke, North Carolina, February 1988.

(Courtesy: Robert Garwood)

Garwood and the author, 1993, just before his return to Vietnam.
(Author's photo)

Garwood and Major Mark Smith, a former Special Forces "shooter."

(Author's photo)

Garwood pointing at Senior Colonel (retired) Pham Van
Thai, July 1993. Senator Bob Smith, New Hampshire, is
wearing dark cap.

(Courtesy: Attorney Vaughn Taylor)

Garwood and Tom McKenney in 1994 at the annual meeting of the Upper Midwest National Alliance of Families in Minneapolis. This photo was taken the day after their first meeting. Attorney Vaughn Taylor is on the left.

(Author's photo)

shadow puppet against the twilight. The other helicopter hovered bravely until all the men were able to snap the lowered ropes onto their rigs. Now came the most dangerous part. They made it up past the treeline but, hanging from their ropes, they invited enemy fire all the way back to the base.

McKenney got the news almost immediately. He was elated. All the frustrations of the past now dissolved and for a time he could feel the anger against the mishandling of this strange war drain out of him.

Then came a wave of intense rage. The man killed by 1–0 was not Bobby Garwood. The same trusted agent who had originally pinpointed the quarry reported a few days later that the man assassinated was a Cuban adviser to the NVA.

A short time after the snatched NVA commander was interrogated by South Vietnamese officials, the information he revealed led to the snatching of a valuable NVA courier. Among the courier's papers, it was alleged, was a souvenir snapshot of a trusted American-run agent named Chuyen. The photograph made a lot of men in the world of special operations go ballistic. Word spread like wildfire that the picture showed a captured Special Forces captain moments before his execution by the VC. Standing next to him on the side of the executioners, it was said, was Chuyen. It was common knowledge among the captain's colleagues that Chuyen had posed as his good friend and that the execution had been singularly cruel. McKenney took a special interest in the case. He suspected that Chuyen, like so many other double agents, had betrayed more than one mission.

As in other cases when a double agent suddenly became suspected of being a spy, Chuyen disappeared. That was the end of the matter until eight Special Forces men with outstanding records were charged with his murder by the United States Army. The recently appointed head of Special Forces, Colonel Robert Rheault, was also charged with conspiracy in the matter. Those who had long suspected that General Creighton Abrams was "out to get Special Forces" regarded this as confirmation. It was rumored that Abrams expected to be questioned by Congress about secret aspects of the war that many critics considered unethical. The arrest of the eight Green Berets was a clear indication to many that Abrams intended to scapegoat Special Forces.

To McKenney, it seemed naïve and ludicrous for the media and politicians to agonize about the morality of assassination in a war like this one, where the enemy did as he pleased and with total disregard for public opinion because his methods were never reported.

Throughout preparation for the court martial of the eight Green Berets, Colonel Rheault maintained that "there had never been substantiation that Chuyen ever existed or that there had been a slaying." The CIA, although it had played a strong hand in the matter, refused to make available documents relating to its record of assassination. The charges were eventually dropped. But the damage to Special Forces was done from the moment the accusations were made. Abrams, and the Department of Defense, made it seem as if Special Forces had engaged in operations that military command considered immoral and would never authorize.

In light of all McKenney knew about orders delivered in ways that protected those who had issued them from recrimination, this was yet another, and perhaps the ultimate, betrayal. Good soldiers were nudged in the ribs, in effect, when handed the names of those marked for assassination. Nothing was in writing. A nod and a wink was the signal to go-ahead. This seemed at the time to be in the interests of U.S. national security. Now it began to smell of political shilly-shallying.

McKenney's frustration grew. When he heard that the dead Chuyen had officially entered the honor roll of

North Vietnam as Hero of the Revolution it only deepened his sense of irony. Perhaps Chuyen had been killed on orders from the CIA. More likely—and more in the style of the Green Berets—he had been set up and killed by the VC as a consequence. Whatever had happened to Chuyen, McKenney was certain of one thing: that his own government had manipulated the situation to seriously undermine, if not destroy, Special Forces, the most effective fighting force it had in this war.

15: The Most Painful Memory

Colonel McKenney was in bad shape physically when the doctors sent him stateside in September 1969. For the previous six months he had been fighting the aftereffects of a concussion he sustained when standing within ten feet of four hundred tons of munitions that exploded during the second Tet offensive and injuries caused by a parachute jump with Vietnamese Special Forces. Both his main chute and his reserve chute malfunctioned. These problems he had been able to deal with by simply ignoring the pain and driving himself harder during those final months. That tactic no longer worked, though, when he came down with five tropical diseases. The worst were hepatitis-A, amoebic dysentery, and sprue, which prevented his body from absorbing food. Some of his nerve endings began to die. Certain muscles stopped working. He volunteered to be a guinea pig in a study of sprue. When he was finally forced by his superiors and doctors to go home, he told them he'd be back. They were dubious, but they had seen other men drive themselves back into action through sheer willpower.

In fact, the emotional scars left by his experience in Vietnam would prove to be more debilitating than the physical ones. Whatever mistakes were made the previ-

ous year, McKenney had no regrets about the secret hunt
to find and kill traitors like Garwood. There were other
secrets, though, that distressed him deeply. One, in particular, was traumatic. Having personally read orders
from Washington to abandon a naval pilot, downed and
drifting in seas from which he could have been rescued,
McKenney blamed himself for not attempting to get them
reversed. Every active duty officer involved, from the
rescue helicopter pilots known as Jolly Green Giants, already heading out to pluck the pilot from his raft, to the
denizens of C-section at Da Nang East, had been furi-
ously vocal in challenging a decision that meant a man
must be left to die.

McKenney had stood silently by. This unspeakable betrayal hit him on his last stretch home on Sunday, September 14th, 1969. As he and his seatmate, an aviator,
watched the approaching northern coast of California and
Mount Shasta, they talked about those who weren't coming back. Then the memory he had buried rose like an
accusing finger, and McKenney's mind filled with the
image of the pilot, sitting in a rubber raft south of Hainan
Island,[1] waiting to be rescued.

That day in October 1968, McKenney was in C-section
at III MAF headquarters. It was during his tenure as order
of battle officer. He had access to the classified world of
those who both eavesdropped on the enemy and communicated to Washington. The situation room, with its
visual display of enemy unit locations in constant flux as
their positions changed, required a special clearance in
addition to his top-secret clearance. Entering the place
always reminded him of the speakeasies in old movies.
Like the mob lookout, the watch officers would visually
identify him through a hatch in the door before allowing
him inside.

As he prepared to get a fix on the enemy unit he had

---

[1] Hainan Island belongs to the People's Republic of China.

come to track, he was asked to wait. Some priority-message traffic was going back and forth over the back-channel communications net, which only high-ranking politicians and generals could use. McKenney gathered this was another case of the Oval Office involving itself. A naval pilot had been shot down in the South China Sea. The Jolly Green Giants—for whom he always stood when they entered a room—were already halfway there. The men in the situation room were visibly relieved to hear the continuing signal from the emergency transmitter of the downed pilot. He was unhurt; he knew help was on the way. "What were those idiots in Washington doing," McKenney remembered thinking as he read their instructions coming over the secure teletype. They demanded the coordinates of the shootdown. What followed appalled everyone in the room: "Abort rescue!"

The communications specialist handling the emergency tore the message off and shouted, "Bullshit!" He kicked the big metal cabinet holding the teletype machine and deliberately stalled communications, obviously not caring which smarmy politician got the message at the other end. The Jolly Greens reacted even more strongly: "Hell no! We're already half-way there." The tension all along the back-channel was palpable. No one could believe such a stupid and inhumane order.[2] Much later,

---

[2] Loss record of the downed pilot is in the author's files. The author also spoke with Maureen Dunn, whose husband, a naval pilot, was abandoned off Hainan Island earlier in the spring of 1968. Ms. Dunn also obtained documents through the Freedom of Information Act that verify that the decision to abandon her husband, and other pilots who were shot down near Hainan Island, was made at the highest level. On April 16th, 1995, Ms. Dunn confronted former Secretary of Defense Robert S. McNamara at Harvard University, where he was giving a speech to promote a book he had written. In her hand she had a record of a meeting he had attended with President Johnson and other top officials on the day her husband was shot down. The high-level group had made the decision to abort her husband's rescue in the same way that McKenney witnessed the abandoning of the pilot in October of the

in 1995, Robert S. McNamara would apologize for a similar case of pilot abandonment, which, at least in retrospect, "horrified" him as well.

The order was repeated. "You will abort. Repeat, you will abort! He is too close to Hainan Island. We don't want to provoke the Chinese." McKenney wanted to kill the man giving that order. The specialist repeated over and over, loudly: "This is unbelievable." He made it clear that he objected. Displaying the same opposition, the helicopter pilots did not turn around until after several repeat orders and only after loud protests. No one wanted to be part of this.

The specialist told McKenney he knew more bullshit would come later, when some of them would be pulled aside and "confided in," told there were more important issues at stake here—political and foreign policy issues that they could not possibly understand. Long years later, McKenney would still wonder why he had not joined the protests, why he had taken no action. He was the highest-ranking officer in the room. He had some pretty powerful friends who might have been able to do something. He could have gone to them. Instead, he had gone to sleep that night, his mind blank.

The diary notes McKenney penned at that time were veined with alarm: as if his very blood spilled onto paper. What had happened to the most basic duty of Americans in wartime, to remain staunch and true to one another, to make every sacrifice to save a comrade in trouble, he wanted to know. This very general question probably served to protect him from what really disturbed his subconscious—his own impotence to help the navy pilot, a

same year. She asked McNamara for an apology. He said he did not remember the incident, but her document persuaded him. He told her: "I'm not just sorry. I'm horrified." Ms. Dunn told the author that she planned a book of her own in which she would present the full documentation to prove that during the Vietnam War at least eight pilots were abandoned in a similar manner off Hainan Island.

comrade, abandoned for cowardly, political reasons—because it justified his loathing for Garwood. The job of finally "getting Garwood," he left to Sam Owens—but only until he himself would return.

As the plane hit the runway with a few bounces and many cheers, flight attendants hid the shoes of a handsome young Marine captain, and asked everyone to help look for them. Vietnam no longer existed. It was time now for fun and frolics. "The troops," McKenney noted in his diary, "were eating it up." It was his last Vietnam entry.

16: Masquerade, or
Limited Distribution
Only (LIMDIS)

Coming home from Vietnam was difficult for Mc-Kenney. Not only did he not receive the hero's welcome accorded those returning from World War II, whom he himself idealized, but no one outside his family seemed to know what sacrifices were being made in Vietnam.[1] Or if they knew, they didn't care. Most frustrating of all, no one seemed aware that at least as he saw it, in military terms, the United States had been winning the war right up until he left Vietnam in 1969. He had believed President Nixon knew this. Now he became increasingly sure that Nixon's policy in Vietnam was motivated by domestic political concerns. As always, "mud soldiers" were left to take the brunt. Troop withdrawals were going so fast—150,000 by the end of 1970—that, as far as McKenney was concerned, it could not but place those left behind in dire jeopardy. In June 1970 the U.S. Senate

---

[1] From 1961 to 1972, III MAF suffered 101,571 casualties—12,938 killed in action and 88,633 wounded in action. In World War II, the entire Marine Corps suffered 86,940 casualties.

repealed the Tonkin Gulf Resolution and passed an amendment barring the use of troops in Cambodia.

Still he fought to get back to the front, never so much as when the classified Pentagon Papers were published in 1971, an act he considered treasonous. He had no intention of giving up, as his doctors seemed to think he should. He insisted on staying in the active Marine Corps, working, when his health permitted, as division training officer. It allowed him to keep alive both his dream of heading the reconnaissance battalion and his obsession to get Garwood. But, always the good Marine, he obeyed orders: he was no longer officially in the loop and made no conscious effort to tap into current intelligence. Still, in the early seventies, McKenney did have news from his Marine Corps friends about his old nemesis that again confirmed his belief that the order to kill Garwood was entirely justified, even if he had to carry it out himself.

It was No Name Island all over again. A Marine patrol near the DMZ had encountered an NVA unit directed by an American who shouted orders in English. One Marine was killed and several wounded. Among retired marines who had worked with SOG, rumor had it that one was blinded. Tom McKenney was certain that such an incident would be highly classified, yet it seemed to have been leaked by official sources. The story first appeared in Pacific Basin newspapers, and was then picked up by British and American wire services. The reports claimed that the U.S. Army was now admitting there were over one hundred deserters, including a number of Marines. This number was more precise than what McKenney had earlier heard from his cronies. The wire reports added that the Marines who were attacked near the DMZ identified the man who shouted orders in English as "a known Marine defector named Bobby Garwood." Most of the Pacific Rim newspapers were regarded by McKenney in those days as holding leftist views that made them suckers for communist disinformation. This made the reports puzzling.

They made no sense as enemy propaganda, or as stories planted by his own side. The accuracy, for Mc-Kenney, who was inclined to believe anything that fit his stereotype of "the traitor," was in the portrayal of the man he believed Garwood to be. And the stories about the one hundred or so deserters tracked closely the CI reports he had been privy to since 1968.

McKenney was very upset by the appearance of this account. He asked himself: Would the Army deliberately leak information so damaging to itself? The antiwar crowd would have a field day with such stories. They further endangered American soldiers—especially those unlucky enough to be prisoners of the North Vietnamese. He had by now heard accounts of Garwood's travels to North Vietnamese prison camps, where it was alleged that the enemy exploited him as a self-proclaimed turncoat, goading and tormenting American prisoners by saying he had chosen to join the NVA to fight against his own people.

It was not until twenty years later that McKenney learned the truth about the leaking of this story. Then it almost destroyed him. He had been right in assuming that the incident was highly classified. He had been right in sensing that the reports had the earmarks of disinformation from his own side. But he had no idea what layers of secrecy here masked the truth. He had always accepted that working in intelligence meant having only the barest minimum of information to do jobs that often required "plausible deniability." This information would be accurate, but there needed to be a cover of deceit that made it possible to deny official involvement. Otherwise an operation could backfire, which might be politically embarrassing and could jeopardize other secret operations. He was thus dogmatic in believing that Garwood was guilty, because this was the information he received, and also that the order to kill Garwood had to be entirely deniable. ''I never questioned the infallibility of my superiors who made the decision on Garwood and similar cases,'' he later recalled. ''I was naïve enough to think that one's own side observed a moral boundary and that common decency prevented us from crossing it. I knew about Soviet 'black' propaganda that harmed their own people but never for a second imagined we might have programs for deceiving our own side in ways that sacrificed Americans.''

This unquestioning belief in a moral boundary was shared by Barry Toll, a young Army operations and intelligence specialist at the U.S. Command and Control Center, Schofield Barracks, Hawaii. McKenney and Toll were not acquainted and they reacted to what they knew about the DMZ incident differently—McKenney was confused, vaguely suspicious, while Toll was in a state of shock. The difference was that Toll knew the entire story, which was nothing like what had been carefully leaked to the American public by the CIA. The leaked information came from a CIA summary that had been classified SECRET. This classification headed ordinary daily war summaries, but was added to this particular summary to impress journalists as to its importance and to its accuracy. Unlike normal daily summaries, this one was planted by the CIA-controlled black ops overseas disinformation program. The CIA was by law allowed to put out disinformation only overseas: but its professionals were skilled enough to make sure this disinformation would be transmitted to the United States if they wanted it to be. The story of the DMZ incident, which McKenney had first heard from his Marine Corps buddies, exemplified this skill. A USMC patrol had been having lunch near the Laotian and North Vietnam border when they spotted an NVA unit approaching from about thirty to forty feet away. The lead soldier seemed to be Caucasian. He was carrying an AK47, which he began firing while shouting orders in English. There had been a brief firefight. Several Marines were wounded. One was killed.

A week after the first newspaper articles in Southeast Asia began to carry articles outlining this summary, they also reinforced it with remarks made by unidentified Army spokesmen who admitted that along with the Army, the Marines had a number of deserters. One of the Marines wounded in the firefight had tentatively identified the Caucasian who led the NVA unit against the Marines as a known Marine deserter, Bobby Garwood.

Barry Toll himself had heard rumors of defectors, including Garwood, and would not normally have been too surprised to hear that a fallen Marine had supposedly attacked fellow Marines. But Toll was suspicious that at some high level of his own government secrecy was used to betray an American soldier because it was the easiest way to deal with a messy problem. Toll was one of a handful of people—perhaps the only one other than high-ranking government and military officials—to establish authoritatively that the SECRET summary of the firefight between Marines and the alleged Garwood-led NVA unit was a smokescreen created by CIA disinformation experts to hide the truth—a truth that had nothing to do with Bobby Garwood and everything to do with sacrificing the rights of ordinary soldiers for "reasons of national security."

Toll learned how this concept could lead to the crossing of that moral boundary based upon common American decency, because he was uniquely placed at the time of these events. A communications specialist, he had special clearances to handle material so secret it was eclipsed from the purview of all but the highest levels of government. Stamped for Limited Distribution Only (LIMDIS) such top-secret messages were sent to as few as eight, not usually more than twenty, privileged and powerful men. The messages were transmitted over high-command or backchannel teletype/cryptological circuits by communications specialists, like Toll, who systematized the restricted dissemination. The lists of receivers were highly compartmentalized. An alpha-numeric coding at the beginning of the message automatically insured that it would travel on a system of secure cryptological circuits to the addressee at his officially designated address *only*. For example, if the commander in chief of Pacific operations needed to report top-secret war intelligence to the president, it would be communicated over secure cryptological circuits to the chairman, Joint Chiefs of Staff, the White House National Security Council, the White House Situation Room, and the National Military Command Center. The acronym LIMDIS was stamped in large, bright red letters at the top of such documents. Some had the added caveat *EYES ONLY*, which meant the contents were never to be spoken out loud by the addressee.

Just such a LIMDIS message convinced Toll that Garwood was innocent of having led the NVA unit attacking Marines near the DMZ. The message passed through the direct chain of command between Vietnam and the White House and the commandant of the U.S. Marine Corps. This chain of command included the commander of U.S. forces in Vietnam, the commander of Pacific operations, the chairman of the Joint Chiefs of Staff, the chief of the military's Vietnam studies and observations group under CIA jurisdiction, the chief of staff of the U.S. Army, the chief of Naval Operations, the chief of the U.S. Air Force, the special assistant for counterinsurgency and special activities, and the National Security Council at the White House. Barry Toll said that some of the commanders may have chosen to further disseminate the message among their staff or subordinate commanders.

More than twenty years later, he was to tell Senate investigators that though he did not remember every detail, there was no chance of his forgetting the main thrust of the LIMDIS message or who had received it. The message explained that the firefight between Marines and what appeared to be an NVA unit led by Bobby Garwood *was in fact a firefight between Marines and a MACSOG masquerade team.*

The MACSOG team, made up of local tribesmen and a Caucasian officer, had been disguised as NVA regulars on a highly classified mission in Laos. Their radio broke down. Unable to call for helicopter pickup, they were making their way back on foot when their point man, a Montagnard, spotted the Marines approximately forty feet away, and mistook them for the enemy. The team went into immediate action, following an automatic drill that was virtually unstoppable: the point man fired two rounds; as he stopped the second man started firing, and so forth.

Toll remembered thinking that once the point man realized they were firing at Americans, he probably tried to shout a warning to his American teammates, who were ninety to one hundred feet behind him. That must have been what gave the Marines the impression that the man they assumed to be Garwood was shouting orders in English to his NVA unit.

Toll, who was the officially designated classified materials custodian and had set up the security procedures for a large volume of extremely sensitive material, understood why this message was given LIMDIS status. The United States was not going to jeopardize its strategic intelligence missions by telling the truth about an unfortunate incident. This would compromise other special-forces masquerade teams regularly infiltrating Laos. Toll did not understand, however, why it was necessary to destroy the reputation of a Marine Corps private named Garwood. The U.S. government might have had something on him but Toll, in his innocence, did not think his government had the right to convict this Marine on trumped-up charges of murder and treason. An enlisted man himself, he empathized with Garwood.

Toll's colleagues would say later that he had a reputation for total integrity, and it was this integrity that
caused his shocked reaction. Senior USMC Colonel Wallace C. Crompton had written at the time about Toll:
"His outstanding abilities permit him to routinely perform the complex duties that are normally the functions
of a commissioned officer. . . . [His job] requires an in-
ordinate degree of integrity [and] responsibility. . . ." The
ironic consequence of having such integrity was that Toll
felt honor-bound to keep his mouth shut, at least for the
time being.

He was not alone in his feelings of apprehension. Silent concurrence came in the form of another backchannel LIMDIS communication from a most unexpected
source. The commandant of the USMC was upset because the merely SECRET memo that had been leaked
along with other disinformation made Marines the scapegoat. The black propaganda distortions, put out by those
whose profession was to deceive, said not only that there
were Marine deserters, but that one of them had led the
NVA in an attack on fellow Marines. Reading between
the lines, Toll had concluded that the decision to slander
Marines had been taken without consulting the USMC.
Now the commandant was trapped by the same codes of
secrecy as Toll himself. The Marine commandant could
not explain publicly that Americans had fought Americans by mistake without compromising the U.S. policy
of sending these special-operations masquerade teams
into countries with whom the United States was not officially at war.

What would remain a mystery to Toll was this: why
had Garwood's name surfaced in the first place? When
he finally spoke about the matter before a Senate select
committee,[2] he offered the opinion that the name had
surfaced at the Joint Staff Level. But there was no ques-

---

[2] Toll testified before the Senate Select Committee on POWs 1991–93.

tion in his mind about the orchestration of the disinformation campaign. Only the CIA had the resources and capability. In those days Toll was first and foremost a man committed to secret intelligence, so he had at the time put aside his private speculations about the incident, just as he put aside thoughts on an increasing number of other incidents of high-level cover-up. He rationalized that better minds than his must have made these decisions to protect national security. The incident weighed heavily on his conscience though, as did other morally questionable incidents he was witness to.

Eventually he opted out of a career he loved, rather than continue to work with those who seemed now to tolerate the abuse of secrecy.

He never spoke of his knowledge of the black disinformation campaign waged against Garwood until he testified before the Senate committee more than twenty years later. But whenever Garwood's name surfaced—as it would over the years and always as the worst of traitors—he felt sick because he had seen no evidence to substantiate the charges at all. Somewhere lost in Vietnam, he used to think, is a fellow American who has been denied justice because somehow we crossed a moral boundary while patriotically following the banners of the deceivers. "Their real intentions have been hidden in folders marked for Limited Distribution only," he thought, wondering about some poor miserable Joe who might never know that in Washington he had enemies banked up, rank upon rank, masked by acronyms and prevented by their own vanity, or by misplaced loyalty to soulless institutions, or by professional politics, from ever allowing a single moment of doubt to disturb the public mind that an innocent man had been sentenced for a crime that mandated a death penalty.

17: Bennies, or Limited Assignments of Assassination

Colonel McKenney had been puzzled by some aspects of the story that Garwood led an enemy NVA unit attack on Marines, but he felt the overall account fully vindicated the assassination work he had husbanded during his tour of duty in Vietnam. To him, the Phoenix program seemed right for traitors.

Some who pulled the triggers were not able later to square their consciences so glibly. Periodically, such men would come to McKenney in his role as elder Marine. They picked up some hint that he'd had experience in this line of work. McKenney himself adhered strictly to his secrecy oaths. But other Marines knew what his formal position at III MAF had been, and deduced some of the rest. The men with troubled consciences came to Colonel McKenney in a blind search for absolution from someone of stature within their own military culture who was also a man of God; at the very least they were looking for reassurance that they had not damaged their souls by following orders to kill men who were American soldiers like themselves. McKenney, becoming more and more fundamentalist in his religion, always prayed with them. He assured them of God's forgiveness. They had, after all, acted as Marines under instruction. He was still so self-righteous, so morally certain that the orders they had followed were justified, that he was able to shore up most of the distressed men. But not always. Some remained uneasy and vaguely apprehensive. And some even began to infect him with a sense that perhaps they had been used, their innocent faith in the infallibility of their commanders exploited far beyond what even in McKenney's rigid view was the Marine way.

One of those troubled Marines was Bruce Womack, who joined the Corps in April 1972, at age nineteen. Originally from Arkansas, his family moved to the Detroit area for a time while he was growing up and then moved back to Arkansas. McKenney at first thought of Womack as a hillbilly who had joined the Marines while young enough to be malleable—one of those decent boys who almost invariably become the best Marines, those he always affectionately called mud Marines. Womack was referred to McKenney by Wesley Keith, a retired Marine captain who had been awarded the Distinguished Flying Cross, the Single Mission Air Medal, and the Navy Commendation Medal. Keith had flown AH Cobra gunships with Marine Observation Squadron 2[1] and Helicopter Squadron 367 from the Marble Mountain air facility just south of Da Nang around the same time McKenney was at III MAF. He knew McKenney had worked with intelligence, but not much else. Keith had become an ordained Southern Baptist minister after retiring from the Marine Corps, often counseling Vietnam veterans. He thought he had heard just about every awful thing he could have about the war, but he found Womack's story appalling. It was instinct that made him think McKenney could ease Womack's obvious pain.

---

[1] Marine Observation Squadron 2 was Tom Selleck's unit in the 1980s TV series *Magnum P.I.*

Womack told McKenney that he seemed destined for the military even though he never cared for any kind of confrontation. Perhaps it was this very dislike of being at odds with anyone, particularly his father, that made him submit to his family's tradition of military service. It came as a surprise to Womack that he was the only one in his recruiting class to be chosen for a highly specialized course in night operations and survival training given at the Army Military Police School at Fort Gordon, Georgia. He was never told why he had been put on an unadvertised and apparently tough and elitist track, but he was acutely conscious of a peculiarity in the way he was informed. The benefits of the course training were described to him by a full colonel, which was extraordinary enough. Even more surprising, the colonel carried a thick folder on Womack that contained more information on his short life than he imagined could exist. The colonel said the class had only eight men. It seemed a kind of compressed sniper course, heavily focused on operating in darkness and on staying alive in hostile terrain.

Womack became skilled in using a .308 Winchester sniping rifle, the M14 semiautomatic rifle, and the M60 machine gun. For months after completing the course Womack wondered what it had all been about. He was assigned as a driver to the motor pool at Camp Lejeune, North Carolina, which certainly did not require any of the skills he had learned at Fort Gordon. No one ever explained why he had received the special training.

Womack figured because the war was winding down, the special warfare skills he had acquired under intense pressure and in double-quick time were no longer required. He was shaken out of his complacency when, in March 1973, after the peace accords had been signed and American prisoners of war were coming home, he and two others were assigned to quarters near the shooting range. Then, for six hard weeks, night and day, he was sent out on the range to perfect his shooting skills under the relentless eyes of reputedly the best marksman-instructors in the service.

His new orders—to report to the Marine Air Station at Kanehoe, Hawaii—were delivered by a full colonel, who told him he would get thirty days all-expenses-paid leave before he was to report for a special assignment that would be explained later. He was also told that chances were good he would not make it back. But if he survived the ninety-day assignment he could choose any duty station he wanted. Womack found all of this a bit strange. ''I was a Marine private, though, and Marine privates don't question full colonels,'' he said later. What was even stranger, although more encouraging, was the order to keep receipts for all personal expenditures. This was unheard of. Whatever he spent out on the town would be reimbursed in Hawaii. It was like being handed an open expense account, and even Womack's father found this puzzling, though, like his son, he didn't think one could question the Marine Corps. His mother, as staunch a Baptist as Bruce Womack would ever know, was full of foreboding. She could think only that such a large sum of money was a kind of payoff for her son's life. It did not strike her as a good deal, but, aside from prayer, there seemed no way out. When Womack said goodbye to his parents, both were convinced they would never see him again. Both held his hands tightly, not letting go until an officer came to usher him onto the plane seconds before takeoff.

In Hawaii he was promptly reimbursed for more than twelve hundred dollars. Not bad for an E-4 corporal who normally made seven hundred a month. It was the first of many substantial payments that he carefully arranged to be deposited in an account with Pulaski Federal Savings in Arkansas. It would give a poor young man a nice start in life when his service was over. If he stayed alive.

His orders, received during a three-day stay in Okinawa, were for ninety days of temporary duty in Vietnam. He was told to let his parents know that he would not be able to communicate with them until the ninety days were over. Womack was full of questions about the assignment. He was told only that he would find out when he got to Vietnam. He was puzzled. Weren't American fighting men out of the war? He thought that perhaps his peculiar skills as a lone-wolf sniper were needed to clean out a nest of die-hard communists. He had once read an adventure story about small Nazi units calling themselves "wolf packs" who continued to fight the Allies, even after their generals had surrendered. Innocently, he thought he might be assigned to find and kill communists who, like the Nazis, were still fighting against Americans. He was flown directly to Bien Hoa Air Base outside Saigon. From there he left almost immediately for an area just outside of Tay Ninh, a few miles from the Vietnamese-Cambodian border. There he joined a compound comprising about fifty to sixty men. The site— approximately six hundred by three hundred feet— looked like a prison camp. It was closed in by a ten-foot high chain link fence topped by razor wire. He was one of fifteen Marines. The rest were Army.

Here, finally, he learned what his job was to be—the elimination of former American servicemen who had turned against the United States or engaged in activities— like drug running—harmful to their country. He would be part of a team of five men who were assigned missions of assassination. Each team lived in a separate, roughly assembled hut with a tarp roof and had no contact with other teams. Every mission was given a dossier on the individual to be eliminated. It included highly personal information like the location of birth marks and scars so that positive identification beyond dog tags could be made. But there were no specifics about their alleged crimes.

Womack had always been a serious Christian, attending Methodist services diligently since childhood. When he saw the dossier on his team's first assigned target with a photo of a young Marine in uniform, similar to the one of himself that his mother proudly displayed in the family room, he recoiled in horror. He told his superior officer, Marine Captain Rodriguez, he would not slaughter a fellow American. The officer had little sympathy for his moral quandary. "These men are vermin," Womack was told. "They are like dogs with rabies. They need to be taken out." When Womack still refused, he was told: "It's either you do that, or you'll wish you'd never been born. With one pull of this little finger," Rodriguez said as he lifted his index finger, "you're gone."

Somehow Womack persuaded himself that God had sent him here. It was important to be a good Marine. The fact that he would always be working with at least two other team members was some consolation, and the five men soon formed a tightly knit unit. It became apparent that the other four were as morally disturbed as he was, but the camaraderie discouraged too much introspection of this sort. The mechanics of the job were easy and never varied. Dressed in the masquerade team style of black pajamas and dyed hair and skin, at least three or more team members were taken to "the site." Significantly, "the site" was always the same Vietnamese-Cambodian border area, always within a nine- to seventeen-mile radius. They were taken there by jeep, by a "drop man," dressed in civilian clothes, whose name they never knew. The drop man told them where the target would be found. They had seventy-two hours to do the job and return to the drop-off point. If they took longer, they'd be stranded, a serious matter particularly if they were inside Cambodia, where the U.S. had no right to be. Womack was never sure whether the missions he undertook were on the Vietnamese side of the border. He suspected that he and his teammates were being sent to Cambodia. Why else would they need to disguise the fact that they were Americans?

Womack's first target was precisely where he and two teammates had been instructed to go. He remembered thinking that it was like a turkey shoot. Three armed men zeroing in from different directions made it almost impossible for the quarry to escape. It was, in loose terms, what had been sometimes called triangular fire during his training. Now, though, instead of three men firing from three points of the triangle at once, only one team member was assigned the kill. Triangular, simultaneous fire worked in clear spaces, not in jungle. Most victims were killed from a distance of seven hundred to nine hundred yards. The weapon most often used was a customized .308 caliber sniping rifle like the Winchester he had trained with at Military Police School, except that it had no manufacturer's marking and could be broken down to fit into a foam-lined aluminum carrying case. Another customized aspect was the large number of separated grooves in the barrel. Womack had learned at sniping school that the more turns to the barrel, the further the bullet would go accurately. Also unusual was the small number of customized rounds he was given for each job. On most military missions you took as much ammunition as you could carry. The unspoken message was that there was no room for mistakes. He was always handed the rifle at the drop off point and ordered to return it to the armory at the base camp as soon as he returned from patrol. Womack found this completely bizarre. As a Marine, he considered the job of cleaning his weapon before returning it to the armory as akin to a commandment from God.

On his first mission Womack was appointed the task of official assassin. His two companions were there for back-up, ensuring there could be no escape. Killing the man turned his stomach—as did undressing him, freshly slaughtered, to look for the body markings detailed in the dossier. When Womack got back to the compound he spoke to no one and went straight to his cot. For three days he floated between deep sleep and semiconsciousness, oblivious to his surroundings. Then he was sent on his next job. It was a routine that never varied—three days off after every kill, during which time the team members were confined to the camp but were free to play recreational games. Womack did not remember a single time when anyone felt like playing.

Somehow the second assassination felt easier. The third even more so. Then Rodriguez called Womack into the camp office for a chat. Womack arrived a few minutes early to an empty office. Curious about everything, he glanced at the papers on the desk. Reading upside down he could make out only Rodriguez's initials on a folder, before the captain came through the door. "Y or T seemed to be Rodriguez's first initial. Middle initial C." It would be the only off-limits information he was able to glean in his ninety days at the compound.

Rodriguez began by complimenting Womack on his work. "Some of you guys are better than others," he said, according to Womack later. "And some just are——." The tone made Womack uneasy.

"How does what you have done make you feel?" Rodriguez continued. The question, filled with innuendo, infuriated Womack. He answered: "What my government did, or what I did? I just follow orders. *I* didn't do anything."

The answer displeased Rodriguez. "Maybe you're getting into this too deep."

That was how Womack recalled the exchange. He did not know what Rodriguez meant. He was aware that some of his fellow assassins had left before their ninety-day tour was over. Somehow the rumor had reached his team that these were men who liked the job of killing too much and had therefore become too big a risk. But Womack felt himself at the other end of the spectrum, utterly helpless to change his situation and yet guilt ridden. Somehow he sensed that he, too, in some other way, did not fully meet Rodriguez's requirements. Disgusted he answered, ''If you can't answer any of my questions and if I can't talk, what does it matter?''

Womack left this meeting with the very clear impression that he and all of his fellow assassins were expendable. If something ''happened to him,'' no one would be any the wiser. He didn't know what Rodriguez had in mind for those who missed their seventy-two-hour deadline, but he didn't want to risk finding out. From that day forward he requested that the drop man pick him up after every mission thirty-five hours from the point of beginning rather than the standard seventy-two hours. In his stressed state of mind he figured, he'd have thirty-five hours to make it back to the compound on his own should his superiors somehow forget to pick him and his ''family'' up. Much later he realized that if his superiors had wanted to ''lose'' him, they could have, no matter what rescue plan he devised for himself.

The nickname for their targets was Bennies, short for Benedict Arnolds. Each successful kill reaped a hefty reward for the assassins—from twelve thousand to twenty thousand dollars to be divided between team members, usually five men. The amount appeared to depend on several factors: the nature of the target, the difficulties created by the impact of weather on terrain, and how long it took to make the kill. The sums paid were handsome in the early 1970s. The financial settlement for killing an American would provide a substantial down payment on a house in those days.

These individual missions were handled like Phoenix missions, McKenney later recognized. ''The project had the mark of the Agency all over it,'' he said after listening to Womack's troubled confession of how each mission was highly compartmentalized. Team members were debriefed separately by different civilian debriefers who compared and analyzed the men's stories. If there was the slightest discrepancy in their recital of events, one or more team members could be grilled for hours. Sometimes neither Womack nor his mates could tell why they were subjected to such grilling. "One time they questioned L. A. Jones until he felt more like a POW being questioned by the enemy than [a soldier being debriefed by] his own superiors," recalled Womack. "They were trying to intimidate him into admitting that his time frame did not match [mine or] that of . . . John Tyler, the man on the mission who had 'dropped that target.' "

Jones never changed his story and the debriefers finally left him alone. When the three men compared notes later they found their stories matched exactly. They were never able to figure out what the point of the exercise had been. If the objective had been to intimidate, it worked. Womack prayed that God would just get him through his ninety days and back to the United States and his real family.

But he could not stop the questions that continued to swirl in his brain. The closest village was seven miles to the southeast. The village seemed to be where the once-weekly helicopter bringing supplies was based. Why couldn't they go to the village? Why was the helicopter pilot dressed in a baseball cap and civilian clothes with a fatigue jacket? What surprised Womack more than anything was that they were clearly surrounded by the enemy. "But," he said, "they never once bugged us."

There was a communications hut with highly specialized and expensive equipment run by men who were not military. McKenney felt it had to have been a CIA project because of the amount of money involved. The Marine Corps could never have afforded the cost of even the bounty payments, much less the whole project.

Womack found that he could remove himself from the reality of what he was doing when he operated with all his highly trained senses on full alert. It was like following a bayonet drill, with the target a bag in the shape of a man. There was an old Army manual for bayonet practice that included the advice: "In—Out . . . Don't think of it as a man." Yet a question nagged each time he got a kill: why did the victims deserve the sentence? He had never been a great student of American history, but he knew everyone had the right to a trial, even in the military.

And he knew he wasn't the only one to nurse doubts. His teammates, who called him Hillbilly because of his accent, knew he was a conscientious Christian. He believed that was why they came to him individually with whispered questions about the morality of their missions. He had no answer to satisfy them or himself. When he took the matter to an Army chaplain on the site, the minister almost bolted. "I don't want to know about this," the preacher said. He advised Womack to just count the days until his tour of duty was over. He would be happy to discuss anything else with Womack, anytime, but he did not want the subject of Womack's mission goals to come up again. Secrecy shielded even the chaplain from personal involvement.

Yet despite their reservations, Womack said to McKenney, neither he nor the others ever consciously doubted the basic premise, that those they killed "like dogs with rabies" had done something indescribably wicked. Perhaps, he conjectured, they had been a rebel army fighting against their own fellow soldiers. After the initial rebuffs, Womack never had the nerve to ask his superiors just what, specifically, his targets were guilty of doing. To his knowledge neither did any of the other snipers.

By the time he spoke to McKenney, he knew that most of his comrades, like himself, had felt their souls in jeopardy. Within two years of returning to the States, L. A. Jones and Quentin Williams blew their brains out. A year later, John Tyler, the teammate Womack had felt closest to, "someone who seemed to have everything to live for," committed suicide by jumping in front of a train.

Twenty years later only one other of Womack's team-mates would still be alive.

What saved him, Womack believed, was a religious experience he had while on a mission in Cambodia. "God," he said later, "helped me." He thought of himself as born again. It was the only way he could get through the ninety-day assignment, which took out thirty-two men. He shrank from thinking about the implications if the other ten or so teams had an equal success rate that meant over three hundred men were taken out while he was there. It was impossible to know how many more camps like his existed or whether he and his mates would be replaced by others who would continue the assassinations.

It would take him a long time to drop the language, in his private thoughts, that disguised what he had really been involved in: a free-ranging execution squad, dispensing rough, frontier-type justice without benefit of courts martial: a kind of disciplined lynch mob, officially sanctioned but mysteriously sworn to a secrecy that made it seem dirty. When the United States finally evacuated Saigon and completed its total withdrawal from Vietnam in 1975, Womack was a driver in Hawaii. He was ordered back to Vietnam on the basis of a *convenience of the government order*. Womack was at the end of his tour. He already had his checkout sheets. He refused.

There seemed to be no adverse consequences for his refusing to go back at the U.S. government's "convenience." But when he was finally discharged, his Vietnam records were missing, removed by an unseen hand. In 1981, after revealing his history as an assassin of U.S. deserters to a Veterans Administration hospital psychiatrist, he literally watched while his service-related file was put through the shredder. When he spoke to Wes Keith and then Tom McKenney he had little documentation to corroborate his story. There was only his record of attendance at the Army Military Police School at Fort

Gordon, his sharpshooter medal, and the record of deposits to Pulaski Federal Savings bank during his ninety days as an official assassin. His mother had had power of attorney and carefully monitored them. Nevertheless, both Keith[2] and McKenney believed him. McKenney told Keith, "From what I know of such classified, compartmentalized operations, everything—including the fine details—fits."[3]

Womack's share of payment for each kill had made him richer by twenty-nine thousand dollars. He began to think of it as Judas money. When he came back from Vietnam, he wanted to be sterilized, to be "fixed," so that he could never have children. He thought that the awful thing he had allowed others to make him do was the result of a genetic weakness he might pass on. Today he is grateful that his family persuaded him otherwise. His wife and three sons make him want to live, despite the fact that he suffers from periodic bouts of severe depression when he goes for psychiatric treatment at the VA hospital. His children are the reason he has broken his vow of silence. If there is anything he can do to make sure American soldiers are never again forced kill their own, he wants to do it.

"I have suffered much guilt over what I did. . . . My job was more like a Mafia hitman than a U.S. Marine," said Womack.

---

[2] Wes Keith included Womack's story in a book entitled *Victories of Christian Vietnam Veterans.* Mountlake Terrace, Wash.: Wine Press Publishing, 1995.

[3] In his position as religious adviser and confidante, Wes Keith was sought out by others who had been involved in assassination projects in the same area and time frame as those described by Womack. The difference was that none of the others had been as inexperienced in assassinations as Womack when they were recruited; all had a special operations background. One man told Keith that he had been wounded during a mission. Ordered never to talk about his wounds, he was advised to get plastic surgery. The U.S. government paid for his surgery.

It would take a long time yet for McKenney to agree. He knew that mud Marines, who actually had come face to face with the enemy and had killed with a knife or gun, always had a harder time living with the memories than men like himself or the desk types. He also knew that contrary to popular belief, time did not heal such deep wounds. Time allowed wounds to fester and made them worse.

Though at first McKenney did not consider the personal aspect of Womack's story exceptional, there were other aspects of it that bothered him, and not because he doubted Womack's memory or integrity. For the life of him, McKenney could not figure out what Marines were doing in Cambodia in the spring of 1973 when the war in Vietnam was over—or, for that matter, what they would be doing there at any time. He said to Keith, "Marines were never in Cambodia." The relatively short, ninety-day tour, too, was unusual. It indicated that someone higher up knew the sniper kids couldn't take much more. "And why," he questioned himself, "were they using kids fresh out of school to do a job that had been done by the most highly trained recon men before?" When his information on deserters had been current, there were large numbers of African Americans among them. He was puzzled that Womack's targets were all Caucasian, just as he was puzzled by the fact that the two or three Womack had to fight face to face had obviously been trained in the kind of martial arts learned in reconnaissance training. This was true of their survival skills as well. Womack's teams had usually spent a day observing their victims before killing them. Most of the men lived in cleverly hidden lean-tos and were well versed in the art of foraging for jungle food. They were nothing like the drop-outs and druggies who had made up the majority of deserters on the 1968–69 hit list.

What really bothered McKenney was the curious concentration of so many deserter-traitors in what was no more than a fifty-mile perimeter near the Vietnamese-Cambodian border, almost as if they had been herded into a slaughter yard. Never, during his tour in 1968–69, when he had made it a point to look at all the intelligence, did he see evidence that placed Garwood or other deserters in Cambodia. Nor had McKenney ever heard of John Sexton, the American prisoner who was set free by the North Vietnamese along the Cambodian border in 1971. So it did not occur to him, as it did to Sexton at the end of the war, that the communists might set free prisoners they had never acknowledged having. Sexton knew his fellow prisoners never showed up at the Hanoi Hilton or came home. He often wondered if the enemy, now that the war was over, would release them in the same casual manner they had released him, along the Cambodian border, where, unbeknowst to him, Bruce Womack completed his ninety-day tour.

McKenney tried to fend off the questions, and even more the possible answers, lurking at the back of his mind. He stayed in touch with Womack. Others came to see him and were even more troubled by their soldier / hit-man pasts. The questions and the logical answers refused to hang back in the shadows. Slowly, reluctantly, he learned more, but always against the grain of everything he believed. Whenever McKenney heard some new fact, offered by some patently honest man, and easily corroborated through his own official contacts, he hid it in a corner of his mind far away from where he nurtured his hatred of Garwood. His certainty about Garwood clouded his judgment of what he heard about any kills—about all those American soldiers who had been given no quarter.

18: Creating a Circumstance

Soon after Russ Grisset was beaten to death by his guards in late 1969, Garwood was moved from the camp. He was not sorry to go. He believed other prisoners had made Grisset the scapegoat for a bad situation. Later Garwood would explain the horror in these terms: "We were all treated lower than the animals. So we started treating each other the same way. The guards built up distrust. We were like spiders in a jar."

He had known the same bitter and abandoned emotions after Eisenbraun died. Then, too, a terrible recklessness had seized him, until he remembered Ike's worldly-wise advice to focus on whatever was within his means to do, from learning the language to scavenging for food or information. It was impossible to explain the mental processes of a prisoner in his situation to anyone who had never experienced the incessant psychological pressures.

What happened after Grisset's grisly death was a combination of an individual rebelling against his caged existence and his captors' determination to set an example to the other prisoners. With come-what-may bravado, Garwood told the camp commandant how he had stolen food and medicine to help other prisoners, and how he had stolen from one guard and surreptitiously planted the

217

stolen goods among the belongings of other guards. Only
Grisset had known about this trickery, and secretly applauded it.

If Garwood had on this occasion remembered Ike's
advice as he did after Ike himself was killed, he might
not have lost his self-control. As it was, he provoked the
camp commandant to march him before a people's tribunal at a special camp. The judges told him he was past
reeducation and would be executed—lined up and shot
by six guards in three days. Garwood did not care. What
happened next, though, persuaded him that Ike was
somehow still with him, and that his fate was truly in
God's hands, not in those of the Vietnamese.

The day before his scheduled execution, the camp was
bombed. Garwood was seriously injured. He hovered in
a nether world of semiconsciousness. This lasted about
four months, he figured later, calculating by the change
in seasons and the Vietnamese calendar. During this
blackout period, he could neither see nor hear. When he
regained full consciousness, he was in a North
Vietnamese-run field hospital in South Vietnam. From
overheard conversations of medical orderlies and doctors,
he deduced that he was one of very few survivors of the
bombing, even, perhaps, the only one. Whoever found
his unconscious body apparently took him for a Cuban
or other communist-bloc adviser.

Because he spoke Vietnamese so well in his exchanges
with hospital staff about his medical and physical needs,
they perhaps had the impression that he was a comrade
of long-standing from another "socialist state." Yet they
treated him with some reserve, and he wondered if you
could talk while unconscious, or if later he talked in his
sleep. Something like this may have happened. It slowly
became evident that senior communist officers were regarding him as an American. There was clearly confusion
and uncertainty about what to do with him. He began to
hope that nobody knew his history as a prisoner, or that

he had been sentenced to execution. He prayed that the record of his travesty of a "trial" had been forever lost.

In June, still heavily bandaged, he was marched by NVA regulars to the North, as he figured, along the Ho Chi Minh Trail. By early September, they reached an army hospital at Nin Binh, where a bed was moved to a storeroom that had been cleared out for him. For the first time in his long captivity, he received what seemed like long-term treatment for his wounds with more than the stopgap medicines they had applied after he signed his one and only propaganda statement soon after capture. He was told that other patients would kill him if he was moved to a normal ward and someone found out he was an American. He sensed that hospital staffers treated him in a relatively more humane manner than their counterparts at S.T. 18 because they were still waiting to be told what to do with him. This did not prevent them from showing him their contempt ("Every injection," he said, "was made straight into the heart of my wounds"), but it may have been that some of their actions were simply those of a tough people responding to tough conditions.

About five weeks after arriving at Nin Binh, nine months after his scheduled execution date, Garwood was moved to Bat Bat prison camp at Son Tay. The camp was famous because it once held American prisoners. Now, with the exception of Garwood, it held South Vietnamese prisoners. From now on, he was to be alone, completely isolated from fellow Americans. The next nine years would be a strange twilight zone. All his information came from a mixture of sources: communist propaganda, the gossip of Vietnamese working in the prison camps, and increasingly, as their country moved toward defeat, from South Vietnamese prisoners. In 1975 they would be the first to tell him about the fall of Saigon. It would be a long time before he knew even that his country was no longer at war.

*   *   *

After the fall of Saigon in 1975, Garwood was joined by many more South Vietnamese prisoners. The administration of such a huge influx of prisoners presented problems. The regular cadres of political reeducation officers, disciplinary troops, and guards found themselves vastly outnumbered by the thousands held captive. It seemed to Garwood that the prison staffs increasingly comprised hastily assembled groups drawn from the ranks of fighting men.

Sixty thousand South Vietnamese prisoners were herded through Camp 5, a hugely swollen facility within a special prisoner-of-war zone in Yen Bai, two hundred kilometers west of Hanoi. Almost the entire Saigon administration was held there. Many of these South Vietnamese prisoners, including General Lam Van Phat, military commander of the Saigon area until the 1975 collapse, would later get out of prison. Somehow they made their way to the United States,—either as immigrants or, like Van Phat, as occasional visitors—where they were to give testimony that Garwood was a fellow prisoner, held under the same conditions as they.

In a letter to President Reagan during his first administration, Van Phat wrote that he felt an obligation to testify: . . . "Seeing Garwood every week over a long period of time, we [Van Phat and other South Vietnamese generals] know him well. . . . I can confirm Marine Garwood was held prisoner and was not a deserter." It seems no South Vietnamese who was in prison with Garwood after the fall of Saigon reported the 1969 "spider-in-the-jar" treatment that had made life insufferable for Americans in the last camp before he was isolated from his own countrymen. Instead, those South Vietnamese who later broke out of the communist prison system would tell stories of friendship and camaraderie between themselves and Garwood that made it easier for them to survive.

After 1975, Garwood's captors repeatedly took pains

to drum it into him that the U.S. government had officially taken the position that no American prisoners were left behind. Garwood did not want to believe this even though a statement made in 1973 to the media by National Security Adviser Henry Kissinger, that all American prisoners had been returned, was played over the camp loudspeaker. He felt that the Vietnamese were trying to trick him into believing he had been abandoned and that in fact America did not know he and others like him were still alive.[1]

Garwood returned to the sanity of religiously following the rules laid down by Ike, now dead for almost eight years. He remembered telling himself, "Garwood, get the hell out of Vietnam anyway you can because none of the bigwigs of the world care. . . . Taking that attitude, I followed Ike's advice again—to avoid confrontations, conserve energy, and learn all I could in order to make my way to Hanoi and perhaps find . . . neutral foreign diplomats. It had to be done without hurting my country or fellow Americans. I was alone anyway, and the war was over. I didn't exist. I grabbed at a chance to help set up a Czech generator at Camp 5, even though I didn't know diddley squat about putting one together." The Vietnamese assumed all Americans had technical skills. What Garwood did have, in place of engineering skills, was a natural talent for working out a mechanical puzzle. He was able to assemble the generator because all the parts were marked and "fit together like a Tinkertoy."

His success led him to deeper trouble. If he could put

---

[1] Although Garwood's guards went to great trouble to prevent him from finding out that he was not the only American still held in Vietnam, he would catch occasional glimpses of or hear snatches of conversation between other American prisoners. Such opportunities would arise unexpectedly. In one instance some American pilots were briefly held in a fenced-off area of huts near Garwood's camp. In another, he silently made eye contact with an American, whose dress and demeanor showed he was a POW, on a staircase in an interrogation center.

a generator together, he could take one apart too. He was obviously more expert than he had let on. Therefore the camp commanders decided that he should break down a different generator from Eastern Europe, for transportation in small sections to another part of Vietnam. He said, "They also wanted me to teach them everything I knew about generators. I thought, the jig's up."

He was in a panic, but he had long ago learned to conceal his emotions from the enemy. News that the war was over had never been confirmed to him by the only authority he acknowledged—his own government. But if those now controlling him were telling the truth, and he had no evidence to disprove their claim, then the official U.S. position really was that all American prisoners had been negotiated home, and his own existence was buried along with uncomfortable memories of defeat. His best buddies now were the remaining South Vietnamese prisoners who shared his feelings of abandonment though retained their faith in America. Some of them were U.S.-trained technicians. "They laughed and laughed when I went to them for help and said I didn't know a thing about generators." Two electricians and three mechanics knew more or less what to do. They quickly took the generator apart, labeling every part so that it could easily be assembled again. They taught Garwood not only how to assemble generators but other valuable information about the running of diesel engines. He said, "that's what saved my butt."

Under the ruse that he was to teach the South Vietnamese prisoners about breaking down the generator, he spent more than a week reversing that arrangement and taking a crash course from his supposed trainees. The guards, impressed by the seriousness of the job, kept a respectful distance. It gave Garwood an opportunity to find out what followed the fall of Saigon. This was precious information. The end to U.S. activities in Vietnam had been until now conveyed only through official communist pronouncements, scraps of overheard gossip, and guesswork. Yet this was the most critical political event of his entire life. The whole reason for his present predicament was that his government had sent him here to fight a war, and now it appeared no longer to matter. His view was necessarily narrow, and he had little hard information on which to base his future moves. From that narrow viewpoint, though, and from what he saw with his own eyes, he would have said that the communists had *lost* the war. Their country was in a shambles.

Now he learned that some of the South Vietnamese generals had behaved with extraordinary courage. Later he would find they received no postwar publicity, no public acclaim for their brave loyalty to U.S. aims from their U.S. allies, whose media, on the contrary, had lost all interest in their fate. He was particularly impressed by one Air Force general who took his own life rather than be captured. Years later, after his escape, Garwood would make it a point to look up the widows and the families of his prison friends who did not survive. The friendships developed here, and later with the families of fellow prisoners, became lifelong and deeply meaningful. Here, his knowledge of the Vietnamese language and culture did not mean he was White Gook or White Cong. Instead it gave him the respect due someone skilled in the language and intricacies of Vietnamese culture.

New-found friendship and solidarity with other prisoners made him want to live again. He did not want to end up like the despised and downtrodden remnants of human beings left behind in Vietnam after the French-Indochina war. His guards referred to them as *ralliers*, people who had converted to the communist cause. Some were not even real Frenchmen, he learned, but lower-rank members of the French Foreign Legion, mostly non-French mercenaries. There had been Germans among them in the days of French military operations; poor devils captured in Europe during World War II and given the option of remaining prisoners or fighting in Indochina. They had made a bad choice. The *ralliers*, according to Garwood's guards, stayed in North Vietnam voluntarily after the French left, but Garwood observed that they, like him, had to ask for permission for any interruption in routine, down to asking if they could urinate.

The American prisoners in camp S.T. 18 had accused him of being worse than a *rallier*. Now, his South Vietnamese fellow prisoners gave him the gift of knowing positively that he was not and would never be one. He also knew that the *ralliers* were perpetual prisoners, for reasons probably similar to those that made the North Vietnamese keep him. No longer a pariah among his own kind, Garwood renewed his promise to the dead Eisenbraun to get out and tell the world what happened to American prisoners. It would take Garwood four more years and every trick he learned from Eisenbraun, as well as a few he picked up on his own.

His new-found prestige as Mr. Electric Generator helped. At Camp 776, so-named because it was opened in the seventh month of 1976, he was made responsible for captured U.S. vehicles. Camp 776 was scattered over one-hundred square miles, and contained twenty-two different camps. Each camp housed two thousand to six thousand prisoners. Attempting to escape meant immediate execution.

Garwood looked for any opportunity that might eventually get him to Hanoi. If it was truly now the capital of a reunified Vietnam, there must be foreign embassies there and some way of getting out a plea for help. His first chance came with an assignment to repair vehicles that broke down on the road. Every vehicle he saw seemed to be held together by ideology and wire. Drivers from the North would talk. He said later, "Drivers know what's going on. They get around. They gossip." Garwood, however, was under tighter security than he had been before he disassembled the generator. Now he was always accompanied by an officer-driver and two guards. He said, "They watched me like hawks. I couldn't do anything. I could not talk to Vietnamese pedestrians, could not take one step away from the assigned task." His new status was both a lucky break and a curse. It got him through the prison walls but it took him into open country where every living soul had been conditioned to inform the security authorities about everything. Any chatter he contrived with drivers had to be discreet. He was under especially strict watch during his out-of-camp runs. He figured there must be individuals like himself who, having something to hide, were equally wary. His most likely marks would be black marketers. They flourished in this poverty-stricken country, and the chance to barter goods to make life tolerable led them to risk draconian penalties, including death. To stay alive, they had to be as cunning as he.

Garwood had to "create a circumstance," the phrase Ike used, to get to Hanoi. If he could only get a message into neutral hands, he still believed the U.S. government would rescue him, somehow. Every time he repaired a vehicle on the road, he picked up some snippet of information. He built up a rough picture of Hanoi as the only place where westerners now came together with diplomats from third world and nonaligned countries. The Soviet Union and its satellites had withdrawn high-profile military and technical personnel. He realized later it was to erase evidence that the late war had been waged with their essential help. They were as eager to wash their hands of the communist regime as the United States was happy to dump South Vietnam. As for China, its troops were rumored to be fighting along the northern border against their socialist brothers.

He heard a lot from the guards and the drivers about a flourishing black market. Everyone seemed to be into smuggling watches, tires, gasoline tanks, and the debris of war, brought up from the south and sold underground in Hanoi. He remembered: "Liquor, sugar, candy, all these little things, any type of clothes. And what they wanted most on the black market—material for making blue jeans." He had now been sent as far afield as Hanoi several times, always under tight security.

There were unlimited numbers of captured U.S. vehicles there in need of repair and urgently required for official use. The communists desperately needed more transport. However, his guards were hungry for other things, which, Garwood knew, would lead them to take terrifying risks. He heard of new hotels built for the expanding foreign community. He began asking the drivers: "Why don't you guys just walk into these hotels and buy this stuff and sell it on the black market?"

Impossible, he was told. Vietnamese hotels were staffed by top-security people. It would mean instant trouble to enter without some official reason. Only foreigners were allowed inside them, or else Vietnamese officials with papers authorizing each visit. Hotels were divided according to nationality. Cubans in some. Russians in others. Garwood was desperate to find which housed people from neutral countries.

His opportunity came just before Vietnam's border skirmishes with China flared up into open warfare in the late 1970s. Tension between Vietnam and China arose soon after the fall of Saigon in 1975 when Vietnam began to seek economic and political agreements with the West rather than with the Soviet Union or China. By late 1976 Chinese-Vietnamese, who were now classed as criminals, were being rounded up and forced to work in labor camps, planting and cultivating the rice fields around Yen Bai. The program followed the pattern of reform-through-labor in China. In the planting and cultivating seasons, Garwood, along with the rest of the other prisoners, had to go to the rice fields. This gave him an opportunity to speak to the laborers. Most of them were middle class and sophisticated. Chinese in origin, Vietnamese was their basic language. Most ran small businesses and needed the "reeducation" that getting their hands dirty would supply. It was, of course, slave labor.

One victim was Nana, a nineteen-year-old girl. Her family had owned a coffee shop in Hanoi. She was shocked to find an American prisoner still in Vietnam. The two became friends. Unwittingly, Nana gave Garwood the information he needed and introduced him to other Sino-Vietnamèse prisoners who knew more. He zeroed in on one hotel reputed to be very nearly up to western standards, albeit built like a concrete Czech bunker, a place to which the government directed neutrals it wanted to impress. This was the Victory Hotel, where the regime tried to create an artificial zone in which the surveillance methods and austerity of a police state were supposedly hidden from naïve outsiders.

His first big opportunity came just before Tet in 1977. It was preceded by unusually hard rationing. He was taken to an old, captured U.S. Army jeep that had broken down near the dikes on the other side of Hanoi. From there he could see the Victory Hotel. With him were an NVA lieutenant-driver and two guards. He had traveled with the trio before and performed well, careful not to create problems. Their cautious friendliness sprang partly from the familiar phenomenon that people everywhere are impressed by those who make an effort to speak their language. Garwood had broken through these cultural barriers. He could joke, use street slang, and make them forget briefly that he was a foreigner. The lieutenant in charge was from Hanoi, and trusted him enough to leave him with only the two guards while he paid his family a holiday visit. Garwood's efficient repairs put the lieutenant in a good mood when he returned. The lieutenant had the sophistication of someone from the big city. The Vietnamese, communist or not, still observed class distinctions that were not in any manifesto. Big-city people were "cowboys." Peasants were peasants. Garwood appealed to the cowboy. He said to the lieutenant, "As a Caucasian, it would be no problem for me to go into that hotel: I could be in and out of there in five minutes with all the booze and candy and cigarettes you want."[2]

He had feared overstepping the mark. The silence following his overture to the lieutenant was one of deep thought. Garwood pushed his luck and said, "What am I going to do, run into a Russian and say, 'please take me to Russia'?"

The lieutenant laughed. He was still in a festive spirit. He understood too well that if Garwood got caught, it would mean the end for all of them. On the other hand, booty could be translated into a small fortune in Vietnamese currency. He considered the odds. They were into the biggest celebration of the year and already there had been a slackening of surveillance by the public-security people. The Victory Hotel was stuffed with what the austerity-plagued Vietnamese interpreted as showcase luxuries, a drab display of bars of cheap western soap in abundance one day, none the next, and a can of western beer displayed triumphantly in solitary splendor on a dusty shelf. The ambience struck "foreign guests," even those from third-world countries, as pathetic. The lieutenant, the sharp city slicker, barely bothered to conceal resentment that a few party chiefs catered to foreign capitalists while ordinary Vietnamese still suffered deprivation as the reward for all their sacrifices. The bleak hotel held out some promise of better times, however brief, for his family. "Foreign guests," the official designation for those who stayed here, including former-enemy capital-

---

[2] His account is taken from the tragically delayed debriefing conducted by retired U.S. senior intelligence officers many years later. Garwood went over the entire incident as if it had happened the day before. He remembered precise details that jibed with what the debriefers knew from other sources.

ists, could buy freely items that were in tremendous demand on the black market, and forbidden to ordinary Vietnamese.

With a nod of approval from the lieutenant, Garwood got between the jeep and the dike and stripped off his blue prison garb. Someone handed him a spare white T-shirt, NVA overalls, and Ho Chi Minh rubber flipflops made from wornout tires. In this guise, Garwood was driven to the periphery of the forbidden hotel. Now he looked like a Caucasian, the kind of foreign guest whose quirks must be indulged. Without looking right or left, he walked into the hotel with a self-assurance he did not feel. He dared not show the hesitation of an interloper. He moved blindly through the dim foyer and spotted a kind of snack bar. He went straight to a counter and in English ordered cigarettes and candies. The lieutenant had provided money, and he handed the worn notes to the salesgirls. They seemed to take an eternity filling out the bill in triplicate. In his anxious impatience, he almost blurted out something in Vietnamese. He could not recall later if there were any guests around. In retrospect, it seemed that he had zipped in and out with his eyes practically closed.

He gave the bounty to the officer. His immediate reward was a pack of cigarettes. He took them, acting the part of trusted prisoner who would harbor no dangerous ambitions and go to any length for some tiny benefit. His style had to be still that of a subdued captive who was content with little. His companion grinned in shared conspiracy. ''I had him,'' Garwood said. ''This guy was my prisoner now although I didn't let him know it.''

The little side runs to the Victory Hotel became a feature of Garwood's working excursions with the lieutenant, who suddenly saw the value of a Caucasian collaborator whose exits and entrances aroused no suspicion. Garwood always scrupulously turned over the things he bought. He kept the receipts.

Then the lieutenant had a sudden attack of nerves, and wanted to stop. Garwood said: "Listen, I'm going to be in Vietnam for a long time, maybe the rest of my life. As an American I crave a lot of things, cigarettes, candy, beer. Do you think it's wrong that I get a little bit of what I want? Meanwhile you can make a little bit of money."

Something else was eating the lieutenant. Possibly he had heard reports of a crackdown by the public-order authorities. He maintained that the business had become far too risky.

Then Garwood showed him some of the receipts and said, "I could go to your camp commandant." The conversation at the motor pool was conducted under cover of checking forms for a trip, and the only way the lieutenant could show his rage was to walk away. That action in itself made him a coconspirator.

He came back, aware of the jeopardy he was in. He was willing to create the circumstances Garwood was asking for—the repair truck would break down every time they went near hotels. There were shabbier hotels that still stocked goods unobtainable in Hanoi's streets. Soon other guards were drawn in, seduced by otherwise unobtainable luxuries like the whiskey Garwood found for them, some of it suspect alcohol from the Soviet Union.

"And so I found myself running what was for them the sweetest little black-market operation. For me, it was the only road out," Garwood told the American debriefers long afterward. One, General Eugene Tighe, the former Defense Intelligence Agency director whose duties had included reviewing intelligence from inside communist Vietnam, said: "Garwood was drawn instinctively to the one major source of information that escaped government controls. In any police state, individuals find an outlet in under-the-counter transactions. This satisfies a basic human need to kick against bureaucratic regulation.

The best professional intelligence analysts were no smarter than Garwood, the amateur, in recognizing this treasure trove. The intelligence professionals lagged behind him in exploiting this. The biggest volume of human-intelligence reportage eventually emerged from black-market organizations running the length and breadth of the country.'' To Tighe and other experts, it would seem Garwood deserved praise for ingenuity. Starting two years after the ignominious U.S. pullout from Saigon, which left hundreds of thousands of South Vietnamese in communist reeducation camps, this isolated American prisoner had applied ordinary American know-how to the job of not only surviving, but also collecting information in an extremely hostile environment. ''All I wanted was to get in and out of those hotels to try to meet anybody who could help me to get out,'' Garwood told the debriefers later. It required enormous patience. He was unsure of his real status in the outside world of humane laws. Was he still a prisoner of war? America's part in the war had ended officially years ago. What should govern his conduct, when his captors insisted that he pay his debt as a ''war-criminal''? He had to improvise, guided by Ike's advice that a prisoner had a duty to do whatever he could to survive and escape. It was incredibly risky. Some of the hotels had KGB and Cuban security men as well as Vietnamese stationed everywhere. He almost got caught several times, once by KGB agents at the Victory Hotel, where they were generally never seen: Garwood had neglected to note the presence of a high-level mission from Moscow. Still, he always managed to escape, having by this time perfected his masquerade as a ''foreign guest'' with two guards and a driver.

The weeks turned into months, and time dragged on. The opportunities for scouting Hanoi came at long intervals.

He did speak directly to a Finnish journalist covering

the border war between China and Vietnam. Garwood passed over his name, rank, and serial number, his address in Indiana, the date he was captured, and the camp in which he was being held. He held his breath. Nothing happened. Years later it became known that the note was destroyed by the journalist before he left Vietnam. The Finn was afraid that it would be found going through customs and that his own notes and tapes would be confiscated.

Later still the Finn swore to one of Garwood's friends that he had memorized the information and passed it on to the U.S. State Department. The State Department denied this, continuing to maintain that there was no reporting on Garwood after 1973 except "reports from refugees who fleed [*sic*] Vietnam [and] confirmed [U.S. government] suspicions that PFC Garwood might still be alive. Significant refugee reporting on PFC Garwood did not really begin, however, until a mass exodus of refugees from Vietnam began in the 1978/79 period, almost a decade after PFC Garwood had gone to North Vietnam."[3]

The second time Garwood tried speaking directly with someone, again with a Finn national, he was entirely successful, but the victory would be short term. On February 9th, 1979, the U.S. State Department was informed that Mr. Ossi Rahkonen, a World Bank official stationed in Washington, had received a note from "a person who claimed to be a U.S. POW. The individual passed a scribbled note to Mr. Rahkonen indicating he was Robert Russell Garwood, USMC, an American in Vietnam."[4] Luck seemed to have turned in Garwood's favor again. It was impossible for the U.S. government to discredit this re-

---

[3] *The Case of Pvt. Robert R. Garwood, USMC*, Final Report, Report to the Assistant Secretary of Defense for Command, Control, Communication and Intelligence (ASD / C³ /), Volume 1, June 1993.

[4] Ibid.

port, like so many they had before. Rahkonen gave the information to the Swedish embassy in Hanoi, from which it was passed, highly classified, to the U.S. State Department via Stockholm. He also passed the message on to the Red Cross and the BBC, which broadcast the news on its world service. The publicity was enormous, and created a furor, especially in the National Security Council, which controlled intelligence on such matters.

Since 1975 two congressional commissions had formally declared, after assurances from the communists, "there are no more Americans left in Vietnam."

From the very beginning, the U.S. government managed the Garwood story. The U.S. State Department issued a caution: It was "unlikely that PFC. Garwood would be free to leave any camp without Vietnamese assistance and . . . it could *not* be excluded that he had acted at the 'request or demand' of the communist Vietnamese."[5] It was more likely, State argued, that Vietnam, in its attempts to achieve normalization, was using Garwood as an agent to manipulate the U.S. In a brilliant display of doublespeak, other U.S. government officials went on the offensive by revealing that senior NVA officers told them during bilateral meetings that Hanoi felt "forced" to make Garwood leave the country. He had been no good to them. Garwood, it was clear, really was the lazy troublemaker that his USMC superiors claimed him to be when they accused him of desertion. The NVA officers told U.S. officials that Garwood was a *rallier*, that he had been involved in black market and other illegal and immoral activities. For these reasons, he was now regarded as persona non grata in Vietnam. American government reports latched onto the communist accusation of "black market activities."[6] Suddenly Hanoi and Washington were in agreement. It seemed the U.S. gov-

---

[5] Ibid.

[6] Ibid.

ernment was no longer worried about the communists; the target of distrust was Garwood.

The worldwide publicity generated by the BBC report left no choice for the U.S. government but to work out Garwood's repatriation with the Vietnamese. In addition there was the unwelcome complication of having to deal with the families of the missing who immediately wanted to meet with National Security Adviser Zbigniew Brzezinski to find out what he knew about other missing men in Vietnam. Memos between the National Security Council, the State Department, the USMC, and the Defense Intelligence Agency released later make it clear that damage control must begin even before Garwood stepped on neutral ground. One NSA memo branded Garwood as "a live American *defector*" (emphasis added), immediately after Rahkonen, the World Bank official, turned his note over to the State Department.[7] Congressman Gillespie (Sonny) Montgomery, who had led a commission to Vietnam and declared afterward that no Americans— prisoners or deserters—were left in Vietnam, now announced at a press conference that it came as no surprise that an American "deserter" might still be living in Vietnam. "If PFC Garwood does come home," he told reporters four weeks before Garwood's return home, "he should be put in jail." Montgomery claimed that he had documents proving "that Garwood led North Vietnamese troops against Americans," but he did not make them available either to reporters, or later to Garwood's lawyers.

Garwood was judged on charges made by Hanoi and accepted in official Washington, which up to that point branded the North Vietnamese as liars. It was the surest way to prevent Garwood from telling his side of the story.

---

[7] Document is in the Jimmy Carter Presidential Library, as well as the files of the author and attorney Mark Waple.

19: Grapes of Wrath

The wrath Tom McKenney felt that day when he first set eyes on Bobby Garwood on the television screen in April 1979 was no different from the blind obsession that had driven his hunt for "the traitor." This reaction shocked him, because he had spent the years after the war pushing himself to become whole again.

After he was finally forced to leave active service, the bottom fell out of McKenney's life. Perhaps because he had no institution making demands on him, he made superhuman demands on himself. Although unfamiliar with the term posttraumatic stress disorder, his family nevertheless had the common sense to know that soldiers coming back from the debilitating war of Vietnam required personal support and time to heal. McKenney denied that he needed any special consideration, and felt only pity and a thinly veiled contempt for those with psychological problems. Military life had instilled in him habits of self-discipline and loyalty. He blocked all the unresolved questions about his actions and his country, and found a challenge that demanded more than even the Marine Corps—a new search for his God.

McKenney was brought up Episcopalian. A regular churchgoer, his approach to religion was ceremonial: he

loved the ritual. After his return to the United States—
prior to the shock of seeing Garwood on television, in
the United States again and apparently unharmed—he
embarked on a course that surprised his military establishment friends. McKenney became as single-minded a
missionary as he had been a Marine. He traveled the
country, then the world, preaching God's forgiveness. In
Haiti, he worked to rescue outcast children. He was
dumbfounded by the custom of locking seriously handicapped children out of sight in boxlike structures that
were little more than coffins, allowing them out only for
life's bare necessities. But he found that Haitians were
willing to respond to his message of acceptance. The
handicapped children, at first hostile, became a healing
force for McKenney's own pent-up feelings about the
shabby homecoming he had received from everyone except his family after Vietnam. By the spring of 1979 he
thought he had expunged what seemed a bizarre sense of
guilt. He was on a slow road to physical recovery. Most
of all, he thought he had regained his peace of mind.

That he was wrong was immediately clear from his
violent reaction to the man on television. Blinded by his
old hatred, one fact escaped him: the man on the screen
did not fit the description of the man he had dreamed of
killing.

The six-foot three, buff and blond character that the
survivors of the No Name Island massacre had described
and the CI men had briefed him on so many years ago,
the White Cong, was not this Garwood. McKenney did
notice that this Garwood clutched a Bible as he stepped
off the plane. This did nothing to soften his feelings. "If
anything," he said later, "it seemed to prove that the
traitorous bastard was smart enough to play on the sen-
sibilities of Americans who took their religion seriously."

What he would not find out for another fifteen years
was that the Bible Garwood hung on to, as if for dear

life, had a meaning for him much like the one it had for McKenney. Garwood's fourteen years as a prisoner of the Vietnamese—more than half his adult life—had robbed him of everything except his belief in God, a belief that had been strongly enhanced by his last conversations about Judaism with his mother. A psychiatrist would tell him later that his prayers in prison must have been similar to the meditation practiced by Buddhists. To the doctor, it seemed that prayer had helped Garwood to travel out of his body when torture and mental anguish became too much to bear. But in Garwood's mind the God who had protected him was the same kind of old-fashioned western God revered by McKenney and somehow like the legendary Marine Chesty Puller, who had always put the welfare of enlisted men above everything else. Like McKenney, Garwood held on to his faith in the Marine Corps. He was a member of "the best military outfit in the world." The thought sustained him in his bleakest moments. The communists had never been able to strip him of his pride in being a Marine. Now that he was home, he was about to be stripped of that pride, of his uniform, and of his honor by his own country.

He had been on his usual round of black-market business, selecting candy, cigarettes, and whiskey at the snack bar in the Victory Hotel when he became aware that four people who seemed at first to be Polish were conversing in English at a nearby table. "Suddenly my antennae went 'bing,' " he later recalled. "I overheard one of them say, 'I'll be returning to Washington in a couple of days.' From that point onward everything happened so quickly, God must have played a hand in it. There was no doubt in my mind."

Garwood tore the flap from the envelope that held the money to pay for his purchases, barely paying attention to the girls who worked behind the bar. He knew better than anyone how such workers were terrorized into reporting on anything even slightly out of the ordinary. Two of the girls walked away to get the items he ordered, and then returned. As they adhered to the bureaucratic rules that required filling out endless bits of paper for every purchase, a kind of reckless giddiness seized Garwood. For the first time, he was separated from his own world by nothing more than the flimsiness of the old envelope in his hand. His instincts for caution, nurtured by years of captivity, vanished in an instant. This was an opportunity far more substantial than the chance encounter with the Finnish journalist. It was now or never. He seized a pen from the counter and hurriedly scribbled: ''I am an American.'' He gave details of his status, rank, and what he knew of other Americans in the same fix. ''Are you interested?'' He wadded the torn envelope into a little ball and walked over to the man he had overheard. Looking back on this incident he said, ''I was so desperate, . . . I didn't know who I was giving the note to.''

It was Rahkonen. He looked up in surprise when Garwood said softly in his awkward, seldom-used American-English, ''Sir, do you have a cigarette?'' Rakhonen offered him not only a cigarette but also a light. The gesture allowed Garwood to drop the ball of paper right into the other man's lap. The action was not observed by others, but Garwood's presence in working garb caused Rahkonen's table to fall silent. The silence spread to the adjoining table. It seemed as if everyone was staring at Garwood. With a boldness he had not known he possessed, Garwood walked back to the bar as if nothing had happened. He stood at the counter and watched while Rahkonen read the note and then looked up at him with a puzzled expression. The seconds crawled. Then the Finn came up and stared ahead at the mottled mirror behind the bar.

''You are American? You don't sound it.''

''Yes. I am in Vietnam fourteen years.''

Rahkonen said, ''Oh, my God.''

"We were both nervous as cats," recalled Garwood. "He just kept looking around. We went over and sat at a table and I told him I was being held in a labor camp at Yen Bai and the date of my capture. When I told him 1965, he did not believe it."

As Rahkonen remembered it later, he had been alarmed by the possibility of a trap. "What am I being set up for?" he asked himself. To Garwood he said, "Nineteen sixty-five? If you are a POW, what the hell are you doing in this hotel?"

Garwood felt the door to his cage closing. He gabbled a brief explanation. He later said, at the long-overdue debriefing with those U.S. senior intelligence officers who risked their own credibility by saying they believed him: "I knew I could not be seen talking to this guy for long. I did not want anything to draw attention to myself because I had already given him the note. Those [Vietnamese] guys would have wasted me right then and there."

Garwood asked, in a sudden return to sweaty caution, "Are you American?"

Rahkonen gave a throaty, uneasy laugh. Finally, the Finn answered simply, No.

Rahkonen continued to be suspicious. Why was Garwood here? Where was he going? He asked, "Aren't you afraid?"

Garwood was acutely aware that his American-English must have sounded broken up and strange. His sentences came out in the stilted style of a prisoner under interrogation: "Am I afraid? I have lost everything. There is nothing more to lose. Will you take this to the American government?"

Rahkonen answered, "Maybe."

Garwood's tenuous contact with the outside world depended upon his story being believed by this privileged visitor from the west, approved officially by the communists as a foreign guest entitled to preferential treatment, and who had no means of understanding what it was like to be deprived of all rights within a country run as one big prison. Rahkonen, though immunized and prevented from glimpsing the hidden universe of police rule, was in fact very well aware that every facet of life was governed by prison rules. He did not believe anyone would dare take a risk like that being undertaken by this gaunt, awkward apparition in worker's garb whose English came out like something learned in a Soviet-funded foreign-language institute. Garwood's approach smelled of entrapment, the Finn thought, and so he responded slowly. The danger of a prolonged exchange was nothing compared with the risk of a diplomatic incident.

Rahkonen broke away, giving no hint of sympathy. Garwood was never able to describe fully the nerve-wracking interlude. Back in camp, he was aware of something being wrong. His usual Vietnamese companions were nowhere to be seen. For twelve days there was an ominous lack of work for him other than his routine duties.

Less than two weeks after Garwood passed his note to Rahkonen in Hanoi, he was abruptly pulled out of the NVA motor pool and put in prison under tight security. He was not allowed to speak to anyone. His meals were brought to him. He did not know whether his note had reached the outside world. The lieutenant-driver he had enticed into the black market was gone. The two guards who'd been made accomplices were now under arrest.

He was numb and exhausted. But at least he had tried. He did not fear his own death. He only hoped it would be swift and merciful. But experience taught him that his captors were likely to play mind games first, so he braced himself for the psychological warfare they were so expert at.

Garwood was suddenly marched to the camp parade ground. Preparations were being made for an execution.

He knew the drill for these ceremonial murders. He was resigned to being the victim.

Then he saw Nana, the Chinese-Vietnamese girl who had educated him about hotels in Hanoi. She was roped to the execution tree.

His vision blurred. He strained to give no sign of recognizing her, knowing he would be closely scrutinized, knowing how mock executions were often staged to trick a prisoner into betraying guilty knowledge. He looked straight ahead, and at first thought the sudden, brutal noise he heard was his own heart thumping out of control. The terrible clatter ceased as swiftly as it began. The normal sounds of the surrounding jungle slowly returned, but there was a menacing silence from the uniformed men around him. Six of them had emptied their AK47s into the bound girl.

"I hadn't even the courage to acknowledge her," he said again and again, later. "I just stood paralyzed. She never realized the significance of the information she'd given me. I had used her."

No one said a word to Garwood. He was hustled back to his solitude and left alone. His nightmares about Nana continue to this day. He is cursed with a near photographic memory and the details repeat themselves exactly. At the center is the face of Nana, distorted with fear and utter astonishment, as she realizes the executioners are really going to open fire.

When they came again to the camp in the middle of the night and took him away, Garwood was riddled with guilt. He did not deserve to live after an innocent girl had suffered a cruel death for something she did not knowingly do.

What he did not expect was to be taken to the Victory Hotel in Hanoi. This time, it was no stolen excursion in the company of men he could coax into collaboration. Instead, public-security men were his escort. "Everywhere I went, they had guards on me," he said. "I mean all over me. They were all in the same uniform—black suits, black ties, white shirts, and black shoes. They all carried pistols.''

At the Victory Hotel lounge he was met by a Lieutenant Colonel Zwen, whose full identity he was not to learn until much later. Zwen questioned Garwood about events on the day he had passed his cry for help to the Finn. But Zwen did not appear to know much, and Garwood hedged. Zwen told him he would be meeting with Colonel Thai, the man in charge of Vietnamese prison security. Garwood knew Thai's reputation for unspeakable cruelty. Zwen smiled as he spoke of the forthcoming encounter but, Garwood remembered, ''Zwen was so nervous, he was shaking.''

''Do you recognize this place?'' asked Zwen.

Garwood did not answer.

''Bob, try to convince me you are not CIA.''

Garwood was dumbfounded. After fourteen years and all he had gone through, they were still asking the same question they had asked at the beginning.

''When you were transferred to us from South Vietnam,'' said Zwen, ''they said you were suspected of being an agent. Do you still deny you're a spy?''

Garwood asked how often must he deny it.

''After what has happened, it's hard for us to disregard your background,'' said Zwen. He resorted to bureaucratic repetition of formula questions. The catechism was endless. Garwood had become a very important prisoner. The paranoid leadership wanted this ''VIP'' to lead them to his guilty associates. Their questions, direct and indirect, continued almost to the moment he left Vietnam.

They would ask, ''How many Vietnamese were working with you? How many Laotians contacted you? How many Palestinians worked with you?''

Garwood by now was clever at seeing through such questions. Clearly the communists were worried about keeping their grip on the locals. Clearly, too, they distrusted allies and foreigners sent to them for training in terrorist techniques. This was true even of allies like the Palestinians who cooperated with the Vietnamese on special torture and interrogation tactics. Moreover his keen awareness and insight honed under the pressures of captivity and the need to stay alive, told him that something was up. He was being handled with an almost gingerly caution, and seemed to have been afforded some mysterious protection.

He said later, "Suddenly they couldn't threaten or do anything to me. They couldn't beat me. They couldn't shoot me."

Taken back to the Victory Hotel again, he asked: "Excuse me, why am I here?" He was doubly careful now to be polite.

"You are to meet American journalists," he was told.

This unexpected, almost off-hand breaking of such momentous news caught him off balance. He remembered Nana, though, and all the many times when an air of patient consideration by his captors had been followed by the disclosure of their hidden motive. He took a grip on himself. He wasn't going to repeat the mistake of throwing caution to the wind at the prospect of normal human contacts.

He gravely accepted sheets of paper with carefully worked out questions and answers. He went through them slowly, pretending to have difficulty understanding the translation. The paper was good quality, possibly foreign, certainly not the usual Vietnamese poor-quality stuff. He made an effort to control his panic. This was a script. It was written to make the Socialist Republic of Vietnam seem like an American defector's paradise and he was afraid of being lured into saying things that would serve his minders' propaganda. Going by past performance, they would bring trumped-up charges that he was an ungrateful recipient of their generosity. He could not afford to forget they were captors, and he was still a prisoner. He knew little about the progression of political events outside; he could not know that his own real world was undergoing profound changes, to which he would later be introduced like a Rip Van Winkle awakening after long sleep.

He was to be filmed, he was told. Americans would follow him around with videocameras. He was taken to what he was told was his future, normal habitat. He would be filmed shopping in the market and lounging by the hotel pool. If circumstances had been different, he would have burst out laughing.

He took the bull by the horns. "Am I going home?"

The answer was evasive: "That depends on you."

So his release was to depend on his acting skills?

Jon Alpert, an American cameraman/director known in the west for his curious ability to win the confidence of socialist guerrillas in various parts of the world for the NBC network, now appeared. The man showed none of the humane concern that would be normal. He was anxious to make his video. The videocamera had come into use after Garwood's imprisonment. There was a Vietnamese-looking woman introduced as Alpert's wife and a technician.

"This American told me I'd be going home soon," Garwood remembered later. "The way he said it, I wasn't sure. He deferred to the security people on everything and kept emphasizing that the Vietnamese government wanted the movie done. He was wearing a Vietnamese-type sampan hat, a black shirt, blue jeans, Ho Chi Minh sandals, and a little Ho Chi Minh button. His wife spoke Vietnamese. The man managing the sound equipment, Victor Sanchez, seemed to be, or at least tried to pass as, Cuban."

Six years later Alpert would give his impressions of Garwood's situation in a research interview for the CBS television program *Sixty Minutes*. He said then that he was not impressed by Garwood because he was "ungrateful" for the many things the Vietnamese had done for him. "The kind of lifestyle Garwood—who voluntarily defected to North Vietnam—led was far more luxurious than that of the ordinary poverty-stricken Vietnamese."

The unedited and uncut version of the videotape shows a vulnerable Garwood who looks like a tall and gangling windup doll next to the Vietnamese. He is asked to show off the "generous" lifestyle given him by the North Vietnamese. Leading questions make it clear that his unseen interrogators want him to say that he defected to Vietnam because he opposed the imperialist policies of the United States. The tape leaves no question that Garwood satisfies neither the man behind the camera nor the Vietnamese security people whose voices are heard in the background. Everytime he begins to answer spontaneously, the visual action is cut but there remains the sound of prompters. Numerous times, after ominous murmurings between Alpert and the security people, Garwood is told to repeat a particular answer. They are not pleased with his appearance. His walk is wrong.

His teeth, according to Alpert later, were too black and rotten: "It would make a bad impression on Americans." Garwood's teeth were fixed and cleaned by a dentist in Hanoi at Alpert's suggestion. Alpert was right. The fresh, white teeth would look like proof to Americans—especially former POWs whose teeth had all suffered—that he had never really been a prisoner.

The tape has never been shown to the American public because, Alpert later alleged, "the CIA intercepted it on its way to America." A copy of the unedited tape is now in the author's files.

In the most moving moment of the tape, Garwood is given one last opportunity to correct himself after his performance has failed to convey the portrait of a happily liberated convert to communism. For the second time, he is directed to give the folks back home a message. His face shows he knows that if he repeats his earlier mistake in saying he loves America, the consequences might be unbearable.

Still he wants that to get across. Close to tears, he pulls himself up and repeats directly to the camera, even more poignantly, what he has said before—that he has always loved America. He adds that he hopes his family will wait to hear from himself what he has to say. His life in Vietnam has not been easy. At this point, he is cut off by voices speaking off-camera, but recorded on the unedited videotape.

Garwood was asked years later how he had summoned the courage to sabotage the full propaganda value of the "interview." He had acted almost in spite of himself, he replied. Even if it meant giving up forever the chance of being released, he could not deny his country. Alpert's response, when Garwood had asked about going home, had made it clear that a positive answer depended upon the prisoner's "cooperation."

After this fiasco, there was a puzzling meeting with Colonel Thai, the chief of prison security. This was the same Colonel Thai who had been in charge of interrogation and torture of prisoners in 1968, and who at that time stopped Garwood from questioning the Montagnard whom he saw wearing Clyde Weatherman's shirt. Thai said nothing about Garwood's message to the Finnish diplomat, yet clearly it had gotten out, and had churned up enough furor to hugely embarrass Hanoi. Garwood deduced this from Thai's wretchedly upside-down manner of telling him that he would soon be released. The prison security chief adopted a bullying, hectoring tone. Garwood was going to find himself a problem to the U.S. government and the military, he said. No one in America would believe he had been a prisoner. He would be watched wherever he went. Thai went so far as to threaten him: the people Garwood cared about most might suffer and die if he was not careful about what he revealed. The Colonel never did explicitly state that Garwood was going home. That would have been admitting defeat.

Shortly thereafter Garwood was taken to another room where a Palestinian named Abu waited for him. Abu told him that he knew where each member of Garwood's family lived and worked in Indiana. There were over two hundred members of the PLO living in the Indianapolis area, he said pointedly. Garwood was to keep his mouth shut when he returned, particularly about any Palestinians he had come across in Vietnam. Abu had apparently been informed that Garwood had seen Palestinians and picked up the rumors about them: they were commandos teaching their brand of terrorist tactics to the Vietnamese. If Garwood revealed this to anyone in the United States, Abu threatened, his family would pay the penalty.

Garwood was touchingly sure that, if he could only make it out of Vietnam, the evil predictions of both Thai and Abu would vanish along with the terrible memories of the last fourteen years of his life.

But almost as soon as he was flown out of Vietnam on March 15th, 1979, Garwood began to get signals that, incredibly, Thai knew what he was talking about. Plans had been made for Garwood to be picked up by a U.S. military plane, but the U.S. government agreed to Vietnamese demands that he leave by commercial airliner. This would save Hanoi's face and demonstrate that communist Vietnam was safe for western private enterprisers. Had the U.S. military stuck to the original plan, Garwood would have been collected like the other POWs in 1973 by U.S. personnel in an American service aircraft. Instead, the impression was given that he had always been free to come and go, an impression that, it turned out, was desired by both sides. Only Garwood did not think he was free. A Vietnamese "security type" sat across the aisle from him. It was obvious he was on the plane to keep an eye on Garwood. This so unnerved the Red Cross official who had joined Garwood just before departure at the Ho Chi Minh Airport that he asked Garwood not to speak to him unless it was absolutely necessary. "You are out of Vietnam now," the official said under his breath, "but I have to go back there. It's where I work."

The crew on the Air France flight to Bangkok, however, did see Garwood as a prisoner suddenly free. They treated him so, and tried to shower him with goodies. Garwood had never even flown in a jet airliner. He knew nothing about the high-tech comforts of modern travel. It seemed like paradise. But he was puzzled when the French captain came to the cabin and tried to persuade him to continue with the flight on to France.

"On this plane, you are on French soil," he said. "No one can hurt you. . . . You should only disembark when this aircraft is finally also on French soil. Only the French people really understand. . . . France will welcome you."

Garwood, who still could not fully believe he was on his way home, said, "I am an American. I want to go home to my family."

The captain turned to the stewardesses: "He doesn't know what is waiting for him." Then he hugged Garwood and gave him two bottles of cognac while the stewardesses pinned a corsage on him.

On arrival in Bangkok everyone except Garwood was asked to leave the plane by a Thai security official. Garwood looked out the window. The plane was surrounded by military vehicles and an army of Oriental men who looked Vietnamese. He went into a state of paranoia. Had a trick been played on him? Was he still in Vietnam? Even when a Caucasian with several aides boarded the plane and introduced himself as U.S. Consul General Andrew Antippas, Garwood was still not completely sure who had control over him.

Antippas greeted him without warmth and escorted

him through Thai customs to a waiting USMC C-130 aircraft. Garwood wanted to touch everything that was made in America and hug or shake the hands of all the Marines who came to meet him, an urge that seemed almost childlike when he thought about it later but which was natural after his long years of bottling up every normal and spontaneous emotion. The response was cold and even hostile. Garwood was not told that formal Preferral of Charges, including desertion and collaboration, had been laid against him three days before he arrived in Bangkok, foreclosing any chance for him to talk about his capture, imprisonment, or escape.

On board the C-130 Garwood was greeted by an expressionless Marine master sergeant who read Garwood his rights with cold efficiency. Garwood's emotions were in such turmoil, the import escaped him. Later he remembered feeling only relief at being addressed by a Marine Corps sergeant instead of a Vietnamese guard. Only the sergeant's obvious hostility prevented Garwood from hugging him. Then a Captain Joseph Composto came forward and said he had been assigned as Garwood's counsel. He immediately advised Garwood not to speak to anyone and that included Composto himself, who did not tell Garwood of the charges laid against him three days earlier.[1] Garwood was stunned. Why did he need a law-

---

[1] From comments made by Composto seventeen years later it appears that he expected Garwood to know of the charges because he was read his rights, given counsel, and generally treated as if he was under arrest. Similarly the government maintained that "the reading of Article 31 which is the military legal equivalent of the civilian Fifth Amendment right was not an anomaly. Article 31 prohibits questioning a subject without first advising him that he has certain rights if the answers he gives might be incriminating. All former POWs who were suspected of having aided or collaborated with the enemy in any way were first read Article 31 and apprised of their legal rights so that they would be protected from self incrimination." (*The Case of Pvt. Robert R. Garwood, USMC,* Final Report, Report to The Assistant Secretary of Defense for Command, Control, Communication and Intelligence. (ASD/

yer who advised him not to talk and acted more like a guard than someone who was protecting Garwood's interests? "That hurt more than anything," he said later, "I wanted so desperately to touch, to hug, to talk. I wanted to make contact of any kind with Americans." The communication Garwood craved was clearly not to be allowed. Even the crew members shunned him although one or two hesitatingly smiled at him. Garwood searched for some way he could show his good will. Then he remembered the Vietnamese currency called *dong* he had been given at Ho Chi Minh Airport to buy lunch. Not hungry, he had kept the money.

Now he asked each crew member in his stilted English, "Are you interested in a souvenir from communist Vietnam?" No one answered but each took one of the *dong*. Then he overheard one ask another, "Can you believe this was once an American?" The question devastated Garwood.

When he asked Composto what about him looked different, the lawyer told him it was that he didn't walk like

---

$C^3/$), Volume 1, *June 1993*.) In other words, Garwood should have realized he was suspected of collaborating as soon as his rights were read because this was a procedure that had been followed with other suspected collaborators who returned in 1973. The fact that Garwood knew nothing about the treatment of *any* returning POWs in 1973 was ignored, just as no one seems to have considered the possibility that Garwood did not consider himself a criminal, but a returning prisoner. The thought that he would be charged for having survived and escaped after fourteen years of captivity did not occur to him. American legal procedures like the reading of Article 31 were so far removed from the reality of his life during captivity, he had no comprehension of their meaning, only an uneasy sense of the hostility directed toward him. In 1992 Composto acknowledged this when he explained to government officials that although Garwood had noted his understanding of Article 31 when it was read to him, he *did not* "appear to comprehend that he was going to be charged." In this he was, according to some military lawyers, no different from thousands of young servicemen who were never POWs, yet still don't understand that when they are read Article 31, it means they are accused of having committed a criminal act.

an American: he shuffled like an Oriental. Furthermore, Garwood spoke like a foreigner, was thin like an Oriental, and his eyes appeared deepset like those of an Oriental.

Garwood consoled himself with the knowledge that however strange his appearance might be to others, he was back where he belonged and if he died right then and there, he would at least be buried on American soil, not in the jungle. That was what mattered. And if he couldn't touch people yet, he could at least touch things. He wandered around the sparse cabin lovingly touching every American-made nut and bolt.

Marine Gunnery Sergeant Langlois was assigned to accompany him on the trip home. Langlois, at least, seemed to understand what he was dealing with. He growled at Garwood, who stood at attention and saluted when they first met, "You don't need to salute gunnery sergeants." Later, as some of the truth began to dawn on Garwood, he was assured by Langlois that if other Marines treated him like a leper, at least they would not physically hurt him.

Hearing his rights read was only the first of a series of events that would drive Garwood, finally, to the surrender he had successfully resisted during captivity—the surrender to hopeless resignation—and to the urge to end it all by taking his own life. The detached hostility in Bangkok left him bereft without knowing why. He said later, "I just wanted someone to welcome me home, to tell me I did a great job." If someone had given him a Snickers bar he would have cried for joy. Instead, he was given cigarettes, but was told he couldn't smoke them on the plane. Ironically, cigarettes were the occasional perk given him even during the worst times of his long imprisonment. There was no physical torture but, just as he had been during the last fourteen years in Vietnam, he was at the mercy of others who demanded obedience. He felt caught in the gears of a machine that was insensible to any appeal for guidance or mercy. His only recourse was to withdraw within himself.

Transferred to the military C-130 in Bangkok, he assumed he would be flown directly to the United States. No one told him otherwise. Unaware that he was already being treated like a top-secret time bomb, he felt as if a huge weight was being lifted as he imagined Asia receding, and with it the nightmares. No matter what happened once he was home, he would at least be safe from his Vietnamese enemies, and with his family. Instead, the plane descended after a flight lasting about as long as his journey from Vietnam to Bangkok. Nobody had told him that he was being delivered to Okinawa. He became convinced that everyone was lying to him: he was being returned to Vietnam.

He was taken to a military hospital that he finally accepted as being American. Nevertheless, due to his experience of the last fourteen years, he continued to distrust whatever he saw or heard. To him, it now seemed as if authority had emptied out a whole section of the hospital to cage a crazed and infectious beast. He had not slept since leaving Vietnam three nights before. Now he was terrified even to shut his eyes. "I thought if I went to sleep, I'd wake up in Vietnam." He was afraid to touch the refrigerator or to lie on the indecently normal bed. The color television was entirely strange to him. He sat on the floor against a sofa, numb with a terror of the unknown that was, in an odd way, more awful than anything he had experienced before. He thought he was surrounded by security and intelligence specialists, and that only their faces and uniforms had changed. If there were humane gestures, he remembered none.

He was in the hands of Americans who, in accordance with orders, would provide creature comfort but abstain from any closer contact, especially the kind of conversation Garwood craved. They treated him, he would recall, like something from outer space, photographing and filming him around the clock.

At some point during the three-day stay at the hospital, the exact moment lost in later memory, questions were posed by nurses and medics about his needs, but they were addressed to Langlois. The Sergeant was told that Garwood's "vitals" needed to be taken and that Garwood needed an injection to get rid of worms. The nurses and medics bustling in and out told Langlois the doctors were worried that Garwood might bring infectious diseases back to the States. When a medic tried to give him an injection, Garwood jerked away. Langlois ordered the corpsman to leave Garwood alone.

Finally a doctor told Langlois, "If we don't give him treatment, he'll die." Langlois, growing visibly more protective of Garwood, said "Give him time. He's still in shock."

A few minutes later a nurse came in and asked, "What does he eat?"

"Ask him!" Langlois responded. She did. Garwood refused to look at her.

Responding to Langlois's unspoken reprimand, the nurse tried harder. She asked when Garwood had last eaten or slept. There was no answer. Not until Langlois gently asked him if he wanted some real American food did Garwood respond and ask for the multiflavored ice cream he had seen advertised on the television screen a few moments before. When the ice cream arrived Garwood refused to eat until Langlois, on impulse, took the spoon and tasted each one of the flavors. Years later Garwood still marveled at Langlois's depth of understanding. The Sergeant had correctly deduced that Garwood was afraid of being poisoned.

Afterward, Captain Composto came in with a photo album. Perhaps because of Langlois's visible concern, the lawyer showed, for the first time, some sympathy toward his client. "I guess there's no other way to tell you this," he said. "Your mother is dead and so is your grand-mother." Garwood felt himself sinking further into con-fusion and dismay. This was irremediable. He had prepared himself for the possible death of his grand-mother and even his father, but not his mother. She had promised they would see each other again, and through-out the long fourteen years of imprisonment that thought had sustained him.

Mechanically Garwood looked at old pictures of his family. He recognized his father and stepmother and brother Don. He could not find his little half-brother and half-sister among the photographs. He had loved them. Were they dead too? Composto showed him pictures of the adults they had become. He stared at the picture of a baby. This, he was told was a new half-brother. It was the first reasonably heartening family event he had heard about in more than fifteen years.

Sergeant Langlois, sticking closer as Garwood's men-tal distress became more obvious, insisted he rest a while. Garwood ignored the bed, more comfortable-looking than any he remembered in the Marine Corps, and crawled under it. There, in fetal position, eyes wide open, he waited to be taken back to captivity. Later he thought the ice cream he had eaten must have contained a sleep-ing potion because, miraculously, he fell asleep for six hours.

Then, incongruously it seemed to him, he was fitted and dressed in a new Marine uniform with four hash-marks,[2] and told the next flight would take him to Chi-cago. Suddenly hope came back to him. Once again he was a Marine. In his most difficult days as a prisoner he had held to the belief that Marines take care of their own. He now told himself that he must have been paranoid about his reception in Bangkok and on the C-130. How-

---

[2] In the Marine Corps service stripes are referred to as hashmarks: one hashmark or stripe equals four years of service.

ever cold his welcome, the uniform, which had been custom made to fit him perfectly, was proof that the old motto was true. It was the reason why the plane was filled with what he decided must be even more security men. It suddenly all made sense to him.

There came a moment, long into the flight, when a member of the flight-deck crew came back and said to him in an easy, conversational tone: "You'll be interested in knowing that we've just crossed the international dateline. You're halfway home."

Those words, or something like them, were the last thing he heard before losing consciousness.

When he came to, he had an oxygen mask on his face, his shirt was off, and someone was yelling, "We're losing him." Someone else thumped his chest. He might have been back in prison. A voice shouted, "Oh, shit, we're in real trouble now." Everyone thought he had gone into cardiac arrest. He was never given an explanation of this incident until many years later, when he was told that his heart had stopped beating.

In Chicago, three black limousines with darkened windows waited on the tarmac to escort Garwood and his entourage of Marine and security officers to the Great Lakes Naval Station. On the short stretch between the plane and limo he was bombarded with questions from what seemed like hundreds of reporters who waited for him. Here, there was no possibility of the U.S. government isolating him as in Bangkok, where he had passively agreed with Antippas, the U.S. Consul General, that it was better not to speak to the press. There, a cordon of Thai soldiers had surrounded him and prevented reporters from getting close.

Now he heard one question yelled over the media din repeatedly: how did he feel about the Marine Corps assertion that he had deserted?

He found the question absurd. How could anyone think the Marine Corps would make such an assertion? Of course they had known about his capture. It had taken place not far from their recon units. In a 1992 interview with government officials, described in The Case of Robert Garwood, U.S.M.C. Final Report, Volume 1, Joseph Composto claimed that just before they arrived in Chicago he "again" explained to Garwood that there were charges laid against him, including desertion. This makes it sound as if Composto told Garwood more than once that charges had already been laid against him but contradicts his earlier statement. He [Garwood] "did not appear to comprehend that he *was* going *to be charged* [author's emphasis] . . . when Article 31 was read to him." Both Composto and his interviewers take the tone that Garwood should have known he would be charged because he was read his rights. "Desert?" he thought as he clutched the Vietnamese Bible someone had thrust into his hand after the cardiac episode on the plane. "Ten days away from the end of my tour?" He was grateful to escape into the limousine.

This was the curtain-raiser to the scene that McKenney watched on his television screen. A motorcade that included armed police cars used all four lanes. Periodically the three black limos changed positions, as if to confuse anyone anxious to know which one Garwood was in. Whenever a strange car overtook the motorcade, a police car would pull it over.

At the naval station hospital, Garwood saw once again that an entire section had been cleared. Ominously, military police were guarding every door. He was in prison. Even Sergeant Langlois could not lessen the blow, though he tried. He told Garwood, "Don't worry Bobby, they're not here to keep you in; they're here to keep everyone else out." It was kindly meant, but it evoked an unfortunate picture of vengeful masses not unlike the brainwashed peasants who had poked sticks up his rectum and otherwise tormented Garwood when he had been on exhibit in a cage.

Garwood had come home, but his reality had not changed at all. He was under suspicion, but no one told him why. He remains certain that he had still not been told of any charges, and yet he was under constant guard. His every word and movement were recorded. The difference now was that the surveillance was being done by the Marine Criminal Investigative Division, with sophisticated apparatus. Here, as in Vietnam, he was an undesirable, a criminal created by a war he still did not understand. The communists had drummed into him that the war had started when the United States launched a criminally illegal intervention, and that the people of the socialist republics were moving forward inexorably on a path to truth and justice, but the campaigns to brainwash him had failed. Garwood saw too clearly that in Vietnam, black was white, slavery was freedom, and all must suffer for the greater good of some unnattainable Utopia. He was made to pay for resisting the enemy's propaganda. Now, having survived fourteen years of inhuman captivity, he was being made to pay still more, but why he didn't know. He sank even deeper into despair.

In the midst of what was, in his disturbed mind, a growing nightmare, Bobby Garwood found a moment of peace. It was something he would have least expected only a few days earlier while he was still in Hanoi: his father came to see him at the hospital with the rest of his family. Jack Garwood made no move toward him when Garwood, accompanied by Langlois, entered the reception room where his family waited. Jack did not recognize the painfully thin man in the spanking new uniform who was his son. Not sure if he was hallucinating, Garwood weaved up to his father, dropped to his knees, and held on to the older man's legs, as if for dear life.

So moved he could barely speak, his father said, "Bobby, don't do that. Stand up." Jack Garwood said later, "I understood everything, right then and there. I'm a simple man, but it didn't take more than common sense to see what they had done to him . . . and what our side was doing to him now. I also knew that what happened to my son didn't happen to the sons of admirals or millionaires.''

Jack Garwood had had many years to mull over his relationship with Bobby. In 1965, when he was first informed that his son was missing, he had gone through an emotional crisis. For the first time he became fully conscious of how much he loved the son he had treated so roughly. He blamed himself for driving Bobby away from home and into the Marine Corps. It was something he would apologize for again and again, now that he had regained his son. For his part, Bobby Garwood was embarrassed by this first apology, and overwhelmed by the unexpected gift of the love he had always craved. He said to Jack, ''I was just as bull-headed as you were.''

Two years earlier, in 1977, the elder Garwood had an opportunity to receive all the USMC monies accruing to his son while he was a prisoner. This was during the Carter administration's attempt to close the books on all Vietnam POWs. The sum, in the neighborhood of one hundred thousand dollars, would have eased Jack's finances considerably. He refused to sign the document that would have declared Bobby dead. He had never been given proof his son was killed, and no amount of money would make him jump the gun. This seemed to him like some kind of pay-off, a sordid business. It sharpened his growing sense of unease about his own past harshness toward Bobby and his suspicion he was not the only one who had been grossly unfair to his son.

A few weeks before Bobby's return, Jack had quickly responded to attorney Dermot Foley, who had given him a sense of the prejudices the government harbored against his son and offered to handle Bobby's defense if it came to a trial. Foley was a bankruptcy and commercial law specialist and had no experience as a trial lawyer, but he had a brother missing from the Vietnam war and seemed highly empathetic to Bobby. Jack, who at any rate had no alternatives, enthusiastically hired Foley. Since Jack had no money to pay, Foley agreed that he would be paid as money became available.

Foley joined up with Jack at the naval station to meet Garwood. After Bobby's emotional reunion with his father, Foley came forward but before he spoke to Garwood, he asked all of the military personnel to leave the room. He told Garwood to listen and not talk because the room was bugged. Then he listed for Garwood the serious allegations that were being made against him: sedition, beating a fellow American POW, and desertion in time of war. Garwood, already in a state of shock from the events of the past four days, was now paralyzed by an overwhelming sense of defeat. He knew now his instinctive feelings of apprehension over the cold and hostile treatment received from everyone except Langlois were not paranoia. How could Colonel Thai have managed to make his threats come true so fast? Worse, he had no idea how he would cope. The words "character assassination" came to mind and he realized how appropriate that harsh phrase was for what was happening to him.

Jack made up his mind at the Great Lakes Naval Station reunion that Bobby would not be destroyed, not if he could help it. And Jack Garwood could help. Family had always been the most important thing to Bobby, and now he discovered he did after all have one that would stand behind him as it never had before. After two weeks of interrogation at Great Lakes, Garwood went home to Indiana for an all-too short stay, courtesy of his accusers. Everyone in that house had been harassed by anonymous threats, via telephone, by letters, and even hurled verbally from cars screeching by the elder Garwood's home. The thrust of these threats was that *someone* would soon uphold the honor of the Marine Corps by taking revenge on the "traitor." Two of Garwood's half-siblings had lost their jobs because their employers could not deal with the constant media attention: one television network had landed a helicopter filled with cameramen and reporters in front of the factory where Bobby's half-sister Linda worked. Jack Garwood did not discuss any of this in front of his son. He knew it was too hurtful. But he made it clear to all and sundry that he believed Garwood totally innocent. "You're home now," he told Bobby, "there's nothing more to worry about." For the four short weeks of his visit, Jack Garwood and his other children acted as round-the-clock protective guards for Bobby.

"That's what saved me," he recalled, "because the questioning I went through at the naval station, which continued after the weeks with my family, was surely going to destroy me."

Still weak from the stress of his last days in Vietnam, and from the cardiac episode on the C-130, and still disoriented by his strange and unexpected homecoming, Bobby Garwood had been given to understand that his own government did know he was a prisoner in Vietnam all along, yet had done nothing to rescue him, or to acknowledge his prisoner-of-war status. He had never been mentioned in negotiations for the return of prisoners.

Instead, he was now asked if he had ever seen a loaded pistol. When he said yes, his interrogators asked: "Why didn't you grab it and take over the camp?" They knew he had stolen chickens to give to some of the other prisoners. Why, they asked, hadn't he stolen all the chickens? Didn't he agree that if he had done more for them, some of his friends might still be alive? This form of prosecutorial examination continued for weeks on end, and he felt he had entered another long tunnel with no end.

The Marine private, who survived fourteen years of imprisonment and finally rescued himself because no one else would do it for him, had walked into a political typhoon. Driving the storm was the outrage of both the public and many veterans at what they were convinced by rumor and innuendo was the commission of that most heinous of crimes, treason. The professional manipulators within the government knew they had nothing besides rumor to offer for public consumption, but this was no deterrent because the slander against Bobby Garwood was not really about treason. It was about the government's own insecurity.

By returning from Vietnam long after his enemies and the United States collaborated to declare all POWs either returned or dead, Garwood embarrassed those in authority. He confounded authority in Hanoi and in Washington. The truth about his long imprisonment and escape threatened to erode public confidence in the ruling bureaucracies.

The memos that flew back and forth between civil servants and the office of the Director of National Security, between the desks of federal politicians and those of military chiefs, were all joined by a common compulsion. What would be the consequences if official pronouncements were judged by the common people to be no more reliable than gossip and rumor? Like Jack Garwood, the families of missing men had strongly protested the closing of the books on those thought to be alive in 1973 when others came home. It would take yet another fifteen years before the U.S. government could bring itself to admit that men had been left behind, and some probably murdered by the communist Vietnamese.

Garwood had become a ritual scapegoat, the single target for all the accumulated hatred and bitterness nurtured by a frustrated military establishment. Like Tom McKenney there were many who were mortified by what they believed was America's ignominious withdrawal. But who to blame? Those who had been POWs in well-publicized prison camps like the Plantation and the Hanoi Hilton focused on collaborators who helped the North Vietnamese in punishing and torturing fellow Americans. These collaborators got away without censure when they were released with other prisoners in 1973 despite the fact that their activities were sworn to by prison leaders. Some returned POWs and their supporters were determined to bring them to justice.

Air Force Colonel Ted Guy had been the highest ranking prisoner at the Plantation, one of North Vietnam's largest prisons, where most of those caught in Laos and South Vietnam were held until they were moved to the Hanoi Hilton[3] in the late 1960s. Guy was courageous enough to take up his responsibilities as the man in charge. He was punished for it and kept in isolation through most of his eight years in prison. He was able to pass instruction to others by code through a small hole in the wall. After the official prisoner return, in 1973, Guy brought court martial charges against eight men who in prison had been among a group of collaborators who called themselves the Peace Committee.[4] They were generally referred to as the Dirty Dozen by other prisoners and functioned in both the Plantation and the Hanoi Hilton. The charges included aiding the enemy; disrespecting a superior officer; disobeying a superior officer; conspiracy; and carrying out conspiracy. According to Colonel Guy, "many men were brutally beaten and tortured in the Plantation, including yours truly for ten days in January 1972, because of the Peace Committee. Some of them [the Dirty Dozen] also sought political asylum and wanted to stay in Vietnam." This was after they had refused Guy's offer "to join us [the rest of the prisoners,

---

[3] When Guy was moved to the Hanoi Hilton he remained a senior ranking prisoner and the man in charge was Admiral James Stockdale.

[4] Guy brought charges against the following members of the Peace Committee: Marine PFC Abel Kavanaugh (who later, after his release, committed suicide), Army PFC King D. Rayford, Army Sergeant Robert Chenoweth, Army Corporal John A. Young, Army Corporal Michael Branch, Marine Corporal Alfonso Riate, Army PFC James Daly, and Marine Lance Corporal Frederick Elbert.

in continuing] to resist and fight as best they could."
Four left the Dirty Dozen during captivity and rejoined
the majority of prisoners. The other eight, according to
Guy, told him to "fuck off" and joined another group
of collaborators at the Hanoi Hilton. This group included
Marine Lieutenant Colonel Edison Miller and Navy
Commander Walter E. Wilbur.[5] Guy had no problem
with the fact that most prisoners—he now believes all—
broke at one time or another and collaborated within the
meaning of the U.S. code of conduct. "They broke me,"
he said. "I sang like a bird." But the thought of prisoners
deliberately harming other prisoners, just to ingratiate
themselves with guards and obtain inconsequential favors, would send him into a fury.

Guy remembered having to reprimand some of the
prisoners who came to the Plantation in 1971 after having
been held with Garwood at S.T. 18. One was Dr. Kushner, who, according to Guy, "had to be pulled up short
. . . bowing nose to the ground to the Vietnamese guards,
without being asked to or threatened in any way." Guy
could tell immediately that there had been no leadership
at their previous camp. At the Plantation, with proper
leadership, "they behaved, like the majority, with as
much decency as was possible in those conditions."

In 1973 Colonel Guy also wanted to bring charges
against those from the Plantation who accepted early release without his permission. He believed that these releasees had collaborated in order to gain their freedom.
In fact he considered that any prisoner who accepted release without being ordered to do so by a superior officer
was by definition a collaborator,[6] which would include

---

[5] Some prisoners, like John Parsels, were under the impression that all
collaborators generally went along with the Peace Committee, even if
they did not actually belong to it. The name Peace Committee was
therefore applied to all collaborators.

[6] The only exception Guy personally made was for Doug Hegdahl,

Ortiz-Rivera and Santos. However, Guy was told that he could not file charges against the early releasees because the statute of limitations had expired. He was assured, though, that other action would be taken. To his knowledge, no measures were ever taken. Some of these early releasees would testify against Garwood at his court martial.

Guy's charges against the eight Peace Committee members were dismissed by Secretary of the Army Howard Calloway and Secretary of the Navy John W. Warner. Calloway said: "We must not overlook the good behavior of these men during the two or three years each spent under brutal conditions in South Vietnam."[7] He also stated that "courts martial would be unduly disruptive to the lives of other [releasees] who would have to testify." Lastly, Secretary of Defense Melvin R. Laird made it a policy to "forgive any alleged offenses by POWs during their captivity."

Guy, who had intended to seek the death penalty for Peace Committee members, was furious. So were the more than one hundred former Plantation POWs who fully supported all the charges, and were willing to give testimony. When Guy refused to go along with the dismissal, he later said, "Calloway delivered the amazing opinion that, 'in prison camps, Air Force officers have no legal authority over Army enlisted men'!" Following that decision Admiral James Stockdale, who was the ranking prisoner at the Hanoi Hilton, brought separate charges against Lieutenant Colonel Miller and Wilbur, who had been upgraded to captain while a prisoner.

---

whom he ordered to accept early release so he could report to the U.S. government on the status of American prisoners. Hegdahl had a photographic memory and was able to memorize the names and situations of all the men with whom he had come in contact.

[7] Calloway referred to the fact that some of those accused by Guy had gone through the same brutal prison experience in VC prison camps as Garwood, before they reached the Plantation and/or the Hanoi Hilton.

Anger gnawed at Colonel Guy and at many of the returned prisoners over what they considered a betrayal of colleagues who had suffered and died trying to uphold the impossible code of honor decreed by Washington. They perceived this betrayal to negate everything they had so painfully striven for. It proved to them that the vaunted Code of Conduct had no force of law in the eyes of those leaders who insisted it be maintained no matter what.

By the time Garwood came out, the resentment of men like Colonel Guy over the unfairness of events in 1973 had festered and grown huge. Without knowing details, many felt it a small vindication that finally, if only symbolically through Garwood, justice would be done. Most knew little about the Marine private, but they had all heard rumors that he had struck another prisoner. Ironically, these stories had come from some of those who had been with Garwood in 1969 and who themselves needed reprimanding for later coming dangerously close to collaboration with guards at the Plantation.

Colonel Guy was upset at Garwood's prosecution, but only because others of higher rank and with more guilt were left out. He called it selective prosecution. He thought Garwood's behavior, as he understood it, should have been better, but that, as a private, he couldn't be held to the same standard as higher ranking officers. Still, Guy had no sympathy for someone he believed had struck another prisoner. Because of the awful charges repeated along the grapevine against him, Garwood was not considered by Guy to have been kept behind, even though he knew it was a common enough practice of the Vietnamese communists. They had kept Chaicharn Harnabee, a Royal Thai Army sergeant who was one of his fellow prisoners at the Hanoi Hilton. Harnabee had courageously served as messenger to his American friends, in the guise of willing Asian servant and sweeper for the Vietnamese guards. After American inmates of the Hanoi

Hilton were released, Harnabee was all the more severely punished because he was an Asian considered to have sold out to the hated west. He was locked in a coffin for eight months with respite only to take care of daily necessities. Led by CIA pilot Ernest Brace, who had been captured with Harnabee when the plane he piloted was dropping off supplies in Laos, the released American prisoners used whatever leverage they could on the Vietnamese and U.S. governments to finally obtain Harnabee's release. Brace, who had been a Marine captain and was highly respected by Ted Guy for his courageous behavior in prison, pulled out all stops and used his connections—including those in the CIA—to push for his old colleague's release. Up to the moment of that release, the U.S. government, in strange unison with Hanoi, maintained that Harnabee had been released with the others. Later, in Thailand, Royal Thai Army and other senior officials made him available to the author, and did not hide their disgust at the way Harnabee had been abandoned by their American allies. Harnabee was promoted to full colonel and given responsibilities in the area of secret intelligence. Harnabee proved to possess an excellent memory and unassumingly told his story with facts confirmed independently by his former U.S. fellow prisoners in the United States.

It would take Colonel Guy more than ten years of painful investigation, leading to an even more painful rejection of his own past assumptions, to find that Garwood had been similarly victimized. Then he would say, ''Why Bobby Garwood was tried . . . even on lesser charges is a complete mystery to me. The only possible explanation has to be that Garwood had to be discredited so that he would not be believed.''

The USMC with its proud and tough tradition of POW heroism had felt itself forcibly silenced and smeared by the fact that Lieutenant Colonel Miller, the highest ranking alleged collaborator to come home in 1973, was one of its own—a man who was not only embraced by antiwar movement leaders on his return, but ran for political office in Los Angeles on an antimilitary platform. When Guy and other former prisoners presented his prison history to the media, he brought an unsuccessful million-dollar libel suit against them. Based on overwhelming evidence that Miller's accusers were telling the truth, the judge ruled Miller could not go forward with the case. The legal costs incurred by Guy and the other former prisoners as a result of the libel suit were covered by their military insurance, but nothing could ever make up for the toll it took on their emotions. The USMC seemed determined that Garwood should not exhibit the affrontery that Miller had. In the process, some thought Garwood was turned into a whipping boy for all those who had gotten off scot free.

Air Force Colonel Laird Gutterson, who had been a prisoner in the Hanoi Hilton said, ''The Defense Department in general and the Marine Corps in particular were reacting to their frustration at being unable to prosecute the high-ranking officers who were clearly guilty of collaborating with the enemy, other officers who made damaging statements in order to obtain early release, or the enlisted men who paraded around Hanoi as 'antiwar protesters.' . . . I still ask myself why people like the Marine lieutenant colonel who beat up his fellow Americans to force them to appear for propaganda purposes in front of Jane Fonda, is not only allowed to retire honorably with full rights but is accepted by high-ranking Democrats as something of a personality.''

By the time Garwood was released in 1979, recalled General Tighe, then the head of the Pentagon's Defense Intelligence Agency, ''the USMC would have preferred Garwood dead, and was determined to bring at least one collaborator to trial.'' It was not publicly known that the USMC had formally drawn up a charge sheet against Garwood three days before his arrival in Bangkok. The government maintained that no decision had been made about charging him and did not inform Garwood that charges had been drawn, despite treating him like someone in custody. When the Joint Chiefs of Staff met to discuss the matter of prosecuting Garwood soon after his return, according to Tighe, he along with the chiefs of staff of the Army and Air Force strongly recommended against it. They were just as strongly opposed by the chief of naval operations, USMC Commandant Robert H. Barrow, who had led a regiment in Vietnam. Tighe was appalled that the USMC presented only "hearsay evidence" that Garwood had deserted or behaved less honorably than other prisoners. Indeed, according to Tighe, "there was considerable evidence that he had behaved with ingenuity and courage, especially in the years from 1973 to 1979, when many sightings of Garwood were reported by South Vietnamese refugees who had been prisoners." In addition, Tighe and the two who advised against bringing charges felt that the emotional costs for the country would be too high. Nevertheless, Barrow insisted on an investigation. If allegations were found to be true, there would be a court martial. Tighe found this "ridiculous," since both the USMC Judge Advocates Division and the Naval Investigative Service already claimed to have thousands of documents of evidence against Garwood. "New evidence," he said, "could only come from those who had everything to gain by lying—the communists." His words had little effect.

Precondemned, Garwood waited four months while the government completed an expensive investigation that involved worldwide travel for the investigators checking on rumors. A typical piece of hearsay that consumed much investigation time and expense was that Garwood had actually been taken out of Vietnam while in captivity and at intervals propagandized against the United States in the Soviet Union and other communist countries. This was obviously a foolish claim. Any such appearances for propaganda purposes would have been, by their very nature, publicized. Communist broadcasts and literature were monitored minutely throughout his Vietnam years by experts working at huge information-collection centers like the BBC bases strategically located around the periphery of the Soviet bloc. Voluminous BBC "takes" were exchanged daily with similar monitoring stations operated by U.S. agencies. There had never been the slightest evidence of Garwood playing a propaganda role and the allegation could have been easily refuted. Garwood had never been out of Vietnam until his escape. The lengthy investigation into this and so many other bits of gossip turned up no evidence on which to base any kind of prosecutorial testimony. And because intelligence bureaucracies are protected from public inquiry when national security is invoked, it was easy to fend off hostile public inquiries into this grotesque waste of time and money. The investigators themselves decided who had the right to know.

General Tighe normally followed the low-key style of an old-fashioned intelligence professional. On this subject he was plainspoken. He referred more than once to "the fanaticism of the Marine Corps." Frustrated at the way his hands were tied, he would make it a personal cause to assist Garwood in clearing his name, at considerable risk to his own reputation. Tighe's character, long record of devoted service to national security, expertise, and even sanity were cruelly called into question by other grandees of the defense establishment.

And so, late in 1979, after a lengthy investigation costing what today would be many times the two million dollars on record, a new charge sheet was drawn up against Garwood. The charges—including desertion, soliciting American forces to refuse to fight and to defect, maltreatment of American prisoners he was guarding, and communicating with the enemy by wearing their uniform, carrying their arms, and accepting a position as interrogator/indoctrinator in the enemy's forces—were read with venom by a sergeant from the Judge Advocates Division who had never been to Vietnam. Two carried the death sentence; three more a life sentence.

20: Dishonored

As Bobby Garwood's case moved toward the court martial that would strip him of his most elementary civil rights and lead him to contemplate suicide, he withdrew more and more into some isolated corner of his mind where he stored those few genuinely good and right things that had happened in his life. Later, doctors would say there was no doubt he suffered from posttraumatic stress disorder. They commented on his "emotional remoteness" when he discussed what had happened to him during his captivity. This was in stark contrast to his nights when, alone, he constantly relived the deaths of Ike and Russ. He was filled with an overwhelming sense of "survivor's guilt," feeling he had no right to live and was of use to no one. Such feelings manifested themselves in an inability to cope with even the simplest daily occurrences, like crossing at a traffic light. Garwood would stand paralyzed at street corners, not knowing when to cross. But at the time, posttraumatic stress disorder, although recognized by some in the medical community and among families of the veterans, was not officially regarded by the military establishment as an illness, and was even viewed by many, like Colonel McKenney, as "a kind of weakness."[1] Consequently Garwood received no treatment for it. Instead he made do with the same comforting mind tricks he had used in Vietnamese prison camps. In the agonizingly long pretrial period during the winter-spring of 1979–80, he relived his reunion with his mother just before he went to Vietnam, his engagement to Mary Speer—who, unbeknownst to Garwood and his father, suffered a nervous breakdown upon finding out from Jack that Bobby was missing in 1965 and later married someone else[2]—his friendship with Ike, and his new, positive relationship with his father. He put himself to sleep by clinging to the good memories, replaying them over and over. Automatically, he was using a device learned in communist prison camps by which he could remove himself from day-to-day ugliness. This, and the unanticipated support from his family, gave him a tenuous hold on sanity during the year and more that he waited for his trial to begin.

At the Great Lakes Naval Station, he was informed that the charge of desertion in time of war carried the penalty of death by firing squad. The government contended that he had not only deserted, but later refused repatriation—thus deserting twice. He was alleged to have voluntarily joined the enemy and engaged in enemy action against U.S. soldiers.

Most cruel and incredible for Garwood were the charges that he had caused the torture of Ike Eisenbraun and Russ Grisset. He could not fathom such ignorance on the part of the government's agencies. He had nourished a conviction that his own leaders had precise and

---

[1] Thirteen years later, when some prisoners came back broken from the Persian Gulf War, posttraumatic stress disorder was accepted as a matter of course.

[2] Mary Speer moved to California. Perhaps because of Bobby Garwood's earlier rift with his father, she did not remain in touch.

extensive knowledge of the enemy at every level, but it was becoming devastatingly evident that either there was no such intelligence or, worse, the information was not welcome if it failed to support an existing mindset. Garwood was beginning to understand that he himself was an unwelcome bit of reality, which crippled his spirit even more severely than did his captivity in Vietnam. In Vietnam, at least, he had assumed his country was on his side. In enemy prisons he had been sustained by his naïve belief that his own people must know he was a loyal American, good enough to drive General Walt, and trusted enough to be treated with respect by this great Marine. Hope had buoyed him during the Vietnam ordeal; hope based on his absolute certainty that powerful institutions in his native land would do everything to rescue him if they only knew of his predicament. Now, he had just enough grasp on reality to know that hope was futile.

The Marine Corps considered him the enemy. Some who analyzed him and his history agreed with his own assessment of his bizarre situation. Colonel James F. T. Corcoran, chief psychiatrist of the U.S. Air Force's Neuropsychiatry Branch at the time, and the military's only forensic psychiatrist, wrote: "Realistically, he is presented precious little for which he can be hopeful. . . . Whenever recognized, he is stared at, chased, followed, and accused. There is little privacy in his daily environment and that will become even less. . . . Those things which separate his Vietnam prisoner existence from a prisoner existence in the United States are blurred. To him there is for now no distinction. It is not even thin or veiled."

Garwood was now subjected to interrogation by a series of government agencies, including the Naval Intelligence Service, the Defense Intelligence Agency, and USMC Intelligence. They appeared and disappeared in his life. The first session of examination and probing at the Great Lakes Naval Station was followed by another and yet another. Naval Intelligence Service agents would come with photos and drawings of Asian men and women and maps depicting specific places in Vietnam. He recognized nothing in all their presentations, neither people nor landmarks. Documents would be slammed down in front of him with knowing looks and direct, silent stares. No questions were asked. The agents of Naval intelligence—who were probably the only people involved in the court martial process who had complete access to Garwood's "criminal file" going all the way back to 1965—would depart abruptly, without saying a word. If they had meant to get some reaction out of Garwood, they must have been disappointed. He was a seasoned survivor of what he now assumed was the way prisoners were treated anywhere.

During the Article 32 Investigation,[3] which ran through the winter and early spring of 1980, the government produced its seemingly one and only trump card—the former POWs who had been in camp S.T. 18 with Garwood during the 1967–68 "spider-in-the-jar" period. Investigators focused exclusively on this period and the incident of Garwood shoving aside David Harker after the Russ Grisset beating.

Publicly it appeared that the testimony of former S.T. 18 inmates, who still harbored their old prejudices against Garwood, the White Cong, persuaded the Article 32 jury to recommend court martial with the possibility of death

---

[3] Article 32 investigations are very roughly analogous to probable cause hearings or grand jury hearings in a civilian court. They were designed to insure that servicemen whose military charges are to be tried by a general court martial have a preliminary hearing to determine if there is evidence to support the conclusion that an offense has occurred and that the person charged with the offense actually committed it. The law had originally come about because low-ranking servicemen invariably felt they had to plead guilty if accused by officers. Article 32 hearings were a legal safeguard of their right to maintain innocence.

sentence. This despite the fact that the five former POWs who testified against Garwood acknowledged that they had themselves "collaborated with their captors" and did other things—"whatever their captors were determined to have them do" similar to what they were accusing him of. Some observers were convinced that the jury's harsh recommendation was based on secret government material that had not been made public.

The press described these proceedings as complex and filled with moral ambiguity. "The public perception," wrote the New York *Daily News*, "seems to be one of confusion, combined with the uneasy feeling that a former POW is unfairly punished."[4]

Most reporters seemed unaware of the fact that the five officers on the jury could, according to military law, ask for a death penalty based in part on material that was not available to the public or to Garwood's attorneys, and that Garwood could therefore not defend himself against the thousands of documents of alleged "proof" of his misconduct collected by intelligence analysts and hunters like Colonel McKenney since Garwood's disappearance in 1965. Almost none of these documents would be declassified and Garwood's attorneys didn't even know of their existence.

The government hinted repeatedly that Garwood committed atrocities against other American prisoners. This would lead to fierce protests from defense attorneys that the government's case was based on hysterical rumors, not on fact. One particularly upsetting example of such rumors were the leaks of disinformation to the international press in 1972 about the Marine patrol suffering casualties in an encounter with an NVA unit being led by "a known Marine defector named Bobby Garwood." Defense attorneys were warned that the government

---

[4] December 21st, 1979.

would produce some of the Marines who would identify Garwood as the one who wounded them.

Nevertheless, when David B. Barker, commanding general of Camp Lejeune, North Carolina, where the tribunal was being held, presented the Article 32 recommendation that Garwood be court martialed, it did not include the possibility of a death sentence. This was a charitable gesture, perhaps made to avert a public outcry. The charges had been modified. Without Barker's intervention some would still have carried the death sentence. The Marine Corps hierarchy realized it would be hard to prove Garwood had deserted ten days before his tour of duty was due to be over. "Unauthorized absence" was substituted for the charge of desertion in 1965. But he was still accused of having deserted in May 1967 when he refused a communist Vietcong offer to let him go if he propagandized for them in the villages. But General Barker had not been informed that Garwood was a short timer at the time of his disappearance. Garwood's attorneys became convinced that Barker never would have taken the crucial first formal step in the long journey to disgracing a Marine who had been getting ready to go home.

The charges that Garwood had been responsible for the torture of Eisenbraun and Grisset were dropped. These were replaced by accusations that he had maltreated other prisoners—David Harker, during the Grisset beating incident, and "Top" Williams, who was said to have been verbally abused by Garwood.

Some of Garwood's lawyers felt that the government had done a good job in preparing some potential witnesses for the Article 32 Investigation. Before the hearing, David Harker expressed the view that Garwood should not be tried, although Garwood had angrily pushed him aside during the Grisset beating. In a *People* magazine article published shortly after Garwood's return, not only did Harker argue against prosecution, citing Garwood's efforts to help the other prisoners, but the incident of Garwood's pushing him with the back of his hand did not come up. On February 27th, 1979, the Greensburg (Indiana) *Daily News* reprinted an article from Harker's hometown paper with a headline that read "Don't Crucify Garwood." Harker was quoted as saying, "I can't believe Garwood was . . . a sympathizer." During the Article 32 Investigation, however, Harker had been persuaded to play a leading role in getting Garwood prosecuted.

His testimony about the shoving incident at Grisset's beating was to prove the key factor in getting Garwood convicted. Vaughn Taylor, who would join Garwood's defense team later and stay on as his attorney, explained how Harker might have been persuaded to change his stance: "Before investigators and prosecutors sat him down and talked to him, he was the victim of an isolated and, in his view, a minor incident. But prosecutors could legally, and probably did, tell Harker about other incidents like the fabrication made up to cover the accidental firefight between Marines and a Special Forces masquerade team, which he himself had not witnessed." Harker was made to feel privy to inside information; he told researchers for the CBS television program *Sixty Minutes* that "the shoving incident was not serious, but there are other things Garwood did that could not be made public." It seemed to one researcher that Harker's sense of importance had been elevated by the sharing of confidences regarding unsubstantiated intelligence reports. The CBS researcher, with no bias in either direction, thought Harker's self-esteem was boosted by his belief that he knew something that others did not.

"Believe me," Harker said, "I know Garwood was guilty of harming other POWs." But he offered no direct eyewitness testimony.

This insinuation of guilt, based on evidence that could

not be presented in the courtroom "for reasons of national security," was the key strategy of the prosecution. There was also deliberate tampering with evidence. Unfortunately it would take eleven years for Garwood's lawyers to prove to their own satisfaction that Garwood had been denied a fair trial because of government misconduct.

As exemplified by the Article 32 Investigation, the U.S. government dealt publicly with Garwood in a coldly proper and even paternalistic manner. Garwood was provided with military counsel, in addition to the civilian lawyer Dermot Foley, whose voluntary services had been arranged by his father with the agreement that Foley would be paid as money became available. Foley was acutely aware that the USMC continued to withhold over 145,000 dollars[5] in back pay that had accrued during Garwood's imprisonment. Furthermore, Foley saw that ten days after Garwood's capture he would have been automatically discharged from the Marine Corps. Instead, Garwood's enlistment had been extended indefinitely. Continuing his pay while he was a prisoner might be considered an act of compassion, but once he was back on U.S. soil, he was legally entitled to decide the status of his enlistment. If he had chosen to terminate his enlistment, Garwood could not have been tried by a military court, but he had no idea that the choice was his. Foley did expect that the back pay would soon have to be made available for Garwood's defense, and he had already filed a writ of habeas corpus that included a deposition from Garwood outlining hampered circumstances due to poverty.

---

[5] This represented the further accumulation of funds that Garwood's father was offered three years earlier when the government was trying to close the books on all POWs, including Bobby Garwood. Garwood Senior would have had to sign documents acknowledging his son was dead. He refused.

The Marines made it clear Garwood would have no say in whether he was still a member of the Corps, but they seemed to recognize his helpless state as it affected his daily physical needs. Soon after his return to the States, they assigned him to sorting mail at Camp Lejeune. He had lodging, food, and was protected from an increasingly hostile public, but not from young Marines who were being instructed in classrooms that Garwood was the greatest traitor of all time. Thus indoctrinated, the Marines shouted their outraged contempt outside his bedroom window, which opened onto the parking lot next to the enlisted men's club. Soon after he was lodged in his room, Garwood's window was broken by a thrown rock. Again he felt he was back in a prisoner's cage and put on exhibition.

This personal tribulation was made tolerable by the presence of two people, Garwood's younger half-sister, Linda, and Sergeant Langlois. Linda, who had lost her factory job because of all the press attention focused on her during Garwood's month-long stay with his family, came to him when he moved to Camp Lejeune. Fiercely loyal and protective of her brother, Linda took on anyone who had the nerve to insult Garwood to his face. Garwood could scarcely believe that this strong young woman who had been his "baby sister" when he left for Vietnam was always there when he needed her. Linda would remain with Garwood until the end of the court martial.

At the commandant's order, Sergeant Langlois continued to stay with Garwood throughout the court martial as a protector and friend. Langlois thought Garwood was being railroaded. Was it the commandant's merciful intention to have this conclusion passed along to Garwood? Garwood could not figure out the answer.

When he left the small world between his room and his job in the mailroom within the camp, he was stared at, followed, and assaulted verbally. Even the Carolina beach outside his windows reminded him of Vietnam.

Most phantasmagorically to Garwood, even some of his military lawyers seemed to harbor the same illusion as his communist jailers—that he was an intelligence agent. The communists thought he was CIA. The Americans thought he was working for the Vietnamese, or—even more surrealistically—as a double agent for the United States. One interrogating officer asked, "Bobby, totally off the record, . . . You know I'm out of uniform here. . . . Who are you?"

Garwood said later that if he had not been so utterly demoralized he would have laughed. Before the court martial began in May 1980, he would be hospitalized for a bleeding ulcer, malaria, and mental stress. In all his encounters with officialdom, he was questioned about himself, not about what he knew firsthand regarding the situation inside Vietnam, a communist country still given a priority intelligence rating as a target in the continuing Cold War. A realistic debriefing seemed as far away as ever, although more and more independent observers who came into contact with Garwood were beginning to think that if he had been inserted deliberately as an American agent, he might well qualify as an ace among spies. One of the great frustrations of his peculiar situation was that he continued to have so much privileged knowledge locked away in his head. Enough fragments emerged under questioning to pique the interest of civilians like his lawyers and psychiatrists. According to DIA chief General Tighe, who would debrief him many years later, Garwood possessed a near-photographic memory. And, thanks to his language skills, he had talked secretly with Vietnamese black marketers in their own language about matters hidden from the more law-abiding majority and therefore had an unrivaled insider's knowledge of the communist system in Vietnam and internal conditions there.

Garwood's mental state at this time was likened to

that of a typical World War II concentration camp survivor by Dr. Emil Tanay, a civilian psychiatrist who interviewed him for the defense. Tanay, who had worked
extensively with concentration camp survivors and was
familiar with the symptoms of disorientation that Garwood exhibited, noted that Garwood's situation in Vietnam had "created unique and urgent psychological
needs that were not met," and that his present situation, "where he was in another kind of mental concentration camp," was serving only to compound his
frustrations and helplessness. Tanay met Garwood when
the Marine had been sent by his attorneys to travel under his own steam. This was, from their standpoint,
good strategy. They wanted Garwood to have the benefit of an expert in the kind of trauma he had suffered,
but did not know how traumatized Garwood really was,
and so made no provision to assist him in finding his
way from the Detroit airport to the doctor's office. The
psychiatrist, an acknowledged expert in his field and
widely respected, immediately recognized Garwood's
symptoms. Garwood was helpless: he did not know
how to function in the society he grew up in; the English language was awkward for him; he had forgotten
how to cross a street. When Tanay spoke to him on the
phone, Garwood needed instruction on how to pay for
transportation by taxi or bus, and he was too helpless
to stay in a hotel. The doctor took Garwood home for
the duration of his stay, an unusual step for a professional psychiatrist, who would normally limit his contact with a patient to the four walls of his clinic.

Tanay, and other psychiatrists called in later by the
defense, warned that additional stress of the kind Garwood endured after leaving Vietnam could be lethal, yet
every day he was subjected to more. His self-esteem was
nonexistent. He was guilt-ridden about surviving when
friends and comrades had not, full of self-recrimination,
and barely recognized that he had done his best to help

his fellow prisoners stay alive. He became passive, as if accepting that all the dreadful prejudgments passed upon him must be true. After all, he felt, those who were judging him were more worldly than he was, and knew more about right and wrong. It never occurred to him that the members of the jury of the Article 32 Investigation, whom he respected because they were all Marine officers and Vietnam veterans, had no understanding of the inhuman system inside which he had struggled. This lack of first-hand experience was exemplified when one of Garwood's lawyers asked each member of the jury in turn what he would do as a captive "if a guard put a pistol to your head and said he was going to pull the trigger unless you signed some innocuous statement . . . like 'all Americans are imperialists.' " "I'd tell them to pull the trigger," each had responded. Men who had been prisoners knew that in reality the situation within communist camps was never reduced to such a simple choice. There had been certain circumstances when you could sign a meaningless piece of paper to get out news of your survival.

Garwood was a man isolated from his own community by an experience beyond articulation. His civilian lawyer, Dermot Foley, who himself had a missing brother, understood this but he had no experience as a trial lawyer and seemed unable to translate his empathy into an effective strategy for Garwood's defense. That the torture and degradation Garwood suffered as a prisoner should have been a primary issue of the court martial was the view of Vaughn Taylor, a brilliant young lawyer, recently out of the Army and hired by Foley after the Article 32 Investigation to bring a new dimension to the case. Taylor had been assistant professor at the Army's Judge Advocates General School at the University of Virginia. He had an outstanding background, having himself written the very specialized instructions for military judges in insanity cases. Taylor took an interest in Garwood's case from the moment he heard of his return, just as Foley had. Taylor was unable to get involved at first because he was not a Marine or civilian lawyer. As soon as he left the Army to join the Charlottesville, Virginia, civilian law firm of Lowe and Gordon, he became part of Garwood's legal team as counsel to Foley, with the blessing of his new bosses.

In the early stages of his involvement, Taylor was not informed enough to judge whether Garwood was guilty of all, some, or none of the crimes alleged. But he believed that if Garwood was at all guilty, it was because he had fallen into an incompetent mental state brought about by torture and duress. Taylor called this "coercive persuasion." As the trial progressed, he learned more of the facts. He also became acquainted with what he came to regard as the government's unethical smear tactics, and grew less willing even to consider the possibility of Garwood's guilt. Taylor was infuriated with the prosecution's attempts to present Garwood as he had always been depicted in the secret "criminal file" kept on him, as a miserable product of his deprived background. Later, Vaughn Taylor would say, "Bobby was not just a product of his background. He did more good than harm to American prisoners in the camps. . . . The courage he displayed in the way he did this makes him the bravest man I know."

The coercive persuasion suffered by Garwood in Vietnam was, to the lawyer, incontestably evident. Even the 121 Board—a panel of military psychiatrists ordered by the judge of the court martial to examine Garwood—did not question the torture and maltreatment he had suffered. But the argument that such coercive persuasion made Garwood mentally incompetent backfired in the courtroom and with the public. It would be twisted by many in the media to make him sound brain damaged or just mentally deficient. It also backfired with Garwood because, despite the effects of posttraumatic stress disorder, he knew he was not guilty of the criminal acts he was charged with and he did not want to be defended on the assumption that he was guilty but "not really because at the time he had been turned into a zombie."

Perhaps it was also pride in the one thing he had accomplished. He had outwitted his clever and cruel captors. A mental incompetent could never have done that. He did not want to be part of a strategy that turned him into a moron.

The three psychiatrists on the 121 Board decided he was mentally competent to stand trial and that at the time of his alleged conduct, he had the capacity to appreciate the criminality of it. No one made much of the fact that Garwood had to be examined twice by the 121 Board because one of its own psychiatrists was disciplined after he had collapsed from an excessive bout of drinking in a Jacksonville bar.

The defense team's cross examination during the court martial demonstrated that military psychiatrists agreed with civilian doctors on one critical point: Garwood's life now hung by a thread and this admission is inscribed in the court transcripts. Only the desire to vindicate himself and to tell the world what had happened to Ike and Russ and others like them, the psychiatrists confirmed, could have kept him alive. Each psychiatric session put him under the stress of reliving what was described as the "grossly traumatic events" of his prison years—the flashbacks to his punishments, the deaths of his friends. He would sob uncontrollably in recalling the deaths of Ike Eisenbraun and Russ Grisset.

Civilian psychiatrists did something the government had not done. They carefully listened to him and studied the "interviews" conducted with the prisoners who testified against Garwood. The consensus of the doctors— military as well as civilian—was that Garwood had ab-

solutely no happy memories of Vietnam. They all believed he told the truth about his imprisonment.

From the limited records available to him, Dr. Tanay
was certain that the rest of the prisoners had behaved just
like Garwood. "They had all engaged in activities which
they, themselves, did not approve of, but had to accept
as the price of survival." Doctors were unanimous in
their opinion that "there was no evidence that Garwood
ever used his Vietnamese language and culture skills to
dominate or harm another American." During the court
martial Garwood would take that integrity even further.
He was aware that those who testified against him were
guilty of actions harmful to other prisoners. But he had
promised himself never to give the North Vietnamese or
Colonel Thai, who had made such dire predictions about
Garwood's future, the satisfaction of knowing that their
"spider-in-the-jar" policy continued to work more than
a decade later. It was a resolution he would not break:
neither during the trial nor since would Garwood ever
accuse any American of harming another American in
Vietnam.

"I seriously believe," testified Dr. David L. Hubbard,
who gave Garwood extensive physical, intelligence, personality, and psychological tests, "he may have conducted himself better than many of his critics who have
come forward here. I believe he is a wounded veteran
and entitled to those dignities granted to his peers." Hubbard's cautious words received little attention.

Bobby Garwood's emotional state left him oblivious
to much of the legal strategy going on. But he had survived prison in great part out of spite against all his tormentors. Colonel Thai and his other Vietnamese torturers
would not have the pleasure of learning that he had finally been broken by his own people.

Thus, when the prosecution hinted at the possibility of
closing the case if Garwood pleaded guilty to at least

some of the charges, he refused to cop a plea. "I was innocent," he said later. "I wanted to prove that. I wanted to do it for my mother and for my father and my brother. I wanted to do it for Ike."

21: Checkmate

Bobby Garwood was upset by media stories that not only distorted the tragedy of his capture and incarceration, but also raised doubts about his intelligence and his family background. Initially he trusted Dermot Foley, who headed his civilian legal team, because his father trusted him. But Foley was a bankruptcy specialist with no experience as a trial lawyer. Garwood also began to suspect Foley was more interested in gleaning information that might shed light on the fate of his missing brother, Colonel Brendan Foley, than on defending Garwood. Almost every meeting between Garwood and Foley was attended by a government official—usually Roger Shields, who had been chief of the Pentagon's prisoner of war task force in 1973. More often than not, Foley would find an excuse to leave Shields and Garwood alone. Garwood would then be grilled about things that had nothing to do with his defense and warned not to talk to anyone else about his experience. Afterward, Foley too would tell Garwood not to talk to anyone other than himself about his Vietnam experience, but for another reason: he had sold exclusive rights to Garwood's story and wanted nothing to spoil his contract with the authors and publisher of a planned book.

It was for this reason that, almost immediately after the court martial began in late spring of 1980, Garwood abruptly dismissed Foley and replaced him with John Lowe, who headed the law firm that employed Vaughn Taylor. When Foley, as head of Garwood's civilian legal team, hired Taylor, he hired the entire firm of Lowe and Gordon, as was customary. Soon after, John Lowe began to assume a leading role. Garwood was impressed by Lowe's take-charge style. Unlike Foley, Lowe was experienced in criminal defense and was a well-respected lecturer on trial procedures. An earlier client of Lowe's had been Robert Robideau, the Native Canadian accused of murdering two FBI agents in Cedar Rapids, Iowa. Robideau had been acquitted by a jury.

Just before Garwood fired him, Foley told reporters that he was moving toward a defense based on "mental incapacity." This tack would require introducing as evidence the head injuries Garwood sustained when he crashed into a bus in Okinawa after having been on driving duty for seventy-two hours. Questioned about this much later, Foley said that his statement to the press had been nothing more than a publicity ploy. He had not really planned such a defense. He was setting up a smokescreen and using the media to confuse the prosecution. Indeed, he continued, he had positive proof in his files that Garwood had always been a prisoner of the North Vietnamese, which included photographs obtained from U.S. intelligence contacts of a bound and broken Garwood after capture. His plan had been, he said, to pulverize the opposition with this material at the most effective moments in the trial itself. He misjudged Garwood's capacity to understand this strategy, or perhaps thought him too emotionally fragile to deal with it. So the smokescreen meant only for the prosecution obscured his intentions from Garwood as well. Furthermore, Foley had persuaded Garwood to do a *Playboy* interview, but instead it was Winston Groom, coauthor of the book about Garwood's experiences in Vietnam, who was interviewed, and who, in Garwood's view, presented just one more distorted version of the facts. Garwood felt he had been used again, and offered up as a victim of a deprived background that made him succumb to the blandishments of the enemy.

Foley's own reason for arranging the *Playboy* interview was money. When asked about this, he said that he had already invested close to 150,000 dollars of his own money on the case with no sign of Garwood's back-pay being released. But Garwood did not care. He did not want to win by means of what he understood to be a strategy that would make him look mentally incompetent, or on false arguments that an unhappy childhood caused him to behave as the prosecution alleged.

There was another reason for firing Foley. John Lowe told Garwood that Foley, a commercial law specialist, was not qualified to defend him and was not looking out for his best interests: Garwood, he said, would have to choose between Foley and the partnership of Lowe and Gordon.

Foley was infuriated at being fired by Garwood. The lawyer told the author that he suspected Garwood had somehow been manipulated into making this decision by Lowe. Foley said his replacement had no interest in the material he had painstakingly collected long before Garwood escaped from Vietnam, including critical documents that would have demonstrated to the court that Garwood was captured; that he was wounded trying to escape; and that he was never anything but a prisoner of the North Vietnamese, undergoing the most severe torture and brainwashing techniques. Foley had gathered this evidence as part of his longstanding interest in the prisoner issue, and more, specifically, the search for his missing brother. He had been certain that if the public was made aware of this evidence, which had cost him a lot of money and time to accumulate, the prosecution would fold up. Without him, he felt, Garwood was certain to lose. He thought if Garwood did lose, he would be rehired to represent Garwood in an appeal. He had therefore saved the documents for that eventuality and had not made them public.

Foley had critics who discounted these excuses. They felt that he, like many others, had been persuaded by the government that Garwood was in fact guilty of such vile acts while a prisoner that only a defense of mental illness could save him from a severe sentence.

Foley's departure just at the start of the trial would have serious consequences for Garwood, and some legal students said later it was the crucial factor in his losing the case. Foley seemed to be the only one who understood that Garwood had been set up from the beginning of his capture—for what Foley said "was probably the most human of reasons. When you make a mistake, blame the other guy—especially if he isn't around to argue." Because of Foley's missing brother, and his interest in veterans—particularly those who had been in covert operations—he had spent the years after the war cultivating military and intelligence sources and assembling information not made public.

He had seen enough official documentation of Garwood's original disappearance in September 1965 to decide that his tragedy really began with the cover-up of mistakes by superiors who failed to recognize the potential hazards of sending an inexperienced and inadequately armed and poorly directed private into the most hostile and dangerous VC territory in South Vietnam. He was convinced that those mistakes were compounded once it became known that Garwood's disappearance was of such interest to the command structure that even the secretary of the Navy was briefed on it. Foley had put together most of the Garwood puzzle in ways the attorneys whom he left behind could not, because they lacked his treasury of documents.

The puzzle would have to be completed much later—too late to influence the court martial—by DIA intelligence chief Eugene Tighe. He and others with a great deal of professional experience formed the opinion, based on evidence they had personally seen, that Garwood's entire Vietnam history had been manipulated, starting with an instinct on the part of his superiors to cover mistakes made on the day of his capture, and continuing with more cover-ups as mistake was piled upon mistake. Most important of all, there was nothing produced at Garwood's trial to make the crucial distinction between the communists' handling of "conventional" prisoners and those they assigned to a more sinister category.

A big Foley discovery was that Garwood had been moved into a separate enemy prison system designed to break suspected intelligence agents, a system known to both sides but kept utterly secret for different reasons. The communists did not kill such suspects because they needed to squeeze information from them about U.S. covert operations and intelligence plans. The U.S. government did not want the enemy to know it was tracking Americans through this secret system.

Foley found that when Garwood was captured, the Victong were returning most ordinary soldiers, but not those suspected of having worked with intelligence and/ or special operations. Regular American soldiers were new to Vietnam, but the communists had been fighting irregular U.S. covert-action groups in Vietnam since the French pulled out in the mid-1950s. The communists regarded these covert operations as cynically contemptuous of international law. They responded with equal cynicism and without mercy to anyone they considered an international outlaw. As a G-2 driver and sometime chauffeur for the commander of American forces in the northern provinces of South Vietnam, Garwood fell immediately into the outlaw category of prisoner.

To the communists, the driver of a high-ranking officer

had to be himself a high-ranking intelligence officer. The fact that Garwood was armed with only a pistol on the day of his capture reinforced that belief. Such drivers in the NVA were tasked with keeping track of the man they chauffeured, even to the point of assassinating him if it appeared he would fall into enemy hands. Such NVA drivers were aware of all intelligence briefings involving the officer they drove around. Garwood's captors assumed he, too, would have a high-level security clearance and be privy to secret information. Foley had been told by his Pentagon contacts that it was highly probable Garwood's capture was in fact not by chance.

Communist double agents kept a tight watch on General Walt's activities. They had already passed onto their superiors, on the day of Garwood's capture, the fact that General Walt was meeting with General Krulak. Krulak, the Pentagon's chief specialist on counterinsurgency warfare, was of special interest to the North Vietnamese. During the first half of 1964, the year before Garwood's capture, he had played a leading role in planning a campaign of highly successful clandestine operations against them.[1]

To the Vietcong, Garwood seemed part of the clandestine world. He was put in the custody of a highly secret and separately administered prison system controlled by the intelligence and security services of the military proselytizing department (Cuc Binh Van/Soviet). According to experts like Bill Bell, the former head of the U.S. office for POW/MIA affairs in Hanoi,[2] Cuc Binh Van/Soviet was loosely the equivalent of the Soviet

---

[1] These operations included air operations against NVA and Pathet (communist) Lao troops in Laos and destroyer patrols sent into the Gulf of Tonkin to collect intelligence and exert pressure on North Vietnam.

[2] Bill Bell was also the former chief of operations of the Joint Casualty Resolution Center in Hawaii and worked for the Pentagon's Defense Intelligence Agency on the POW/MIA issue. He currently heads the National Veteran's Research Center at Fort Smith, Arkansas.

KGB. It was Cuc Binh Van/Soviet that took charge of all Americans suspected of having been involved in covert action or intelligence, and to which highly trained interrogators, graduates, like Mr. Ho, of the Soviet Union's specialized schools, were assigned. Almost no one held by Cuc Binh Van/Soviet returned from captivity unless they escaped through a fluke bombing, like Issac Camacho, or were traded back to the Americans through the CIA for a Vietnamese of similar value.[3] All reports on the capture, detention, and exploitation of U.S. personnel regarded as spies were hand-carried by party couriers to the interministry/national defense council in Hanoi.

American intelligence knew a great deal about Cuc Binh Van/Soviet's highly secret and labyrinthine prison system, which spread throughout Vietnam, and tried to keep track of those it held; this was almost impossible, however, because prisoners were constantly moved from camp to camp to prevent their being rescued.

The North Vietnamese handled Garwood's case in a markedly different way from that of American prisoners who were judged to have been performing normal military duties when they were captured. Although he and other "secret intelligence and criminal prisoners" were sometimes held with "regular" prisoners, they were subject to a separate administration.[4]

---

[3] After Cuc Binh Van/Soviet prisoners were evaluated and "sorted," they were evacuated to a camp of the regional party committee (Khu Uy), operated by security section personnel and directly controlled by the national defense council of the Politburo in Hanoi.

[4] Those considered strictly military prisoners were placed in the enemy proselytizing department (Cuc Dich Van Soviet) patterned after a section of the Soviet GRU (Soviet Military Intelligence). The prisoners destined for bases administered by Cuc Dich Van Soviet were initially evacuated to a camp of the military region Quan Khu. Subsequent to "exploitation," they would be evacuated to the main American prison in Hanoi—the Hanoi Hilton.

The majority of "secret intelligence" prisoners under Cuc Binh Van/Soviet never ended up in the Hanoi Hilton and were never repatriated. This belated knowledge was to lead a former national security adviser, Zbigniew Brzezinski, to say publicly in 1993 that it was likely most of these prisoners were killed shortly after the end of the war in a massacre similar to Nazi and Soviet massacres at Babiy Yar and Katyn Forest respectively. Fearing such a fate for the special category of U.S. prisoners, American intelligence had always been as secretive about the Cuc Binh Van/Soviet prison system as the communists themselves.

The general U.S. prejudice against Garwood and others held in custody by Cuc Binh Van/Soviet was a consequence of the success scored by this security branch in exploiting U.S. and foreign personnel for propaganda purposes, especially in the United States itself. The organization's true purpose as a top-secret dirty-tricks outfit fashioned on the highly skilled Soviet model was known to a select few in Washington. Its ingenious propaganda about Garwood always made him appear to be working for the communists out of conviction; never that he was being held as prisoner.

The effectiveness of this subterfuge was proven by the American prisoners who were persuaded by their VC captors that Garwood, dressed in NVA uniform, had visited their camp and contemptuously challenged them to follow his example. It was not until these men saw pictures of Garwood during the court martial that they realized he was not the man who had been pointed out to them in prison camp.

This was how misconceptions arose about some American early releasees, like John Sexton, who was left by the Americans to wander near the Cambodian border even though they had been alerted to his release, and perhaps also the so-called "Bennies" Bruce Womack was sent to assassinate. Once American intelligence learned that a prisoner had been associated with Cuc Binh Van/Soviet, and used for communist propaganda purposes, the usual assumption was that the man had either turned after being taken prisoner, or had voluntarily defected to do propaganda work.

Dermot Foley had managed to pry from his intelligence contacts a secret known to many of America's South Vietnamese allies, but to only a handful of American intelligence operatives who were in Vietnam when Saigon fell in 1975. He discovered that almost all of American intelligence during the war had been compromised and manipulated by a North Vietnamese agent who managed to infiltrate both the South Vietnamese intelligence superstructure and the American CIA. This was cartoonist Huyn Ba Thanh, the powerful liaison between the CIA and South Vietnam's President Thieu. Thanh worked at Saigon CIA headquarters on Pasteur Street and had access to almost all CIA files, including those kept on American prisoners, because the CIA was responsible for prisoner rescue.

Not until the war was over did privileged Americans realize that the South Vietnamese intelligence chief they had trusted with most of their secrets was in reality a hard-core communist and intelligence (Cong An) captain. Thanh had always been suspect to some South Vietnamese intelligence experts who had plenty of raw evidence to suggest that he had used the Phoenix program as a cover to destroy good people loyal to South Vietnam and the United States. In the days when U.S. intelligence groups were first becoming involved in Vietnam, experienced French security officers had warned the Americans about Thanh. They said he had been a protégé of Mai Chi Tho, the powerful North Vietnamese Politburo member and minister in charge of Cong An, and was unlikely to change his allegiance.

No one listened to the French "losers" after 1954, but in 1975, as Saigon was falling, French warnings proved to be well-founded. Thanh, the double agent who had worked closely with the CIA in trying to bring down the Thieu government, was left in charge of destroying sensitive American records, including the lists of South Vietnamese who had worked for the CIA and other American intelligence units. After completion of this crucial task, he was supposed to leave on one of the last American planes for the United States. He never showed up for his flight.

A few days later, photographs of a smiling Thanh as People's Revolutionary Hero appeared in the North Vietnamese media. He had just been promoted to Cong An colonel and publisher of the secret service journal *Tat Chi Cong An.* Foley discovered that Thanh had handed the sensitive American records, supposedly destroyed by the CIA, to his superiors in Hanoi, thereby sentencing thousands of America's most loyal South Vietnamese allies to death or to Camp 776, one of North Vietnam's harshest prison camps. Some of the betrayed South Vietnamese were the men who helped Garwood become Mr. Electric Generator in that same camp. These were facts, Foley said later, that would have done much to vindicate Garwood.

The few high-level American intelligence officials who knew of Thanh's massive treachery saw no benefit in making any of this public. The facts about Thanh, however, would have explained the complicated web of disinformation, double crosses, and betrayal in which Garwood had been trapped. Now that Foley was gone, Garwood's defense, too, knew none of this history. From the court records, it appears the prosecution did not, either.

Thanh had played a key role in confusing the Americans. Now it seemed probable that he and Colonel Thai had themselves been unwittingly misled into believing Garwood was an intelligence expert by the high-level U.S. interest in his disappearance. Thanh, having access to CIA records, knew that ordinary noncommissioned deserters did not generate the frenzied activity that followed Garwood's disappearance on September 28th, 1965. Most telling for him was the briefing that General Walt himself had given the secretary of the Navy about Garwood's disappearance. It was ludicrous to think that a run-of-the-mill deserter warranted such top-level attention and crisis management.

Thus Garwood was not only suspect to his captors but a challenge that became greater when they discovered his unique fluency in their language and customs, and his skill in the art of survival—actually taught him, of course, by Ike Eisenbraun. The communists had turned their psychological warfare plans up a notch. They were no longer just out to break Garwood but to make use of what they regarded as new-found knowledge about him to toy with American intelligence. They succeeded beyond their wildest expectations, while Thanh's duplicity remained undiscovered. Their American opposites, who for the most part did not know the plain facts regarding Garwood's last driving assignment and the significance given it by the enemy, fell hook, line, and sinker for the enemy's deceptions—none so hard as Colonel Tom C. McKenney.

The North Vietnamese were masters at the art of propaganda. Their announcement of Garwood's capture was designed to persuade the Americans that Hanoi considered Garwood an intelligence catch. Radio Hanoi's broadcasts, as transcribed by western monitors at the time, make this clear. This in turn caused the Americans to wonder whether Garwood knew more than they realized and had spilled the beans about Walt and G-2 immediately after his capture. The broadcasts became more provocative as time wore on and the enemy drew fresh conclusions about Garwood's importance. Other methods were designed to convey to the Americans that Garwood was a goldmine of information. This eventually played into the hands of Garwood's USMC superiors, who needed to prove that no mistake had been made on their part. If the brass could be persuaded that Garwood defected, they would not ask why he had been ordered on an ill-considered mission into dangerous territory, alone, unprepared, and inadequately armed.

Foley also knew that when Garwood was captured, the Marine Corps was still smarting over the rumored defection of several other Marines. Clyde Weatherman appeared to have "crossed over" some months before Garwood's capture. It was easy to persuade the USMC brass, who had no knowledge of Garwood's short-timer status, that Garwood had also crossed over. This was when top-secret memos first began to fly that would later pile up in Garwood's file.

Foley had learned enough about the voluminous, but what he called "flimsy" evidence collected on Garwood's defection to feel confident it would never stand up in court. He had sufficient documentation of his own to refute any claim by the government that Garwood had gone over, but this documentation never became part of Garwood's defense. Lowe and Taylor said Foley did not pass it on. Foley maintained that there was no interest.

In the end, Foley's conclusions were vindicated. Captain Werner Helmer, the tall, almost skeletally thin prosecutor whom some reporters described as looking more like a POW than Garwood, never even referred to the alleged criminal acts in Garwood's secret file during the trial proceedings. Instead, following the pattern established by U.S. intelligence, he built a secret case against Garwood behind the scenes of the trial while in front of judge and jury relying primarily on the testimony of former Garwood prisonmates who had themselves been manipulated by the enemy.

That the prosecution would resort to such tactics was at first inconceivable to Taylor. Taylor would remain Garwood's attorney after the court martial, but it was years before he fully understood how government manipulation and interference had made it impossible for Garwood to prove his innocence.

It did not take long, though, for Taylor to feel outrage in general at the government's way of playing rough with Garwood's constitutional rights, particularly in confronting the defendant with alleged evidence that was never explained. "They would say 'here are photos or documents you are allowed to see,' never what it meant or how they planned to use it," he said later. Taylor questioned Helmer about the ethics of this behavior: as in any trial, the prosecution was required to share evidence with the defense, especially if it could lessen the charges or lead to acquittal. Taylor knew the prosecutor well. Although they were about the same age, Helmer had been one of his students when he taught at the Judge Advocates school.

Now Helmer answered, "The law only allows you to see the evidence."

Still, Taylor thought, despite the hardball tactics, the prosecution was within the law. They had to be. A military trial does not allow for the same kind of dazzling showmanship often seen in civilian celebrity trials. Both prosecution and defense were under the microscope for unethical conduct. Even hand gestures had to be described for the court record and, if inappropriate, could be used to justify an appeal.

In the courtroom Helmer was technically proficient, doing everything by the book, but both Taylor and Garwood were aware that he carefully avoided meeting Garwood's eyes. The only emotion he ever showed was in a comment made under his breath to Taylor, before assistant prosecutor Teresa Wright made her final statement. With a grin he whispered, "Wait until you see this. Hell hath no fury like a woman!"

Taylor felt Helmer was deeply prejudiced against Garwood, but he did not know why. Privately the prosecutor kept up a continuing barrage of innuendo. This seemed intended to turn Taylor's sympathies against his own client. Throughout the court martial, Taylor would allege later, Helmer grabbed every opportunity to take Taylor aside and tell him of Garwood's horrendous record in harming other troops in Vietnam. Taylor said, "You almost had to believe Helmer knew something the rest of us didn't." Helmer told Taylor he had a Marine who had been blinded in a VC attack led by Garwood and was ready to testify. The Marine could identify Garwood by his voice, said Helmer. Later, when Taylor learned about the firefight in 1972 that allegedly involved Garwood, he recognized it as the source from which Helmer had gotten his information. Helmer promised to produce the blind Marine on the witness stand.

"I didn't know if Helmer had the stuff, and didn't want to produce it because he didn't want to show his hand," said Taylor afterward, "or if he was empty handed and just bluffing."

Helmer began telephoning Taylor in his Charlottesville office. During one of Helmer's long-distance harangues, Taylor blew up. "Look, Werner," he said, "both you and I know the military has a completely open disclosure system. Either show me what you've got or shut up!"

Helmer replied: "I really don't have anything in particular . . . but I've studied the historical traitors like Benedict Arnold. These 'Bennies' are all alike—and I've learned that once they start, they go to the nth degree."[5]

---

[5] The government has not abandoned its strategy of character assassination by innuendo against Garwood. Helmer's insinuations about Garwood derived from the same misinformation that had influenced McKenney, and were totally without merit. Garwood was not formally charged with any of the crimes attributed to him in the government's file of classified intelligence reports. Nonetheless, authorized accounts continue to assert his guilt. The following is an example from *Marines and Military Law in Vietnam: Trial by Fire* by USMC Lieutenant Colonel Gary D. Solis, published by the History and Museums Division,

Taylor became concerned that there was a kind of arrogance to Helmer's convictions that made him oblivious to facts. Although no one, not even Colonel R. E. Switzer, the trial judge, took the AWOL charge seriously anymore, since it had been brought out that Garwood had only ten days more to serve when he was captured, Helmer did not let it go. He put Lieutenant Colonel John A. Studds, Garwood's company commander, and Charles Buchta, Garwood's battalion motor-transport officer the day he disappeared, on the stand. They swore that no stone had been left unturned to find out whether Garwood had a legitimate reason to leave III MAF, and stuck by their original story that Garwood had no authorization to go.

To prove that Garwood had no plans or reason to desert days before his tour was due to end, Garwood's attorneys called his long-ago fiancée, Mary Speer, to the witness stand. Speer, now married, testified that Garwood and she had been in the midst of wedding plans when he was captured and that she suffered a mental breakdown when she learned of his disappearance. Her testimony was backed by Kenneth Banholzer and his wife, Vicky, friends of Garwood who like Speer had corresponded

---

Headquarters, USMC, in 1989: "In September or October 1969 . . . Captain Marin L. Brandtner commanded Company D, First Battalion, Fifth Marines in an operation in Arizona Territory. During a firefight he saw a Caucasian who appeared to be pointing out targets for the enemy. Even though the Marines fired at him, the Caucasian did not appear to be hit. Captain (later Brigadier General) Brandtner was aware of reports that Garwood was suspected to be in that area and believed the man he saw with the enemy was indeed Garwood." On the basis of such hearsay, the book concludes that the magnitude of Garwood's crimes is unsurpassed in Marine Corps history. The final paragraph in this official statement is unequivocable: "Garwood was the only former prisoner of war of any armed service convicted of acts committed while with the enemy—not for acts committed while a prisoner, for his prisoner status ended the day he refused release and asked to remain with the enemy. Robert R. Garwood *was* the enemy."

with Garwood just before his disappearance. The two couples had intended to have a double wedding. Garwood's letters had stated emphatically that he couldn't wait to get back to the States. This testimony seemed to make little impression on the jury or the press. One reporter, seemingly unable to understand the relevance of Speer's testimony, said it seemed only "to prove that Garwood had a girlfriend when he disappeared in 1965." He knew nothing of the emotional scene that had taken place between Garwood and Speer in Vaughn Taylor's office before her court appearance.

Speer had come all the way from Covina, California, to testify. Her husband, who knew how much Garwood and she had been in love, had encouraged her and accompanied her. When Garwood and she met, they ran to each other, embraced silently, tears streaming down both their faces. For a long time they clung to each other.

Despite the fact that Speer's testimony was considered inconsequential, the testimony of Studds and Buchta was invalidated by irrefutable evidence. Billy Ray Conley, who wanted to take over Garwood's assignment on the day of his capture, was called by the defense. Conley, at this time a warehouse worker in Detroit, had watched Garwood's return to America on television in April 1979. Glued to the set, he understood at once just how lucky he was to have been denied Garwood's last assignment: "God looked out for me that day," he later said.

Conley knew that a lot of things could happen in fourteen years, but one thing was unalterable. Garwood had not deserted, and Conley could prove it. Conley had vied with him for the same assignment. Conley waited to see if the U.S. government would go through its records and find the interviews done with him and Garwood's other colleagues at the time of his disappearance, which validated Garwood's claim that he was on an official assignment when captured. The government failed to get in touch with him during the lengthy investigation and pretrial hearings and even after the desertion charge was changed to "unauthorized leave of absence." Then news reports showed the government still maintaining that Garwood had no assignment on the day he disappeared. And so Conley came forward, a witness nobody expected.

Conley's testimony left the prosecution with a severely weakened case. As they had during the Article 32 Investigation, the prosecutors now focused exclusively on Garwood's "spider-in-the-jar" prison experience with other Americans in 1967–69, that most painful period when the enemy had made him an outcast to his own people, and Russ Grisset was beaten to death. It was a weak strategy but singularly effective against Garwood because, on the advice of John Lowe, he did not take the stand in his own defense. This was against all his instincts. He wanted desperately to tell the world what had really happened to him in Vietnam. But Lowe recited a long list of criminal cases won because the defendant did not take the stand, including that of Robert Robideau. He said that 90 percent of cases were lost because the defendant became too emotional under cross examination. Still Garwood insisted. Finally, Lower said: "the prosecution has over three thousand questions for you. They will put you on the stand for four to six weeks. They will ask a question. You'll answer it truthfully. Then they'll rephrase it. If your answer is only slightly different, they'll call you a liar." Lowe asked Garwood to consider what this would do to Jack Garwood and the rest of his family. Garwood acquiesced. He said later, "I was actually confused. There was only one certainty about the trial: I had no control at all."

It was at this point that Garwood would have benefited most from the services of the departed Dermot Foley. Foley had planned to use testimony from Dr. Edna Hunter, a psychologist and the head of the Pentagon's POW unit in 1973, when the prisoners came home. A published expert on torture and manipulation by the communists during the Vietnam war, she had interviewed all the former prisoners who testified against Garwood. Hunter, who wanted badly to testify, thought the jury should know that every one of Garwood's accusers felt guilty about having behaved exactly as Garwood had, or in some cases worse than he had, while being held prisoner. She passed no judgment on any of them. "They were all tortured, tricked, and manipulated by the communists," she had said to Foley. "They all tried to survive." This was something the judge and jury would not have a chance to hear.

Consider the example of Dr. Kushner. During his debriefing after his release in 1973, he spoke of the terrible conditions and torments the men had had to live through. Six men he knew in fact did not survive, he said, most of them dying in his arms. He talked about the physical and psychological torment, as well as the disorientation and psychoses suffered by the men. He talked about himself being brought to the edge of insanity by the awful, coercive, life-threatening conditions.

At his debriefing Kushner did not describe Garwood even once as excluded from the suffering of American POWs in general. Now, at the trial, he gave what was, because of his rank and profession, grave testimony against Garwood.

Much had been alleged during the preliminary hearings and in the press about Garwood's being armed and guarding American prisoners in Vietnam. Yet no one who testified could remember him ever acting as a guard without himself being under the watchful eyes of Vietnamese guards, or pointing a gun at another prisoner, or firing a gun. Indeed no one had been close enough to see whether the gun they alleged he carried had a firing pin. That was true of Kushner as well, yet Garwood's attorneys were very much aware of how persuasive he seemed in convincing the jury that Garwood had done the worst, even when they cross examined him. So John Lowe questioned him further on the stand:

Lowe: "During all the time that you say PFC Garwood was acting as a guard or otherwise carrying weapons you never saw him point a weapon at any American POW, did you? You never saw him display live ammunition for a weapon did you?"

Kushner: "No."

Lowe: "In fact, if you get right down to it you have no way of knowing whether any of the weapons he was seen carrying had firing pins or were otherwise operable, do you? Personally?"

Kushner: "No, nor do I know if the guards' weapons had firing pins."

In fact, making prisoners carry arms had been a ruse commonly used by the enemy. Dr. Hunter would have been speaking knowledgeably in court if she had been able to testify that prisoners were often required to carry useless weapons in order to arouse suspicion and sow dissension among the prison-camp population. None of the guilt-racked men she had interviewed, forced to carry a weapon in full view of other prisoners, was ever given one with a firing pin. Garwood himself said under intensive pre-trial questioning, over and over, that he had never carried a weapon that could be used to fire ammunition, and that he had never been given ammunition.

There was testimony from Jose Ortiz-Rivera, the Puerto Rican who was given early release by his captors because his "people were exploited by America just like the Vietnamese," and who persuaded American intelligence that Garwood had in reality deserted when he refused "liberation." Now living in Puerto Rico, Ortiz-Rivera was flown back and forth four times to testify against Garwood. At the court martial, Ortiz-Rivera required an interpreter for his testimony. Just as Garwood had remembered from their time in the same prison camp, Ortiz-Rivera spoke almost no English. Nevertheless, the Puerto Rican claimed now that he remembered having lengthy conversations with Garwood—in English. Ortiz-Rivera swore under oath that Garwood told him in the camp "that he felt better with them, with the Vietcong, and they treated him better than the U.S. Army [sic]." Had Ortiz-Rivera been even slightly better acquainted with Garwood, he would have known that the Marine never referred to himself as having been in the Army.

Many of the witnesses brought forward by the prosecution were, like Ortiz-Rivera, early releasees. This had made them suspect to men like Ted Guy, who thought they all should have been brought up on charges. Guy had felt that by accepting early release they had collaborated, seriously harming their fellow prisoners in the process. Had Guy and the one hundred other prisoners who backed him not been prevented from bringing charges by the government, these witnesses might have been robbed of credibility by the time of Garwood's court martial. When Garwood did not take the stand, however, their testimony stood uncontested.

Garwood's lawyers now did their best to present him as a sick man, someone who had been coerced and brainwashed into committing the crimes suggested by former inmates of Camp 4 and S.T. 18 like Ortiz-Rivera and Kushner. The Washington *Post* reported that "his [Garwood's] attorneys do not deny the substance of the charges." In fact Garwood admitted to his attorneys that he was guilty of some of the charges brought against him, but, he explained, they were things that all prisoners were guilty of. He cited the example of having to verbally castigate other prisoners. This, he explained, did not mean he had been driven to insanity. He asked John Lowe, "what's wrong with using duress as a defense?" Lowe replied that, legally, duress would only work if a gun had been held to Garwood's head every moment of the fourteen years he was a prisoner.

Garwood asked, *"literally?"* When Lowe replied "yes," Garwood knew the die was cast. Lowe tried to be ameliorative.

"Bobby, we are not saying you are insane. We are saying you did things because of the horrible conditions in the camp."

"But I never hurt anybody. There were many times when I put my life on the line for others."

Garwood's sister Linda was outraged at the way his defense lawyers ignored her brother's pleas to be defended on the basis of duress and in a way that demonstrated his integrity. Every day something was said by his own attorneys that betrayed their belief that he would not be vindicated in the only way that mattered to him. As in a Shakespearean tragedy, each day "crept in its petty pace" toward the dishonor John Lowe, his lead attorney, foreshadowed in his closing summation. Even if the jury found Garwood not guilty, said his own defense lawyer, "he'd still be a sick man. . . . There would be no vindication." Garwood lost his trust in Lowe, the lawyer and former Army intelligence officer who had been so optimistic when he persuaded him to fire Dermot Foley. Lowe often told Garwood that he had staked his entire reputation and that of his law firm on this case, but Garwood felt he was being patronized. There was no sign of empathy. Above all Lowe wanted to hear nothing "personal," nothing about the stress and torture his client had been subjected to in the camps.

Years later Garwood remembered that Lowe had paid very close attention to him only once. The lawyer had been in the process of lecturing him about not taking the witness stand. "What will you do," he had asked, "if you're convicted and sent to federal prison? How will you deal with that?" It seemed to Garwood that his lawyers thought of "a possible guilty verdict as being like a switch in my head, bring it up and memories of prison would light up and I'd do as they asked." Lowe expected him to try to avoid such a fate at any cost, but not in the way his client was planning.

"I'll ask for the death sentence," Garwood replied. "In Vietnam I was the enemy. I will never allow myself to be put in the position of being the enemy of the American people. I only asked one thing of God—that he would allow me to be buried here on my native soil—and he has already granted me that wish."

Garwood did not tell him that he expected to be convicted, or that he was just looking for an excuse to kill himself and had already obtained a 9-mm automatic gun. It had been made clear to him that there was to be no opportunity to tell the truth and defend himself. Ike and Russ, the only people who had known the truth, were dead and he felt an almost overwhelming desire to be with them. He had it all worked out. During breaks in the court martial he wanted to find a place to be by himself and to pray. Sergeant Langlois suggested nearby Emerald Isle, which was uninhabited. When he went there, Garwood sat cross-legged under a tree, facing what he believed was Southeast Asia, and found a measure of peace and comfort in the thought that he would soon be with the two dead comrades who had really cared about him. "I was going to go to Emerald Isle," he said later, "to my tree, strip, and shoot myself under my chin."

Garwood kept these plans to himself, but his sister Linda was by now so finely attuned to her brother that she instinctively knew he planned to take his own life. She also understood the reasoning behind his decision and confronted him. She told him that she knew he thought his family had assumed he was dead for over ten years: "But there is no way you can turn back the clock, expect us to go back to that time and just get on with our lives," she said, "because we love you. . . . You have to be a fighter for us." Garwood said later that Linda must have known her argument was the only one that could make him hesitate.

For Garwood, the judgment, when it finally came, was worse than death. Found guilty of informing on his comrades, interrogating them on military and other matters, serving as a guard for the VC, and simple assault against a fellow American prisoner, he would have to stand condemned before the world of the one thing he had never done, harming a fellow American prisoner of war.

Most damaging had been the testimony of David Harker, the only witness able to report that Garwood had struck him a blow: "As I recall, he hit me with the back of his hand, I don't know whether it was in a fist or whether it was an open hand that he hit me, in the rib. I remember he had a disgusted look on his face . . . and he made the statement, something to the effect that 'you're gonna have to pay for what happened to Russ.' " Harker qualified it by saying the blow neither hurt nor harmed him, but "merely surprised him." He allowed it was the eating of the guard's cat that led to the fatal beating of Grisset, and this had triggered Garwood's "assault." But even as he described the horror of Grisset's beating, he seemed unable to connect Garwood's action with the pain and rage he felt over what was being done by their captors to his only friend.

Harker never explained just what had made him change his original and strongly worded opinions when Garwood first came home: "Don't crucify Garwood," and "He should not be prosecuted if nobody else was." So many questions were left unanswered by the court martial, even Judge Switzer could not help but remark on the apparent injustice done the plaintiff. "It is not the way I would have handled the defense," he told the author. "We never got at the truth because we never heard Garwood's side of the story."

What Judge Switzer did not know was that the government had actively tampered with at least one witness who would have been able to verify that Garwood had always been a prisoner of the Vietnamese, suffering the same torture as those who returned in 1973. That was a fact Vaughn Taylor would find out only years later. The lawyer never changed his mind that coercive persuasion was a relevant and important defense in the court martial, but he concluded that evidence showing Garwood was a victim of these communist pressures was not enough to counter the government's deliberate strategy of character assassination. Taylor would dedicate himself to clearing Garwood's name.

On the face of it, the jury came back with a minor verdict: Garwood was to be reduced to the lowest rank, forfeiting pay and allowances, including 148,000 dollars due him from his fourteen years in prison. In reality Garwood was sentenced to the purgatory of nonbeing, a state of wretchedness that western democracies often self-righteously accuse communist countries of inflicting upon their political, religious, and social dissidents. Not released from the Marines, but not paid by them either, suffering from posttraumatic stress disorder and a host of other illnesses resulting from his long imprisonment, he received no medical benefits. He had no rights as a private citizen of the United States, not even the right to vote. As a Marine, he was not entitled to find civilian work. He owed hundreds of thousands of dollars in legal bills for a sentence he would just as soon have traded for a firing squad. That at least would have been clean and quick.

Perhaps sensing that Garwood's resolve to live was at best tenuous, his defense attorneys whisked him into a waiting car immediately after the sentencing. He was driven to Harrisonburg, Virginia, where Dr. Robert Schowalter, a psychiatrist who'd established good rapport with him during earlier sessions, waited for him. There, for a few weeks, he was able to do what he had been so desperate to do during the court martial—tell his own side of the story to an impartial listener.

Since he had no alternative but to support himself and

begin paying his legal bills, Garwood soon began looking
for a job. He was relieved when John Lowe, intrigued
by Garwood's history of working with cars, offered to
take him on as his personal driver and handyman me-
chanic. In this way Garwood was able to work off some
of what he owed his lawyer and to put food in his mouth.
Under the terms of his sentence, Garwood was still in
the USMC, and legally allowed to work on a part-time
basis only. However, he often put in more than a full
work week and that seemed acceptable to the Marine
Corps. He was still under strict surveillance and required
to report to the local USMC headquarters at regular intervals, but no one questioned the number of hours he
worked. After some months, he found low-paying work
as a gas attendant general-helper in a Virginia service
station, where nobody asked questions about his right to
employment.

Slowly he made friends and began dating. There were
many women who sought him out because of his experience in Vietnam. Some had relatives who had been prisoners or were missing. Others heard about him through
the media because periodically he was called before various congressional committees, ostensibly to give testimony about those still listed as missing in action, but
seemingly more to remind America that he was a traitor
and could not be trusted. "I felt like news reports about
Bobby Garwood were not about me, but about an evil
Garwood clone," he said later. The women who sought
him out were usually generous, full of sympathy, and
anxious to help him exorcise the ghosts of his past, but
his relationships with them invariably fell apart. Garwood
wanted to separate his current life from the horrors of his
Vietnam experience.

"For a long time I felt like an alien in my own country," Garwood said later. "I just wanted to be normal,
do normal things, and talk about normal things. I was
jealous of couples who would go to a movie and just talk

about the movie and the day's events." He would have to wait until 1986 to meet Cathy Ray—the woman he would marry—who would instinctively understand this need and provide him with the kind of normal and loving relationship he craved.

Surprising to him, some veterans of the Vietnam War sought him out and offered their friendship and support. They were usually men with outstanding war records who had worked in reconnaissance. Like the various congressional committees, they too were interested in obtaining information about missing comrades from him, but unlike most of the government representatives Garwood dealt with, these men did not automatically accept the court martial's ugly findings. Garwood felt dutybound to cooperate, but it was not easy to keep reliving the past.

To his father and others who were close to him, it was amazing that Garwood was able to cope at all. He did cope, though, perhaps because he had no alternative, perhaps because, finally, he had his family behind him and was not alone. Just before court martial proceedings began, Jack Garwood had come to Camp Lejeune to be with his son. To Bobby it was "like a vitapack." He said, "All the love I'd been missing all those years was there." Jack Garwood intended to stay with his son throughout the trial, but Bobby made him go back after a week. He said later, "By then I knew what the prosecution would do. I knew I didn't have a chance. My dad had a heart condition and I didn't want him to witness the tactics they had employed during the Article 32 Investigation." But father and son had stayed in constant touch and Bobby was convinced that's why he survived. Jack Garwood's parting words had been. "Come home to me, son. Don't leave me again."

It seemed later to his father that Bobby had shown too much integrity. He was manifestly not guilty on any charge. The judge, among others, had expressed sympathy for him in published remarks during the trial. It was for this reason, his father surmised, that the ultimate powers, those with real control over his fate, had taken a stab at him so unfair it could not but have been intended to destroy all his credibility, to keep him from ever convincing anyone of significance that the abstract entity known as Authority had made a mistake.

Having been dissuaded by his lawyers from testifying in his own defense, Garwood's withdrawal into a shell of exhausted resignation was almost complete. During the last week of June 1980, however, he suddenly perked up, thinking he still had a chance to be acquitted because of the unheralded appearance of one potential witness. The government must have thought so too, because it pulled out all stops to prevent this witness from being heard. The potential witness was a masked Vietnamese man who, according to newspaper accounts that Garwood saw, had just testified before Congress. The man was masked to protect his identity and it was generally assumed that he was in a witness protection program. He told lawmakers he had until recently worked as a mortician for the Hanoi government and had personally seen the bodies of four hundred Americans. In secret testimony he also reported he had seen some living U.S. soldiers in Hanoi after the war. The Mortician, as he was billed by reporters, appeared before Congress with his features concealed by a motorcycle helmet, but Garwood immediately recognized him as Colonel Tran Van Loc, the communist secret-police chief who sat on a five-man tribunal that determined each prisoner's fate. Of Chinese descent, he fled Vietnam when another border war broke out between China and Vietnam in the late 1970s. For Garwood, there was no mistaking the obese half-Chinese. The figure was burned in Garwood's memory, not only because of the power he had wielded over himself and other prisoners, but because Garwood had several times, long after the war was over, begged him to be allowed to return home.

He had never imagined vindication coming from a source that had once tormented him, but the fact that the Mortician had sought refuge in the United States convinced Garwood he might be willing to tell the truth about Garwood's fourteen years as a prisoner.

There were others who recognized the Mortician's true identity. This included Pentagon intelligence analysts, but that did not help Garwood.[6] His attorneys were never allowed to find out who the analysts were, or to get the Mortician to testify during the court martial.

General Tighe, director of the Defense Intelligence Agency, on the other hand, had seen the intelligence analyses and enough corroboration from South Vietnamese refugees to know the Mortician was the man Garwood claimed him to be. Later, Tighe said he had found it impossible, as director of an intelligence agency, to openly assist Garwood's efforts to have the Vietnamese testify. Without success he tried to do so sub rosa. "The court martial," Tighe said, "was completely controlled by the fanatical elements of the Marine Corps." It was a matter that weighed heavily on his conscience until the day he died in 1993. He recorded the agonizing choice between making public all he knew and observing the rules of official secrecy. Above his desk, in his DIA director's office and later at home, he had hung a quotation about the abuses of government secrecy and the need for integrity among those entrusted with such burdens of classified information, adding: "Absolute secrecy corrupts absolutely."

---

[6] Congressmen Lester Wolff and Benjamin Gilman were quoted in news reports as saying there were other official sources who backed Garwood's claim that the Mortician had been a powerful figure in Vietnam's secret police hierarchy. But it was almost as if someone had persuaded them that this had no relevance to Garwood's claims. Congressman Gilman said: "He [the Mortician] has been asked specifically whether he was ever aligned with a POW camp or whether he had ever been to a POW camp and he has denied that."

The Mortician took Vaughn Taylor by surprise. Taylor was trying his best to win acquittal on grounds that torture and imprisonment had impaired Garwood's judgment and ability to live up to a tough code of conduct that men of much higher rank and experience had also violated, but he was flexible enough to see other possibilities. Taylor was disturbed by the insensitivity of the prosecution and he was affected by Garwood's obvious sincerity. Now for the first time since Garwood had insisted on taking the stand and been talked out of it, he was showing interest in his own defense. Taylor believed Garwood was telling the truth about the Mortician. If the Mortician verified Garwood's status as a fourteen-year prisoner there was a chance for real acquittal. He wanted him subpoenaed. The prosecution immediately objected.

"What really made me mad," recalled Taylor, "was that they played this constant game with Bobby—silent confrontations, attempts to trick him into revealing who he knew in Vietnam. Yet when Bobby really did know something in a case as important as the Mortician, they not only refused to listen, but made it impossible for us to subpoena him." Taylor continued, "What I would not learn for another eleven years was that the prosecution had gone far beyond refusing to listen. It was smack in the middle of subornation of perjury and obstruction of justice."

Taylor moved to subpoena the Mortician. For the prosecution, Captain Helmer objected strenuously on the grounds that Garwood could not be telling the truth. When Taylor insisted on Garwood's right to every relevant witness, Judge Switzer ordered a lineup. Garwood was to be given the opportunity to identify the man. If he identified the Mortician, a meeting would follow. The lineup took place in the office of John Drake, director of the International Rescue Committee. The IRC is officially a nonprofit, nongovernment association reputed to have strong ties to the Defense Intelligence Agency. It was an ordinary office interior except for the one-way mirror through which Garwood would be able to screen the lineup.

When a number of balding, Oriental men with similar body types appeared behind the one-way mirror, Garwood immediately identified the Mortician. Taylor was impressed. Unexpectedly—at least for Taylor and Garwood—the meeting with Garwood and the Mortician came just fifteen minutes later. It took place in the same room where Garwood had observed the lineup. It seemed as if the government had anticipated Garwood's quick identification. There was even a translator on hand whom intelligence sources later identified as working for the Naval Investigative Service, the same agency that had been investigating Garwood since 1965 and interrogating him since his homecoming. He also seemed ready for the Mortician and Garwood.

Before Garwood and Taylor sat down across from the Mortician and translator, the man who claimed to be simply an undertaker exchanged a few words under his breath in Vietnamese with Garwood. To Taylor it appeared the two recognized each other. He noted that Garwood suddenly paled before he slumped back into the pose of removed indifference he had shown throughout most of the court martial until the Mortician appeared on the scene.

When the formal interview began, the Mortician, through the translator, denied knowing Garwood and said he had never seen him in Hanoi. He had simply been an undertaker for the NVA with no connection to live POWs. He knew about the four hundred prisoners' bodies only because it had been his job to embalm them.

Under close questioning by Taylor, he admitted that at various times he had also seen three live Americans whom he thought were pilots, under guard, being moved around at 17 Lynam Day Street—the Vietnamese equivalent of the Pentagon—in Hanoi.

"Were they prisoners?" Taylor asked. The Mortician answered, "It did not appear to me that they were free to leave." As if to make certain it was on the record, he reiterated: "Garwood was not one of the three."

Taylor reported back to Judge Switzer that the defense had no grounds to call the Mortician.

The young lawyer, who had hoped briefly that his client would be completely vindicated, was frustrated beyond words. In strict privacy, Garwood told Taylor what the Mortician had whispered before the meeting began: he and his family had been threatened with deportation. The man pleaded for understanding; if they were sent back to Vietnam, they would all be killed. He could, under no circumstances, acknowledge that he knew Garwood.

Taylor was dumbfounded. Garwood seemed so certain, and the two did seem to know each other. But the story his client now attributed to the Mortician was so outrageous, he could not believe it. Who would have threatened the Mortician when only a few people involved with the court martial knew he would be meeting with Garwood?

Ten years later, long after Garwood's case was lost, Taylor obtained proof that Garwood had been telling the truth. In November 1990, the Defense Intelligence Agency called Taylor. It was a matter of urgency having to do with the possibility of collaborators coming out of Vietnam. Taylor was asked to bring himself and Garwood to meet with Gary Sydow, a Vietnam specialist/analyst, as well as Colonel Millard Peck, who headed the POW unit, and the DIA general counsel.

At this official meeting, Peck showed Garwood three sketches, including a likeness of Garwood. They were composites DIA had put together of the three men the Mortician said he had seen under guard in Hanoi and had assumed were American pilots. Peck told Garwood: "The Mortician says that's you."

It hit Taylor immediately. "I thought: My God, here's proof that the Mortician knew Garwood. I knew then that I had been lied to." He informed the Senate Rules Committee, which he knew was small consolation for Garwood.

Taylor remembered Helmer's vehement protestations, ten years earlier, that Garwood was fabricating his connection to the Mortician. "I knew," Taylor said, "that the federal government had not been honest, but I still asked myself, 'Had the prosecutor too been fooled?' "

He got no answer to that question but some months later he was given access to evidence that specifically linked the government to the abrogation of Garwood's rights during the court martial.

He received a call from Senator Bob Smith, a member of the Senate Select Committee on POWs. The Senator told him that the committee was deposing the Mortician at an unnamed federal office. Smith knew that Garwood and Taylor had been summoned by the Defense Intelligence Agency the previous year to verify the sketches identified by the Mortician. Taylor's help in providing senators with intelligence that Garwood had collected on the communist hierarchy in Vietnam did much to persuade them to form the committee. For these reasons Smith invited Taylor to sit in on part of the deposition and provided him with transcripts of the entire interview. The questioning was done by counsel to the committee. The proceedings were recorded by a court reporter.

Smith wanted to know exactly how and why the Mortician had perjured himself eleven years earlier, so that he could judge his trustworthiness on other matters the committee wanted to question him about.

Taylor did not know if the Mortician remembered him when they were introduced, but it appeared as if he did not. Taylor did not identify himself as Garwood's lawyer. Although the Vietnamese seemed more at ease than he did ten years earlier when he denied knowing Garwood, he made it clear that he was beholden to the U.S. government and would do anything that was asked of him if the request came from a government institution.

There had been new delaying tactics in letting him give this fresh testimony. Senator Smith recalled that DIA had reported, for instance, that the Mortician was suffering from cancer and did not have long to live. He was unfit for travel and should be left to die in peace. Senator Smith, at the risk of appearing hard-hearted, reminded all that even secrecy institutions came under civilian control. Smith persisted with the request to see the ''dying'' man.

Now the Mortician proclaimed emphatically that he was not sick.

The committee reassured him that he was in a protected setting and could be completely frank and honest. This official reassurance was obviously important to the Mortician. He now admitted that he had not been honest with Taylor and Garwood ten years before. His excuse? He had been ordered to lie.

Because the Mortician seemed not to have learned any more English than he knew ten years earlier, the committee provided a translator for him. Senator Smith and committee counsel J. William Codinha's careful questions, repeated several times when necessary, brought out the true story of how this key potential witness for Garwood had been intimidated.

It now appeared that the day before the lineup in which Garwood identified him, the Mortician had received a morning visit from a Mr. Phong, assistant director of the International Rescue Committee (IRC). The IRC, at the time, was a lifeline for the Mortician. It provided him and his family with their daily living allowance and other administrative help to settle in the United States. Phong gave the Mortician instructions that came directly from the director of the IRC.

Later that day, Phong told him, he would be visited by a lawyer from the Defense Department about meeting

Mr. Garwood the next day. The Mortician complied. The Defense Department attorney arrived in military uniform and introduced himself as "a lawyer working with the Defense Department." The Mortician now told the committee he had assumed the lawyer held the rank of captain because he remembered being told this by the IRC director.

According to this fuller version of events affecting Garwood's trial, the Defense Department attorney, apparently not advised that the Mortician required a translator, quickly called the IRC to get one. When the translator arrived, the attorney provided the Mortician with specific instructions, advising him that he would be seeing Robert Garwood the next day: "If he [Garwood] picks you out of the lineup, you are to deny having seen him in Vietnam."

The Mortician had never discussed this since, he now told the committee; neither with his family nor with anyone. He feared for his family and himself. To Senator Smith this was obvious from the variety of ways the Mortician responded to the same repeated questions. Smith was quite sure the man was deeply afraid of the consequences if he said anything about this to anyone, and that the fear still lingered. The Mortician emphasized he'd had no problems obeying the "attorney-captain" because it had been made clear to him by the Defense Department that denying Garwood was vital. To such a witness, this implied many things having to do with U.S. national security. That point must have been underlined by the fact that the lineup where Garwood identified him had taken place in the IRC director's office. Both the director and assistant director had been present. Under the circumstances the Mortician had felt compelled to promise, "Okay, tomorrow, I will do whatever is asked for."

With the same anxious compliance, the Mortician had later worked with the Defense Intelligence Agency. For DIA, he firmly identified Garwood as one of the three

Americans he saw under guard in Hanoi and had assumed were pilots. He made the unequivocal statement because he was no longer in fear of compromising himself and his family, and he was giving information that was required by a U.S. government agency. Now, in front of the select committee, he admitted again that he had seen Garwood being held against his will in Hanoi.

Taylor now had proof, sworn testimony before a U.S. Senate committee, that Garwood's witness had been tampered with, enough to win an appeal—if the money could be put together.

In later years when Garwood was asked how this had affected him emotionally, he could only say, "I don't know myself how I survived." The feeling that there had been a cold and calculating obstruction of justice destroyed his hope.

Right after the court martial, even his lawyers seemed to think his mind was so disturbed that he had fabricated what he said about the Mortician. But there was one uniquely informed group of people who did not need to be persuaded about the Mortician and knew the truth as Garwood knew it. These were some of the South Vietnamese officers who had been together with him at Camp 776 and had helped him to become Mr. Electric Generator.

Now they and their families took him under their wing. They contacted him to say they knew he had been abandoned and betrayed, that his betrayal was part of their betrayal. Just as before in Camp 776 the knowledge that he was not alone kept him sane. He had the outspoken respect of men of integrity. They had been America's best allies, and they had paid for it. His prisonkeepers and torturers had also been their keepers and tormentors. He needed to prove nothing to them. They knew those who resisted the hardest were the ones that the communists kept the longest.

Many of Garwood's loyal Vietnamese friends were do-

ing all they could to keep track of their fellow countrymen still in Vietnamese prisons. They made Garwood
honorary chairperson for their cause. It was the only
honor he received and he treasured it.

This group of men provided for Garwood another gift:
friendship with Mrs. Le Hung. Mrs. Le Hung was the
widow of South Vietnam's last Air Force chief, whose
heroic behavior had so impressed Garwood when he
heard about it from his fellow prisoners at Camp 776 in
1976. In the last weeks before the fall of Saigon, General
Le Hung had managed to get his family safely out of
Vietnam. With an American promise of support and the
guarantee that if Saigon fell, he would be evacuated, he
had stayed to lead his men and fight until the last seconds
of the communist takeover. When it became clear that
the United States would not keep its promise to get him
out, he committed suicide just before capture.

Mrs. Le Hung had come from one of Vietnam's oldest
and most patriotic families. She had idealized the American democratic system. During South Vietnam's heyday
as an important ally of the United States, she and her
husband had had dinner at the White House and with
then-Defense Secretary Robert S. McNamara. Now she
supported herself by cleaning the houses of Washington
bureaucrats. She did not mind the work and considered
her problems miniscule compared to those of most people
in her country. However much her former hosts now discounted what she and her husband had stood for, her
values had not changed. She still cared for the people
who had been loyal to the cause, and the two nations for
whom her husband had sacrificed himself. Mrs. Le Hung
heard from General Lam Van Phat, who had been military commander of the Saigon area until the 1975 collapse, how Garwood was being treated. She knew he had
been a prisoner with General Lam Van Phat and other
South Vietnamese generals at Camp 776. Now he was in

America, but being treated as an enemy. She invited Garwood to visit her.

As Garwood entered her modest apartment in Falls Church, Virginia, his eye immediately caught the altar that dominated the entry: American and South Vietnamese flags, incense, fresh flowers, and photos of her husband. Mrs. Le Hung told him that he was the only American to have crossed her threshold since she came to the United States. She had invited him because she wanted him to know that she knew he had always been a prisoner and behaved with honor. She had talked to many people who had been in the camps of North Vietnam, she told him. They had all said the same thing: Garwood had been one of them—a prisoner despised and vilified by the communists, who had tricked the U.S. government into betraying him. Had she not been totally convinced of this, Garwood would never have been allowed across her doorstep. She had invited him because he had been betrayed just like her husband, for political reasons. There were others—South Vietnamese officers who had been good, brave, and loyal allies—willing to testify to Garwood's real status as prisoner and to his staunch character. The last American helicopters to leave Saigon had shoved away former allies as if they had become a nuisance. That's how the United States now seemed to view Garwood, she said. Once he had been needed as a soldier. By surviving fourteen years as a prisoner, he had become a nuisance.

Mrs. Le Hung then said something to Garwood that returning veterans often said to each other because no one else would: "Welcome home." And she added, "On behalf of my husband and myself, thank you." It was as if the husband who had died in Vietnam to avoid capture spoke through her; as if General Le Hung were offering Garwood the spiritual sustenance he needed to find hope again.

For Garwood, Mrs. Le Hung's welcome meant more

than the one he had received from another general of the Vietnam era. Long after the court martial was over he had received a postcard from his old boss and idol, General Walt, who was by then retired. Walt had addressed it to Garwood at his father's Indiana address. The General had written: "Welcome home, Marine."

22: Creeping Doubts

Although Colonel McKenney had by 1980 spent a good deal of psychic and real energy wishing for a silent, hard death for "that traitor, Garwood," he was curiously pleased to have the ugly matter brought into the open with the court martial. It was a kind of vindication of the darker aspects of his military career and his obsession with Garwood. It reinforced all his pride in being a "jarhead" to see the Marine Corps deal with such an ugly matter so judiciously and fairly. He felt as if a great weight had been lifted from him. He felt free, for the first time since 1968, of the desire to get Garwood.

McKenney kept track of the proceedings leading up to the military trial, but he was surprised at the sparsity of media coverage. He noted contradictions between what he had been told of Garwood's history and what was coming out at the trial. The Article 32 hearings determined that Garwood should actually be court martialed but they seemed to deal entirely with Garwood's prison experience, about which McKenney knew nothing.

Small doubts began to nag at him. Garwood was charged with desertion. That jibed with what he knew. But Garwood a prisoner? That meant he could not have functioned as a turncoat. The proceedings made it appear that Garwood was not where he had been placed by the intelligence McKenney received in 1968. If Garwood was in the camp with David Harker, the man he allegedly assaulted, he could not have led the attack at No Name Island. On top of that, there were observers who felt that Garwood was guilty of nothing other than being a prisoner who had survived to embarrass politicians and brass alike.

Although one of his best friends was an old-fashioned war reporter who had covered Vietnam since Dienbienphu, McKenney had little regard for most of the media coverage given to events having to do with Vietnam. That made it easy to rationalize that the media, not well informed about the Garwood case, was distorting the court martial. McKenney assumed that a lot of reporters who had been sympathetic to the North Vietnamese were pro-Garwood and would now want to present "the traitor" in a sympathetic light.

Then his rationalizations were suddenly turned upside down. Early in the court martial, Garwood got all the news coverage McKenney had expected but it had little to do with Vietnam. The headlines blazed from every supermarket tabloid: "Garwood Accused of Child Molestation."

Garwood easily disproved this charge in court, but not before he was another twenty-thousand dollars in debt to lawyers. Uncontested evidence put Garwood hundreds of miles from the scene when the crime was alleged to have been committed. But the fact that he was completely cleared at this trial, which immediately followed the court martial, was mentioned almost nowhere in the media, and the original tabloid slur festered on.

"They've cut the legs right out from under him," McKenney told his wife when he read the first awful headlines. She was stunned by the sympathetic reaction and the way her husband seemed dejected by the news. He knew too much about dirty tricks and Garwood's his-

tory to believe the molestation charge. A famous senator
once told him that it was always easier and cheaper to
get someone on a sex charge, even if it was trumped up,
than on a real crime. He felt this was what had happened
here. Garwood had been set up and it offended Mc-
Kenney's sense of honor. He wanted the toughest sentence possible meted out to Garwood. (Privately, he felt,
even the firing squad was too good.) He wanted to see
Garwood punished for what he had done against his fellow Marines. But these heinous crimes had not come up
during the court martial, and in McKenney's mind, Garwood's sentence had been as nebulous as the entire proceedings.

McKenney lived the good life now. He was a gentleman farmer on a modest scale, preacher and missionary
without pay, and unofficial Marine Corps booster. There
was not a deserving old Marine in the South who would
not eventually get the citation he deserved, if McKenney
could help it. By the mid-1980s, he was also becoming
a sought-after speaker in many southern states on national holidays.

Despite this, he was caught up in "outsider" malaise.
He compared it to the narrow, tall houses you could find
in parts of old southern cities. These houses always nes-
tled against much bigger houses. The narrow house was
called a spite house. It was where the man of the family
was relegated when marriages fell apart in the old days.
That way, the errant father was near his children, but
fundamentally separated from family life. McKenney figured that was what happened to Vietnam veterans. They
had been divorced from the American family and moved
into the spite house of society. He did not wish to be an
ingrate, though. He had much to be thankful for. He had
pretty much recovered from injuries and illnesses con-
tracted in Vietnam and felt he had been literally saved
by a miracle.

His belief in an old-fashioned God of miracles got him

into trouble with some friends who had no sympathy for his "Jesus freak streak." McKenney had heard that Lewis Puller's family thought it better if he did not speak to Lewis—who was having problems adjusting to his severe handicaps—about religion. He thought it might be a rebuff from the Puller family and a criticism of his missionary work. Marty, his wife, told him he was silly even to think people were critical about his religious work. People, she said, were just too busy coping with their own problems. Marty knew, too, that although her husband had courageously battled to regain his physical health, he had never dealt with mental stress and deeply buried emotions from the war. He maintained an affectionate, postprofessional relationship with many wartime colleagues—especially the generals who supported and promoted him in difficult times—but he had lost touch with most of the men he worked closely with under Phoenix. McKenney had even lost touch with Sam Owens, to whom he had entrusted his personal file on Garwood when he left Vietnam.

Periodically, he felt pangs of guilt for not doing the paperwork required to get citations for Sergeant Bob Hyp, the courageous translator/interrogator who, under dangerous circumstances, went to meet the second in command of an NVA regiment in April 1969. The NVA officer offered invaluable information about the enemy's plans, but there had been a strong possibility the rendezvous was an enemy setup and that whoever went to meet him would be ambushed. McKenney never forgot how Hyp's courage paid off. The NVA officer provided Hyp with information that resulted in an important victory for the Americans.

Everytime he heard the term posttraumatic stress disorder McKenney cringed. He felt deeply sorry for the vets he imagined crying in front of the Vietnam Veterans Memorial in Washington, but the Wall itself offended him. He did not consider himself a Vietnam vet but rather a veteran who served in Vietnam. He said, "It was part of my history, but not my identity." Yet his family and friends were aware that he was a deeply troubled man whose problems had their origins in the war. They were also concerned that, earlier, he had started to use alcohol to deaden his pain. When he again chose to abstain, he apologized for drinking bouts that had seemed to assuage the effects of the war. Later, he admitted that his drinking may have been related to Garwood. "In truth," he said, "Garwood's court martial opened such a frightening possibility for me, I dared not confront it."

The frightening possibility began with all those contradictions between what he believed as absolute certainty about Garwood's activities in Vietnam and what little had come out at the court martial. He found that some of the people he admired most had strongly disagreed with his original views on Garwood. Issac Camacho, the Special Forces sergeant who had been captured by the Vietcong in the early 1960s had no doubt that Garwood was captured and had suffered as many prisoners who were captured later had not. He said "no one who has not experienced the horror of one of those early VC camps has the right to point a finger at Garwood. And no one who has experienced those horrors *would* point a finger." Camacho cut short those who accused one of his own prisonmates of being a collaborator like Garwood. He remembered the man, half beaten to death, his body so starved and ravaged that maggots were crawling out of his mouth. Obeying his Vietnamese captors in such a condition, as long as he didn't harm Americans, did not constitute collaboration—not in Camacho's book.

Camacho's sentiments were echoed by USAF Colonel Laird Gutterson, a former Hanoi Hilton prisoner whom McKenney put in his gallery of heroes. Gutterson publicly endorsed Garwood during and after the court martial. He wrote, "I ask myself if I could have survived as well. I had two wars and several skirmishes under my belt, a lot of education, and was imprisoned not in the primitive conditions of the South Vietnamese jungle, but in the structured prison system of North Vietnam, where pain and deprivation were a daily occurrence, but death was seldom faced.'' The words were like a slap in McKenney's face, especially when Gutterson asked why ''men who lived in comparative luxury demean themselves by continuing to deny the inescapable truth of Bobby Garwood's status, an American hero, and the scapegoat for the collective sense of 'not being quite tough enough'—an attitude hidden in the private darkness of those who survived.''

McKenney tried to force himself to stop thinking about his own ''private darkness.'' He simply could not believe that he was mistaken, or worse, misled, about the target who had taken up so much of his time and energy. Gutterson and Camacho were letting their own integrity blind them to the evil of Garwood. Nevertheless, their words, and those of a growing number of other veterans, both South Vietnamese and American, began to invade the darkness, and to undermine his equilibrium. Later he said, ''I must have had a desperate need to find out the truth without ever admitting this to myself.''

Nineteen eighty-five marked the beginning of real turmoil. McKenney heard about General Van Phat's letter to President Reagan in which he confirmed that Garwood ''was not a deserter.'' Van Phat, military commander of the Saigon area until the 1975 collapse, had been a prisoner with Garwood at Camp 776. He wrote, ''As a prisoner of the communists myself, I can confirm Marine Garwood was held prisoner. . . . Seeing Garwood every week over a long period, we [Van Phat and his fellow South Vietnamese prisoners] know him well. . . . I feel an obligation to testify.'' McKenney could not dismiss this voluntary statement from the former Saigon military commander, now a resistance leader who had dedicated his life to defeating the communists. McKenney had to find out more.

His special operations friends, again both South Vietnamese and American, educated him about Cuc Binh Van/Soviet, the communist Vietnamese secret system of camps that Dermot Foley had at one point planned to introduce into Garwood's defense. They told him that Garwood ended up in that system with many of their own lost colleagues—ground personnel on intelligence missions who were counted among the missing in Laos and Cambodia where secret wars were fought simultaneously with the Vietnam War. McKenney now discovered that by way of secret channels even he had not known about, United States intelligence had tracked this communist system and many of its prisoners. His contacts explained how ingenious the enemy had been in setting up camps in dense jungle, a skill little understood even today in the west. It seemed inconceivable, to anyone who had not been there, that trained U.S. observers could pass within a few meters of primitive camps holding a large body of captives and not see them because of the thick foliage, through which even light could not reach the ground.

On that score, McKenney didn't need much persuading. He remembered how one of his hunter-killer teams had discovered a POW camp in the hills. "It had been made of two-inch bamboo, narrow, low cages, about two feet off the deck," he said, "so the prisoners couldn't sit up straight." The camp held twenty-six ARVN POWs. The Marine recon team, a crack outfit, watched the camp until they were sure of what they had, then killed the guards and called in helicopters to lift out the POWs. "That camp, near Chu Lai," McKenney said, "was in our TAOR [tactical area of responsibility]. We kept patrols out in the area at all times, had permanently manned observation posts deep in the bush, plus aerial recon, infrared airborne radar, surveillance, agents, electronic intelligence, you name it. And we had no idea that there could be an enemy POW camp in the area. It was a total surprise. We kept wire taps on their telephone lines, tape-recording their telephone traffic. We knew lots about them. We were good. But they could have had twenty or thirty POW camps of the size we found, right in our TAOR, and go undetected.''

McKenney became engrossed by the recon veterans' detective work. But he still did not know—or consciously want to know—what all this had to do with the deserter and traitor. If Garwood was what these men seemed to imply—not just a prisoner, but one of the hardcore prisoners the communists were toughest on—what did that make of McKenney, of Sam Owens, and of all the brave men who had hunted him?

In the years following his court martial, Garwood was sought out by veterans who wanted to know if he could provide them with information of lost colleagues. They found that Garwood, because of his language skills and curious ability to pick up the mannerisms of his captors, had been able to memorize information on the prison systems. Garwood had done this consciously because he had been trained by Ike Eisenbraun, within the very narrow limits of imprisonment and time running out, to think like a special operations soldier. He had wanted to share his knowledge with U.S. officials from the moment he set foot in Bangkok, but except for a few very terse questions asked by Marine officials in a threatening environment, there had been no debriefing. He continued to hope for one, though it was made clear to him by Vaughn Taylor that by giving any testimony, even before congressional hearings, he risked further prosecution for collaborating even after 1973, when the peace accords were signed. Taylor, afraid that any new trial would be a repeat of the first, requested immunity for his client before Garwood testified or cooperated with any government debriefers. Garwood remained willing to cooperate with government agencies, even without immunity.

McKenney now learned that the detective work of his new veteran friends was backed up by an unofficial but professional debriefing of Garwood done by the now-retired General Tighe, who served at first as deputy director and then director of the Pentagon's Defense Intelligence Agency from 1974 to 1981. Tighe had done his best in 1979 to persuade his peers that Garwood should not be court martialed. Garwood finally received a dishonorable discharge in 1986, so there was no possibility of USMC interference with the unofficial debriefing.

The former DIA chief, working with Dr. Chris Gugas, the polygraph expert who had set up the CIA's polygraph system, was astounded at the extent of Garwood's knowledge. It so closely matched the information collected by U.S. intelligence agencies in the same time span, and more. He said "it would have been impossible to make it up." During Tighe's tenure at DIA, the agency responsible for collecting and analyzing military intelligence, including that on POWS and the missing, there had been more than two hundred live sighting reports on Garwood. "Those reports," Tighe said, "never gave the slightest indication that Garwood behaved in any manner that was illegal or even embarrassing to his country." Although aware of rumors spread by USMC intelligence that Garwood had shot at his fellow Marines, Tighe never saw any proof of it or any documents repeating the allegations. He said, "American intelligence *did* know that Garwood was a prisoner and they had a pretty good idea where he was held." This was passed on to the Marine Corps without any judgments attached because that would have gone against policy. "At DIA," he continued, "we just directed the information like good traffic cops. Officially, we didn't pass judgments or do any interpreting."

Unofficially, the DIA director thought Garwood served as scapegoat for all those Marines who rigidly believed that "Marine prisoners in Vietnam should have adhered to the old-fashioned name-rank-serial-number code of conduct that actually ceased being official U.S. policy after Korea: That they should have escaped or died trying."

Why had Tighe not spoken out at Garwood's court martial? He had been too steeped in the habits of secrecy to break his oath. All those sighting reports were highly classified. The DIA chief had done his best to be persuasive behind the scenes and, later, to report the truth to appropriate congressional committees. After he was introduced to Garwood in 1985, when both were being interviewed for *Sixty Minutes*, he finally made the decision to debrief Garwood himself, because the matter weighed heavily on his conscience. He felt that all of his dire predictions about the more close-minded members of the Marine Corps controlling Garwood's court martial had been borne out. "They had been determined to get Garwood and they destroyed his life," he said.

McKenney, having read Tighe's remarks in a veteran's newsletter, recognized himself in Tighe's description of Marines who continued to adhere to the old code of conduct, but he felt that there had to be a mistake somewhere. Otherwise, his faith in the institution he had idolized since childhood would be shattered. He needed affirmation from some of those who had been with him in Vietnam, and who were party to the "dirty Garwood secret." But he had lost touch with most of them. What happened next, he believed, surely had God's hand in it.

Sergeant Bob Hyp, the linguist interrogator who in 1969 had risked his life to meet an enemy NVA commander at night in dangerous territory, now, almost eighteen years later, tried to get in touch with McKenney. He left a message with McKenney's secretary. McKenney had not seen or spoken with the sergeant since Vietnam, though he had wanted to recommend him for a Silver Star. Now, if the strange message was not a hoax, Hyp wanted McKenney to phone him back at Edwards Air Force Base in California. He wanted to talk to McKenney about Garwood.

When McKenney tried to call the number given, no one admitted to knowing who Hyp was. McKenney was in a fever of frustration. He tried to trace Hyp through USMC and other government channels. Unlike the quick results McKenney usually got through the Marine Corps finder service, which sends letters on to the intended recipient, he received neither a reply from Hyp nor the usual note sent by the USMC when the addressee was known to be deceased. After almost a year more of detective work he was told Hyp had ''died of a heart attack.''

Hyp had gone to work as an analyst for DIA after the war. In that capacity he had debriefed Bobby Garwood over a period of two years beginning in 1986 after General Tighe's informal debriefing had prodded DIA brass into finally undertaking a full and official procedure. The results were so successful that a secret DIA report (the Gaines Report) suggested, ''Supervisors must optimize plans for Garwood's cooperation and availability. Planning should include consideration of hiring him as a consultant.''

Someone at DIA had leaked portions of the report to McKenney's recon veteran friends. They sent him a copy, along with the videotape of Garwood in Hanoi, made shortly before his release.

Jon Alpert, the director of the videotape, had made it available to the author for possible use in a *Sixty Minutes* program. It was shown to a small group of veterans by the author to get their reactions. They had been stunned by what it revealed of Garwood's character. They told McKenney, who was intrigued. He wanted to see it, and yet also he didn't.

He was in Washington on the eve of the official Marine Corps birthday, 1990. This was the most important day of the year for him, devoted to the memory of all the good Marines, "officers and mud Marines alike." Perhaps it was fitting, he thought, to be reminded of what they had fought against. His friends loaned him the videotape. Sequestering himself in his hotel, he turned it on. He was grimly prepared for a communist propaganda masterpiece, celebrating a Marine gone bad.

What he saw put him in a state of shock and he needed to watch only a few minutes to realize that whatever the original intent had been, this was no propaganda film. The tape was rough, completely unedited footage. Even the instructions to Garwood given by Alpert and the Vietnamese and English chatter behind the camera had not been edited out.

The man who appeared on screen looked nothing like the Garwood envisioned by McKenney: neither the 1968 Garwood that counterintelligence had told him of or the clean-cut Garwood with perfect white teeth that he had seen depicted in magazines and newspapers during the court martial. This Garwood was painfully thin, with sunken eyes and rotting teeth. With his ill-fitting, baggy suit and broken English, he resembled nothing so much as the survivor of a Nazi concentration camp. He looked helpless as the people behind the camera paraded him up and down the streets of Hanoi, and through a market. McKenney knew from the wonder in Garwood's eyes that this apparent freedom to wander amiably among the austere foodstalls of the market was in itself a luxury.

To McKenny, one sequence, a visit to Garwood's "regular barber," was a crude set-up. Everyone seemed to have the sense of unease that amateur actors display during tryouts for the yearly local play in high school. McKenney said later, "That barber had never seen Garwood before."

McKenney was so tightly focused he did not hear the ringing telephone. Family and friends later told him they had called. He was in the world on the screen. Unwittingly, the producers of this farce allowed him to feel what Garwood was experiencing.

In one scene Garwood was surrounded by attractive, obviously smart and well-connected young Vietnamese women who spoke excellent English. Theirs were the same voices McKenney heard off-screen being helpful to Alpert and advising Garwood on what was wanted. The women reminded McKenney of the female communist intelligence operatives he had himself encountered in Vietnam. They were attractive and their Americanized English, complete with slang, could only have been learned in the kind of specialized "charm" schools run by the communists for their trainee spies.

Alpert seemed to have great rapport with them. When they wanted to do things that wouldn't sit well with an American audience, he told them so. Alpert teased Garwood about which of these girls was his girlfriend. Years later Alpert told the author that he believed Garwood had deserted to the communist side and then become unhappy with his meager living conditions. He had no reason for doubt, since that information had been given to him by both the Vietnamese and his intelligence contacts in the United States. Alpert admired what he thought was Garwood's defection, but not the fact that he wanted to return to America. Like many Americans, the director's sympathy toward the Vietnamese went back to the war. He felt the United States was responsible for the miserable circumstances of their country. "Despite the fact that Garwood's conditions were sparse by American standards," Alpert said, "he always had more food and better living conditions than his hosts." To Alpert, this was a fact Garwood did not seem to appreciate. He admitted Garwood was thin but "he looked as fit as most Vietnamese."

As McKenney watched in fascination, the women in the film giggled at Alpert's suggestion that they were Garwood's girlfriends. "Like cats playing with a mouse," McKenney thought, "they considered the wreck of a human body in front of them was incapable of functioning sexually." The camera closing in on Garwood's face showed a kind of tortured humiliation McKenney had never before seen in a human being. Involuntarily, he turned away his eyes as he felt Garwood's degradation. He knew from other prisoners that the hardest thing they had to deal with psychologically was the peculiar pleasure their captors got from insulting their manhood, knowing that conditions deprived the men of all sexual drive and instilled a fear of permanent impotence, made worse by the personal indignities visited upon them. Then shame and a red-hot anger began to well up in McKenney. He felt he was seeing an utterly defeated, and most probably brainwashed man. He didn't know whether to laugh or cry. Is this what the Vietnamese did to Americans who had supposedly given their all to the communist cause? It was no wonder the film had never been shown in the west.

Then he saw the sequence where Garwood, asked to give a message to the folks back home, said he loved his country. McKenney understood what was going on when the camera abruptly stopped and the disembodied voices suggested that Garwood try again. This was not the attempt at self-exoneration McKenney would have expected before viewing the tape and the noises coming from behind the camera made it clear that neither was this the kind of thanks the communists had expected in return for their magnaminity. Garwood was supposed to talk about his "reformation through education" and the crimes committed by the United States during the war. "Yet he faced the camera directly again and said he loved his family," McKenney later told his wife. "Garwood said he hoped they would not judge him until he could tell them his side of the story."

When the camera stopped a second time, McKenney thought the voices speaking in Vietnamese sounded quietly ominous. "Garwood's duress was palpable. Everything was at stake. Another wrong answer meant no release." The director told Garwood to do the last bit again.

McKenney watched in fascination, expecting to see his old nemesis crumble. He had never, during the days when he had jurisdiction over such things, seen coercion applied with such cruel finesse. It was agonizing to watch Garwood's face. His eyes showed he understood what was expected of him and what was at stake. He showed the paralysis of a wild animal caught in the glare of headlights. Then Garwood pulled himself up slightly. With a flicker of defiance he looked behind the camera and said what he had said before. McKenney could not believe it.

"I am a true American," Garwood said in his Vietnamese tinged, broken English. He had always been a true American and he loved his country. His life in Vietnam had not been easy. . . .

McKenney was stunned. Garwood had ignored his captors. He had only to repeat their words—few enough and obviously fabricated—to ensure his freedom. The toughest men would rationalize such a compromise. The war had been over for so long that nobody in the west would have cared if Garwood had delivered an entire litany of praise for Hanoi's merciful enlightenment. All of it would have been recognized as propaganda. Yet Garwood would not pay this trivial price for his ticket out. McKenney had once read a description of Winston Churchill that he thought fit Garwood perfectly: "He was brave, and that was all that mattered." In that one moment, all the convictions that drove McKenney in Vietnam, and long afterward, fell apart. McKenney spent the rest of that year's USMC birthday celebrations in a kind of horrible trance. Forever after, he would remember nothing of the events attended, the people he spoke to, or the trip back home to Kentucky.

"The communist propaganda was crude," he said

later. "Any fool could see Garwood's physical distress. Garwood got out in spite of refusing to cooperate, and my government spit-and-polished him to erase evidence of ill-treatment by the enemy. In Hanoi, he was a wretched survivor. In the United States, he was turned into someone who had done well out of the communist system. I realized that my government had done the un- thinkable, not only in betraying Garwood but in using me and others like me as murder weapons. How many other innocent and brave men were made to look like traitors? My last threads of trust parted and I passed into a horrible nightmare I still can't express. I nearly lost what was left of my mind. I had an irrational compulsion to get back into jungle dungarees, put on my killing knife and pistol, and withdraw from everyone but the others who'd been betrayed by those who never knew the sweat, the tears, the mud, and blood." He began to pick fights, always with strangers: "I challenged anyone who looked at me the wrong way," he said later.

Some months after watching the video, McKenney lost twenty-four hours. In that missing time, "I did awful, insanely violent things I cannot fully remember." He would forever be grateful that no family member was in the house during his blackout because he was not certain that he would not have physically attacked them. "When I came to," he said, "I was lying on the floor of my house, blood-stained, surrounded by broken glass and furniture. Apparently I had smashed most of the furni- ture. The entire house looked like a war zone."

Most shocking of all, he saw the charred remains of his beloved "blues," his formal Marine Corps uniform, along with ribbons and badges. Only a few weeks before, he had worn them with pride to his daughter's wedding. It seemed as if he had tried to destroy himself. He had no recollection of committing what he now thought of as almost an act of sacrilege.

Unaware of the events that had shattered McKenney,

but realizing that he was in serious trouble, three of his friends, one a veteran, virtually set aside their lives for him. They knew his scorn for the "posttraumatically stressed" excuse, and searched for someone who could help without injuring McKenney's self-esteem.

John Steer, a fellow "charismatic Christian," fit the bill. Steer ran a retreat and healing center for troubled veterans. Deliberately built like a military installation, Fort Steer was in remote, rural Arkansas, in the foothills of the Ozarks. It had a headquarters building, mess hall, dayroom, showerpoint, and a row of small barracks. The sense of Vietnam was everywhere. The guys called the barracks "hootches."

Steer, himself, was larger than life, with a hook for the arm he lost in Vietnam. A preacher like McKenney, he was also a golden voiced baritone country singer known to Vietnam veterans throughout the United States. McKenney had in the past been moved by his rendition of "Don't Let Another Wounded Soldier Die." When they met, Steer immediately recognized what was at least a part of McKenney's problem. He reached and took McKenney's hand with his own good left hand and asked, "Has anyone yet said: 'Welcome home?' " McKenney was surprised that tears filled his eyes. Had anyone said this to him earlier, he would have thought it embarrassingly trite.

Now he said, "No."

"Then, welcome home, brother."

It was what McKenney needed, although this new association kept raw the wound opened by the Garwood video. Through the extended network of veterans informally associated with Fort Steer, he learned, finally, the whole truth about Garwood. The brief flash of recognition he experienced when he viewed the Garwood tape had been prescient. "Bobby Garwood," he said now, "was a man abandoned just like the aviator off Hainan Island, punished for being a politically embarrassing survivor.'' It was a truth he accepted with great difficulty, but one he had to accept because it came from men he admired most—those who were involved in the dangerous work of behind-the-lines reconnaissance during the war, and those who had been prisoners themselves, like Laird Gutterson. Even Ted Guy, who had wanted to bring charges against repatriated prisoners suspected of collaborating during the war, and who was judged by McKenney to be a soulmate in his hatred for Garwood, now openly wondered if Garwood's court martial was politically motivated. Guy would be one of the first among those McKenney had considered ''fellow hard-core haters of Garwood'' to write open letters of support for Garwood.

McKenney needed Garwood's forgiveness and he needed more than anything to get it in the true biblical sense. It was more important to do what was right before God than it had ever been to satisfy the tough standards of the Marine Corps when McKenney was doing his best to get Garwood assassinated. His second hunt for Garwood would be more difficult for the proud Marine Corps officer. It was a humbled and deeply sincere man at the annual meeting of the Vietnam Veterans Coalition, on Veterans Day 1991, who asked the author to carry a message of repentance to Garwood.

23: Semper Fidelis

Garwood asked the woman he loved to listen in on the call about McKenney. They heard in silence the story of this retired Marine lieutenant colonel who, they were told, wished to ask forgiveness for having been ready over so many years to kill Garwood by fair means or foul.

It was a lot to be hit with so suddenly and by a long-distance telephone call. The two functioned as a unit. Cathy Ray had not met Garwood when she first began to suspect that he was a man of integrity and courage despite the charges of treason and the wild accusations of molestation made against him in the American tabloids at the time of the court martial. Common sense told her that these charges had not been proved.

The two were introduced at a 1986 dinner party quietly honoring Garwood's birthday at the California home of Chris Gugas, the retired CIA polygraph expert. Gugas had then just finished helping General Tighe to debrief Garwood, who had recently moved to California. At first Garwood was wary of the woman described to him as the sister of an MIA. He expected, as was usual in such cases, to be inundated with questions about her brother or the larger issue of the missing, but he had completely misjudged the intentions of Cathy Ray. The dinner turned out to be jolly, with lots of conversation about almost everything but the issue of POWs or Vietnam, and Garwood was charmed by Cathy's open and friendly manner. He said later, "She treated me like a human being—not Bobby Garwood, ex-POW." By the end of the evening the two had established a friendship that deepened over the next few months. They took long walks on the beach, exchanging their thoughts about life in general but avoiding those specific matters that remained as painful to him as raw wounds. They shared quiet dinners, pooling their few resources. She discovered that he was handy around the kitchen.

Eventually they fell in love: each was drawn to the other's humanity. Cathy marveled at the fact "that a man who had been deprived of everything for so long could have such a strong sense of what really mattered in life." She admired his attempts to keep his promises to friends dead and alive, no matter how difficult; that he was a loving son, and brother, and a good friend. "For someone who had been betrayed so often," she said, "he had a very fine sense of justice, easily forgiving those who had hurt him by mistake. Most of all," she said, "I loved his strength and integrity." At one point Ross Perot, the Texas billionaire, offered him a lucrative and secure position to work on Vietnam prisoner data. Garwood refused the salaried job, offering his service for free: he did not want to make money on such an issue. Similarly, Garwood admired Cathy's integrity. She had been very much troubled by questions regarding the missing, but the subject of her brother would not come up, not until he questioned her, years later, after they married.

Cathy Ray was the sister of a fellow Marine, Staff Sergeant James Michael Ray, an MIA who had disappeared in Cambodia. Jimmy Ray had been one of those who volunteered for the most dangerous special operations,[1] so secret that the real facts of his capture had to be "plausibly deniable" by the U.S. government. It was almost certain he had ended up in Cuc Binh Van / Soviet, Hanoi's secret prison system. The family had evidence of this because they had two death certificates listing different times and places for his death. One month after his first "official" death, according to U.S. government records, Ray had received the Silver Star for a heroic attempt to escape prison. Five months after his "first death" he was alive enough to win a Purple Heart and Bronze Star. When Ray's family contacted those persons said by the government to have witnessed his death, they claimed to know nothing of it.

Cathy had enough experience of government manipulation of her brother's case to understand perfectly what had been done to Bobby. She never tried to discuss his prison experience in Vietnam, leaving that to the doctors Garwood continued to see. But she knew, from his nightmare-filled sleep and cold-sweat awakenings, that the past was always with him. Garwood was still suffering from an overwhelming survivor's guilt. She could tell without his saying a word how often his mind was with Ike and the others he had left behind: not just when there were news reports about the return of missing bodies, but on almost every happy occasion. There were times when Garwood, needing to be alone, took up a friend's offer to make use of a remote mountain cabin. Such times revitalized him and gave him the strength to face a world that allowed him none of the benefits automatically available to other veterans.

Garwood continued to make a modest living by repairing automobiles. Until 1986, when he was dishonorably discharged from the Marine Corps, he was officially denied the right to gainful employment or the usual service benefits, in addition to having no status as

---

[1] Ray was with the 525th Military Intelligence Group—Team 38.

an American citizen. He was never paid for any Marine Corps service beyond the day of his capture and did not receive any veterans' medical benefits. Making the best of things, the Garwoods formed a very tight and very private family unit that included Cathy's child from a former marriage. They got on with their lives as best they could, but they never entirely put out of their minds the wrong that had been done Garwood. Cathy was very protective of Garwood: she meant to see him cleared, no matter what powers were still amassed against him.

So Cathy was cautious about McKenney's request, as was Garwood. McKenney was not the first to seek forgiveness for targeting Garwood during the war, but he seemed to be the highest ranking officer who had ever tried to contact him with a message of sympathy. Just the same, Garwood remained noncommittal. In the ten years following his court martial, a number of men claiming former assassination assignments had approached him, always secretly and sometimes anonymously, to tell him he had been their number-one target because they had then believed the rumors and innuendo circulating in their secret world. They had believed that Garwood led NVA attacks against his fellow Marines; that he took pleasure in killing and maiming them. Most of these callers were like Bruce Womack, former enlisted men who had been assigned the highly secret and financially lucrative work of assassinating other Americans. Like Womack, they were usually from poor backgrounds not unlike Garwood's, and were patriotic and deeply religious in a fundamentalist way. Most had been troubled over the contradictions apparent in their assignment from the moment they had killed their first American. At least initially, they had all shared a particular similarity: an innocent and zealous belief that their government and the branch of service to which they were attached could do no wrong.

Garwood recognized himself in them, and he could

give any number of examples of his own naïve zeal. For years he had been haunted by memories of an awful event that happened during his Marine training. He and fellow recruits were warned to stay low during a simulated firefight because, they were told, real bullets would be used. One young Marine did not stay low enough and appeared to be killed by a bullet. Garwood's training officers then lectured the trainees on how the dead man could have avoided his fate by following the order to stay low. Garwood still felt guilty about the young Marine's death when he talked to psychiatrists during his court martial. He remembered the blessed relief he felt when the psychiatrists finally persuaded him the entire episode had been faked to teach young recruits a lesson. Such relief, however, would never be available to the troubled men who came to see him now. They now lived in the shadows of society, ashamed of what they had done. A lot of their fellow assassins committed suicide, became alcoholic, or otherwise went under. Usually, the survivors who came to see Garwood appeared to have been kept alive by a strong belief in God and supportive families. Garwood easily forgave them.

McKenney, with his intelligence background, was different. He smacked too much of the official resolve to keep Garwood discredited. Ever since the court martial, all of Garwood's efforts to clear his name had been opposed. Dishonorably discharged and humiliated before congressional committees, he had been called deserter and traitor by powerful politicians who had access to the truth, if they were interested in it. Those who struck the most patriotic poses demonstrated voluble ill-will, and continued to speak of him publicly as a deserter when even the court martial established he had not deserted. For example, in July 1985, the powerful chairman of the U.S. House of Representatives Committee on Foreign Affairs, Subcommittee on Asian and Pacific Affairs, Steven Solarz, denounced Garwood in a Washington speech before the League of Families: "We have the spectacle of someone who betrayed his nation, somebody who worked for the enemy, somebody who deserted the institution he was pledged to support. . . ."

The following year Garwood agreed to be formally debriefed by the DIA even though he had no guarantee that he would not be prosecuted again, as U.S. government officials had threatened, this time for collaborating after 1973. The more than one hundred hours of debriefing by specialists began in the Washington office of then-DIA chief Leonard H. Perroots and ended almost three years later at a quiet retreat at Okrakoke Island, North Carolina. This was the marathon interrogation that prompted DIA to suggest that Garwood be hired as a consultant. The reports concluded that "there was a lot of information [DIA had] . . . which tends to substantiate what Garwood says. Despite this, it was made clear to Garwood that he would have to live with the stigma of being a traitor. Those who opposed him made certain that the suggestion of his being hired by DIA was never followed up.

Garwood had hoped that his long nightmare might soon end. From what DIA had asked him, he could tell they knew the truth. He said later, "They had precise intelligence on every camp and prisoner. They showed me photographs of myself in some of the camps. They told me highly individual things about my prison guards and black-market bosses. Only someone who was there could have described their traits so precisely." One of the men DIA wanted to know about was the Mortician. There was no question in Garwood's mind that they knew precisely what role Colonel Tran Van Loc had played in Vietnam. Nor was there any question that Garwood's own movements were known. For a long time, the debriefers now told Garwood, U.S. intelligence had tracked him through the prison system known to specialize in psychological duress, and were certain he would end up in the Soviet Union as a propaganda tool for communism. No one could figure out why this had not happened. Garwood just kept moving from camp to camp. Apparently no one had felt it necessary to research Garwood's history from the beginning to find out what was really going on.

Garwood felt that some of the debriefers empathized with him. One sought him out near the end of their session at Okrakoke Island. This was Bob Hyp, coincidentally the same staff sergeant who had worked with McKenney in 1969 and distinguished himself by his bravery. Of course Garwood had no idea that his interrogator of 1988 had been closely associated with this Marine colonel now asking his forgiveness, or that McKenney had overseen the efforts to have Garwood assassinated in 1968–69.

Also, and ultimately the most important piece of information withheld from him, Garwood had never been told that Hyp was one of two DIA interrogators who had subjected the Mortician to six weeks of interrogation in Hong Kong in 1979. The Mortician said in later testimony before the closed U.S. Senate committee hearings that this questioning had been so intense, it had gone on "day and night." Only Sundays were left free to sleep.[2]

Hyp revealed to Garwood that he was a former "jarhead" himself. The interrogator impressed Garwood with his fluent Vietnamese. Hyp said, "We never had reservations about you. We knew for a fact you were a prisoner of war. . . . We knew how they broke you and we knew how they used you—often you, yourself, didn't know how. There was never any doubt about you. I checked all the rumors about you, the bad ones. There was absolutely no validity to them."

Garwood had been a necessary sacrifice, Hyp told him.

---

[2] Deposition of the Mortician, Select Committee on POW / MIA Affairs, December 12th, 1991.

It was important, at the time, to discredit him because it
sent a signal to the communists that they could not use
Garwood or any others like him to blackmail the United
States. Of all the things that had been done to him and
said to him, Garwood probably found this the most difficult to accept. He asked, "Sacrificed for what? . . . and
why can't it end?" Hyp only replied, "Bobby, there isn't
a day when I don't feel bad about all of this."

At the end of the debriefings, another debriefer expressed different sentiments. Garwood was lucky, he
said, because he had made it back. He pointed out others
were not so lucky. "You're in the clear now, Bobby,"
he said. Then, more ominously, he seemed to correct
himself. "You're on the plus side now . . . but be careful
because contact with the wrong people can put you in
the minus."

"What wrong people?" Cathy asked. She had not
been part of the debriefings, but she had gone to Okrakoke with her husband. She said afterward that she could
not understand the callousness. She answered her own
question. "The wrong people are those who refuse to
stick to the secrecy that requires an eighteen-year-old soldier, for whatever twisted reasons of wartime security,
institutional pride, and foreign policy, to sacrifice his
whole life."

A short time after the Garwoods returned home, Bob
Hyp telephoned. Cathy Garwood's heart jumped at the
message. Hyp would be sending them a package of documents in the mail. Discreetly, but leaving no doubt
about his intent, he said the contents of the package
would give Garwood the proof he needed to win an appeal against the court martial's finding.

About the same time, someone who gave his identity
as Hyp called the Canadian publishing house McClelland
and Stewart, and left a similar message to be passed
along to the author by senior editor Pat Kennedy: a package of documents would be sent that would clear Gar-

wood in any court of law. No one knew then who Hyp was. When the call was returned, those who answered at Edwards Air Force Base said no one by the name of Hyp worked there. During later interviews with McKenney, it became clear that this had occurred about the same time that McKenney had received a message from Hyp, which ''drove me crazy.''

The documents, promised by Hyp with the assurance that they would irrefutably exonerate Garwood publicly, were never delivered to any of the intended recipients. Later, Senator Smith confirmed that Hyp had died of a massive heart attack. It occurred to Smith that the documents Hyp had promised pertained to the Mortician's testimony, which had been kept from the public by the U.S. government. The Mortician must have told Hyp during the intensive 1979 debriefing in Hong Kong that he knew Garwood was a prisoner in Vietnam. That could explain why Hyp had told Garwood, ''We always knew you were a prisoner. We never had any doubts about you.'' Hyp must have known, as Vaughn Taylor would later find out, that the government had prevented the Mortician from testifying at Garwood's court martial and that Garwood would certainly be cleared on those grounds in an appeal.

Briefly, Garwood had allowed himself to believe that he would finally be vindicated in an appeal. When Hyp's unexpected death shattered those hopes, Garwood took a deep breath before resuming his stolid effort to take each day one at a time. The experience of his recent debriefing had taught him that officially the government was going to continue to sacrifice him to a policy he still did not fully understand. It made him wary of any approach that began with, ''I know the awful truth of what was done to you. . . . Could you forgive?''

Garwood agreed to receive a letter from McKenney, but only if it was forwarded through the author. The call asking him to deal yet again with such a hurtful part of his past could not have come at a worse time. His father had just died. Garwood had wanted more than anything to give him the gift of seeing his son cleared. He was anguished that the debriefing that he had hoped would accomplish at least this much had only exacerbated his father's disillusionment with institutions he had once revered.

Jack Garwood, true to the oath he made when Bobby came back from Vietnam, had not let "authority" run over him. He had always loved his oldest son, but from the day Bobby had fallen on his knees and embraced him like the biblical prodigal son, Jack never again passed up an opportunity to show this love. Until Cathy Ray came along, he was the single most important factor in Garwood's slow climb back to physical and mental health.

The father had resented the way he was made to look like a crude buffoon by the media during Garwood's court martial. Garwood Senior had been convinced that the majority of Americans were made up of his sort of people. Never without a sense of humor, he would point to the success of the television program *Roseanne*: "The American people," he said, "are smart enough to know what's genuine." But the fact that his son had never been given a chance to place his case before the public ate away at him. Bobby was certain that grief and rage over his own helplessness to restore his son's honor had hastened Jack's death. Now Bobby was more determined than ever to give his father, at least in death, what he had coveted most in life—the restoration of family honor. A year after receiving McKenney's request for a meeting, he would risk his life in one more attempt.

In the spring of 1993 Senator Smith was planning a trip to Vietnam in his capacity as vice chairman of the U.S. Senate select committee on POW/MIA affairs. He wanted Garwood to accompany him so that he could verify for himself the accuracy of Garwood's testimony during the earlier DIA debriefings conducted by Hyp.

From Garwood's description of the location of some of the prison camps where he was held, combined with evidence in the committee's possession, Smith believed other Americans had been held in the same camps.

It was a difficult decision for Garwood. Senator Smith had become his strong supporter. He had ended his opening select committee statement with the words, "I am here today because I believe Robert Garwood." He wanted Garwood to travel with him in a protected status, with appropriate "red" passport and travel documents. But other Senate committee members were incensed by the idea of U.S. tax dollars being spent to send "a convicted collaborator on a vacation to Vietnam." Those who opposed Smith prevailed. Garwood now had to decide whether he would travel with Smith without protective U.S. documents, albeit with Smith's promise to raise a ruckus if the Vietnamese arrested Garwood. The situation was exacerbated by a more personal dilemma. Garwood's beloved younger brother Don was dying of cancer and begged him not to go. The fact was, doctors told Bobby, Don could die any day. The strain of worrying about Bobby could hasten his brother's death. Don knew that General Tighe had warned Bobby not to go back to Vietnam, telling him it would be extremely dangerous for him. Many of Garwood's former captors would have no compunction about having him killed, Tighe said, and the United States would probably not make an issue of a convicted collaborator dying in such a way on foreign soil.

Despite the warning, Garwood traveled to Vietnam in early July 1993, having married Cathy just a few days before. Garwood wanted to make certain the American government would be legally obligated to report to Cathy if Tighe's worst predictions came true. Reluctantly, Cathy agreed that returning to Vietnam was something Garwood had to do. He decided that this would probably be the only chance he would ever have to keep the last

promise he made to Ike Eisenbraun when he lay dying—
to bring him home. Garwood knew precisely where Ike
was buried and was determined to ask his former captors
for that one favor, even at the risk of incensing them to
his own detriment. He knew nothing could mean more
to Ike's daughter Elizabeth. She had done everything,
including an attempt to enlist President Reagan's help to
bring her father home, all without success. Bobby Garwood was godfather to Ike Eisenbraun's grandchildren.

Garwood's request to the Vietnamese for Ike Eisenbraun's remains got *no* press coverage, even though he
had preceded it with requests for assistance from appropriate U.S. agencies like the Joint Casualty Resolution
Center. Senator Smith's strongly stated verification that
Garwood had told the absolute truth about prison sites
during his debriefing was received with press skepticism.
Instead, most western reporters uncritically repeated the
Vietnamese propaganda line. One American news service
quoted Ho Xuan Dich, director of Vietnam's MIA office
as saying that "Garwood socialized with other Vietnamese officers." Dich accompanied the Senator's team. He
denied that someone named Eisenbraun had ever existed
or that Garwood had been in a prison camp. Yet he lost
no opportunity to needle Garwood:

"You were free to go everywhere," Dich said. "You
were a low-ranking officer of the People's Army. You
were my friend." That last was too much. Garwood,
pointing his finger at Dich, shouted "You were never my
friend." That, with an accompanying photograph, did hit
some newspapers.

Vaughn Taylor, who accompanied Garwood and
Smith, photographed a similar scene reporters either
missed or thought irrelevant. Garwood and Smith made
ready to leave one of the sites that Garwood identified
as a former prison camp, despite the fact that his former
captors had torn down the buildings. A diminutive male
figure in white shirt and old-fashioned green helmet ap-

proached Garwood, who immediately recognized him as
Colonel Thai, the man who had warned him just before
his release that he would be watched wherever he went,
and that the U.S. government would not believe he had
been a prisoner for fourteen years. Garwood had never
supposed that Thai, which is also the Vietnamese word
for war, was the man's actual name, but he could never
forget the face that had ordered the torture and execution
of his friends. Colonel Thai had always taken a personal
interest in Garwood, endlessly interrogating him about
his language skills. He had never believed that Garwood
learned the Vietnamese language in an ad hoc manner.
Feeling uncontrollable rage, Garwood now pointed his
finger at Thai and said, *"You* tortured and killed my
friends.''

Thai went white. Taylor said later that it seemed to
him the closest they had come to fulfilling General
Tighe's prediction that Garwood would be arrested. Taylor was convinced it was only Smith's obvious intent to
stand his ground that saved them. Some months later
Thai was still so angry over Garwood's audacity that he
publicly contradicted Ho Xuan Dich's statements to reporters that Garwood had always been free in Vietnam.

During a meeting with Patricia O'Grady-Parsels, the
daughter of a missing American pilot, the man formerly
in charge of prisoner interrogation and torture emphasized that Garwood had been arrested and was a criminal
from the start. Thai said the Americans released in 1973
from the capital region had been successfully reeducated
and their sentences commuted. He told O'Grady-Parsels
that Garwood had always had a "bad attitude." He had
needed to be separated from the others in order not to
contaminate them. Garwood remained a "criminal,"
Thai continued. For that reason his sentence was not
commuted in 1973.

Back in Bangkok, a brief stopover on the way home,
Garwood received Colonel McKenney's letter. It was

again a very poor time to catch him with such a matter. He felt defeated because he had not been able to bring back Eisenbraun's remains. He looked exhausted and vulnerable. He was not at all the strong figure in cowboy hat and jeans who was pictured pointing an accusing finger at the Vietnamese director of MIA affairs in Bangkok newspapers just days before. But he was not alone. With him was a friend—a retired American Special Forces officer and former POW who had at one time believed the worst about Garwood and had been willing to shoot him on sight if given the chance. Now, sharing a late dinner at the Siam Intercontinental Hotel, there was an easiness between them, a camaraderie that came out of the shared horror and inside jokes of having been POWs in Vietnam. The presence of his friend seemed to infuse Garwood with strength.

His face became a mask as he was handed the letter. He betrayed no emotion as he read it.

11 June 1993

Dear Bobby,

I have delayed for a long time writing to you because it is such an important, terribly significant thing for me. You are such an important, terribly significant person in my life. I have said to Monika [the author] that "I'm not ready . . . it's too important . . . it has to be right." But the devil's time is always "later," since "later" never comes. So the big moment doesn't have to be a big moment. I'm too tired to think straight tonight, but so what. . . . I'll just do it.

As one idealistic Marine to another, I want to say that I now know the truth about you, I respect you and want to be your friend. I am that now. I look forward to meeting you face to face, and it looks like it may not be much longer; but I am your friend now.

She [the author] has probably told you that at one time I believed the lie about you and was part of the effort to kill you. I didn't just want you dead, I wanted the pleasure of killing you myself. I wanted to kill you so badly that I actually dreamed about doing it. I believe that if our roles had been reversed, you would have felt the same way about me, because we were both totally gung-ho Marines, true believers.

I've been pretty crazy for the past five or six years anyway, living more and more in my Marine Corps past, feeling alone, not belonging here and wanting to go back to Vietnam where I did fit in. I was always ready to fight, often in a kill mode, a growing menace to those around me. When I found out the truth about you and realized what it meant, it nearly finished me. I'm coming out of it now, doing better and better. I don't know about you this moment, but it is the Lord's job to square away all the wrong of it; in the meantime we can only ask Him to heal our hearts and minds as we pick our way through the emotional and political minefields around us to get on with our lives. We can exercise caution as we move ahead; but only He can heal us, and He will if we will just ask Him. You're not alone, and there are still a few we can trust. . . . Maybe we can finally get the truth out to the American people. So Jarhead, this letter isn't the masterpiece of incredible climactic summary that I thought it had to be, but it is a start. Let me hear from you. I want to know you. I want to help. We need each other. There aren't many people I trust anymore, but you are one of them.

I'm praying for you.

Semper fidelis,
Tom C. McKenney

When Garwood finished the letter he got up without a word and disappeared for more than an hour. He said nothing about the letter when he returned. Much later, as he talked long into the night about this last, bizarre visit to Vietnam under an American senator's protection, he paused for a moment and said he would meet Colonel McKenney, but he needed time. It was another year and a half before the meeting took place.

Garwood turned down more invitations than he could keep track of from Vietnam veterans groups. Almost all veterans knew who he was and they were all curious about the man whose name had become synonymous with traitor. Most had come to believe that of all the horrors that had befallen Vietnam veterans during the war and its aftermath, those that he had suffered were the worst. Garwood declined most invitations because it was still difficult to speak of friends tortured and dead. He did agree to address the Upper Midwest National Alliance of Families in Minneapolis, in late November 1994, because, Vaughn Taylor told him, to get the money they would need to appeal his conviction—including a hundred thousand dollars just for the paperwork—he would have to accept some speaking engagements. The strategy did not really work. Garwood still could not handle repeatedly conjuring up his past as a prisoner, and he was not the kind of man who could simply recite the same preset speech.

On the afternoon of November 28th, the large reception room at the Minneapolis Holiday Inn was packed with veterans, many, if not the majority, former Marines. The gathering and the hotel where Garwood was staying were guarded by off-duty policemen. They were all Vietnam veterans who had volunteered for the job, in itself an extraordinary demonstration of how the tide was turning. After Barbara Sworski, the regional director of the

Alliance, introduced Garwood to thunderous applause, the room became totally silent. Garwood spoke, quietly, slowly, at times in a whisper, yet every word was clear. Audience members later remarked that Garwood had been able to transport them back to Vietnam, to the prison camps where Ike and Russ had died. There were long, painful moments of silence while Garwood tried to collect his emotions. No one moved. It was clear that Garwood was reliving his imprisonment. In the hushed aftermath of the speech, veterans presented Garwood with a miniature of the Minneapolis Vietnam War Memorial. A long line of men queued up to offer Garwood their hand in friendship. Many said they had hated him because they believed he had betrayed their comrades, and asked for his forgiveness.

Colonel McKenney arrived in Minneapolis the night before. He was not in the crowd. His meeting with Garwood took place immediately after his arrival and lasted until the early hours of the morning. McKenney had barely taken the time to drop off his bags and check in. Garwood had checked in earlier. It was as if, having waited so long to finally meet face to face, neither man could stand to wait any longer.

Cathy Garwood opened the door. Bobby stood behind her. The two men greeted each other in a low-key, casual manner, as if they were two ordinary Marine Corps veterans thrown together by chance. No outsider would have guessed the long history between them. If Garwood had expected an immediate apology from McKenney, he did not show it. Cathy did. She watched the two men silently, with a tight expression.

After they sat down with nonalcoholic drinks, Garwood began talking—not McKenney, as Cathy had expected. The two men seemed to revert to their former ranks: Garwood, the Marine private, totally respectful to his superior; McKenney, the lieutenant colonel and in-

telligence officer, listening courteously and professionally. Garwood began with the day of his capture,
mapping out carefully how he got his assignment and
how he was captured. It was as if floodgates had opened
in his mind. He could not stop talking. He carefully outlined the names of each building at III MAF, each officer,
each roadblock, and bridge.

Then McKenney began to ask tough, specific questions: "The small bridge you crossed," he asked, "did
you know it would be there? Did you know about its
history?" McKenney knew the bridge had been of major
interest to the enemy. There had been tunnels leading up
to it when Garwood was captured and it would be blown
up countless times by the VC over the next three years.
It was negligence, McKenney had thought privately, that
the question did not come up at Garwood's court martial,
just as someone should have asked what an inexperienced
driver was doing in enemy-infested territory alone.

McKenney concluded that Garwood's memory was
phenomenal. On the few minor details about which
McKenney had doubts, he checked with friends like Sam
Owens,[3] who had been camped not far from where Gar-
wood was captured on that fateful day. McKenney found
Garwood's memory better than his own.

When McKenney asked Garwood to take off his shirt
so that he could check for scars, Cathy Garwood suspected he had come to catch her husband out. To her he
seemed to have again become the hunter-interrogator and
perhaps worse. Something had gone awry. Her husband
did not agree to meet the man who had unfairly targeted
him simply to be judged again. If anything, she thought,
the roles should have been reversed. Garwood should be
the judge. But something silenced her.

---

[3] McKenney had renewed his friendship with Owens after the two met
by chance at the San Diego airport the year before.

"Why not let him see the
"They were always there an
Bobby's interrogations and exa
the court martial and later during
ever showed the slightest interest."

Cathy Garwood suddenly underst
pening. This was the trial Garwood al
never had. McKenney, the tough profess
his prey no quarter, was the judge Garw
These were the questions Garwood had w
asked during the court martial, to prove his
He had begged his lawyers to put him on the
stand, arguing that he could answer any question
fully. He had only refused to defend himself wh
meant resorting to the backbiting "spider-in-the-jar"
tics the enemy had forced on American prisoners to mak
them accuse each other.

Up until this moment, even after he wrote his letter of
repentance to Garwood, McKenney had continued to believe that at least Garwood's court martial was conducted
fairly, according to Marine Corps ethics. Later Mc-
Kenney said he felt awkward playing doubting Thomas,
but a sixth sense prodded him to continue. He still had
not seen proof that Garwood was wounded when he was
captured. If he had lied about that—even if he told the
truth about everything else—it would have tempered
McKenney's regrets about the injustice Garwood had suffered. Once he saw the scars on Garwood's right forearm
and wrist, he said: "Garwood should have been given at
least a Purple Heart. He fought off his captors until his
injuries prevented him from picking up his gun. That's
when he was captured. He resisted until he was not able
to resist any more."

It was almost daylight in Minneapolis when Garwood
reached the part of his story that dealt with his return to
the United States. Both men were now gray with fatigue,
yet neither wanted to stop. McKenney's face was set in

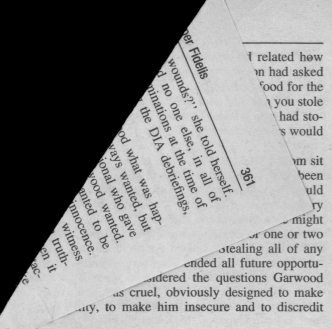

l related how
on had asked
food for the
you stole
had sto-
s would

m sit
been
uld
ry
might
or one or two
stealing all of any
ended all future opportu-
sidered the questions Garwood
as cruel, obviously designed to make
ity, to make him insecure and to discredit

The image of the spite house sprang to mind. More than any other veteran, Bobby Garwood had been put away in a spite house. It had been built, block by rotten propaganda block, to envelop him, destroy him, and obscure from public view the ugliest secrets of the war. McKenney understood now that he himself had been as much a part of the attempted destruction as the interrogators at Great Lakes Naval Station.

When he arrived at Garwood's door earlier that evening McKenney knew Garwood had been done a great wrong, but he had not known what category of man he really was. He had no doubts now. Garwood was one of those mud Marines who had gone face to face with the enemy, for fourteen years, armed with nothing but his own ingenuity and integrity. He was, as far as McKenney knew, the only American who had beaten their system. Throughout his fourteen years as a prisoner Garwood had remained a good Marine in a way only real jarheads

could understand. Even in the most constricted and dehumanizing circumstances, he had gone out and
"whipped butt," without getting caught. McKenney
could think of no better example than the night Ike Eisenbraun was suffering from severe stomach cramps and
Garwood had risked his life to steal a small can of condensed milk for him. The style in which he had managed
this—spreading muddy clay all over his body and crawling through the gate right past the guard post to the
kitchen and back—was classic leatherneck. The same
was true of the times he had stolen food and medicine
for the other POWs and managed to turn on the Voice
of America for only fifteen to thirty seconds at a time
with guards just around the corner. And though he was
never caught red-handed the enemy had fully understood
how big a threat someone like Garwood was to a totali-
tarian system that prided itself on being able to fully control human beings. They did their best to break him, but
they did not succeed.

All of this hit McKenney harder than the four-hundred
ton explosion that had given him a concussion during Tet
1969. Garwood was the kind of man he had himself been
at one time. McKenney, too, had disregarded regulations
when he went on booby-trap patrols as an overpaid rifleman, or borrowed the general's helicopter in a hot zone
in pursuit of an urgent goal. Garwood had remained that
kind of a Marine. McKenney, on the other hand, had
eventually traded in his own freedom to think and act
according to his conscience for blind loyalty to an institution.

It didn't make him feel better when Garwood admitted
he would have reacted the same way as McKenney if
given the same limited information.

"No institution is deserving of blind loyalty," Mc-
Kenney wrote later in the notes he kept of this unique
encounter. "There has to be room for the moral scrutiny
of one's own conscience." He had always had two mot-

tos. The first—''When it gets too tough for everyone else, it's just right for me and my guys''—now rang hollow. It was the second motto McKenney would try to live up to: ''*Real* Marines take care of their own.'' Whatever it took, he wanted justice for Bobby Garwood from the Marine Corps. It was the only way future Marines had a chance.

Cathy Garwood thought: ''McKenney will be fighting against the spirit of McKenney past.'' It had taken a quarter century for him to win the first crucial battle within himself. She wanted to believe he would win the second battle.

She only hoped it wouldn't take as long.

Epilogue

Bobby Garwood lives with his family on the west coast of the United States. He makes his living doing mechanical repairs.

Tom McKenney heads Words for Living Ministries, an independent church, and publishes a Christian newsletter. When he is not teaching the Bible, he lectures and writes articles and books on historical, military, and religious subjects.

Sam Owens retired from the Marine Corps in 1977. After a stint as a computer analyst and executive, he switched to a career in high-intensity law enforcement. He retired as a deputy sheriff in the Warrant Division, Columbia, South Carolina, in the fall of 1996.

Werner Helmer was promoted to colonel. For a period of time he was a military judge. He is a Professor of Military Law in North Carolina.

General Eugene Tighe died of cancer in 1994.

Chris Gugas is committed to helping Bobby Garwood get an appeal.

The Mortician works as a cook at an undisclosed location in the south.

Vaughn Taylor practices military law in Jacksonville, North Carolina. He continues to head a defense fund for a Garwood appeal.

General Lewis Walt was appointed Assistant Commandant, USMC, after his stint as head of III MAF, and retired in 1971. His critical view of the Vietnam War was perhaps best expressed in the title of his book, *Strange War, Strange Strategy*. He died at the US Naval Home, a military retirement home in Gulfport, Mississippi, on March 26, 1989.

John Sexton was honorably discharged as a disabled veteran after his release in 1971. He communicates regularly with Jean Ray, Cathy Garwood's mother. In a curious twist of fate, he is the last known American to speak to Cathy Garwood's brother Jimmy Ray in prison, in August 1969. He was not allowed to see Ray, who was held behind a screen of bushes, but the two called out to each other and exchanged basic information during the time they were briefly held in the same camp. Sexton was subsequently moved to another camp.

Don Garwood died two months after Bobby Garwood returned from his trip to Vietnam in 1993.

Linda Garwood died just before Christmas 1995.

Index